A History of the ANC
South Africa belongs to us

FRANCIS MELI

Zimbabwe Publishing House
HARARE

Indiana University Press
BLOOMINGTON & INDIANAPOLIS

James Currey
LONDON

First published 1988 by
Zimbabwe Publishing House
Harare

© Francis Meli 1988

This edition published in Britain 1989 by
James Currey Ltd
54b Thornhill Square, Islington
London N1 1BE

and in North America by
Indiana University Press
10th and Morton Streets
Bloomington, Indiana 47404

The photographs are reproduced by courtesy of *Sechaba* and the
International Defence and Aid Fund for Southern Africa
The cover photograph is from the Cradock funeral in 1985
and is by Rashid Lombard

British Library Cataloguing in Publication Data
Meli, Francis
    South Africa belongs to us: a history of the ANC
    1. South Africa. African nationalist movements.
    African Nationalist Congress, to 1988
    I. Title
    322.4'2'0968

    ISBN 0-85255-331-5 (James Currey Cloth)
    ISBN 0-85255-332-3 (James Currey Paper)

Library of Congress Cataloging-in-Publication Data
Meli, Francis 1942–
    South Africa belongs to us: a history of the ANC / Francis Meli.
        p.   cm.
    Bibliography: p.
    Includes index.
    ISBN 0-253-33740-2.   ISBN 0-253-28591-7 (pbk.)
    1. African National Congress – History.   2. Blacks – South Africa – Politics and government.
    3. South Africa – Politics and government – 20th century.   4. Apartheid – South Africa – History.
    I. Title.
    JQ1998.A4M45 1989
    322.4'2'0968–dc19   88-39946

        1   2   3   4   5   93   92   91   90   89

Typeset in Zimbabwe by Chrystal Graphics and printed in Britain.

To the youth of South Africa who, through their actions and thinking, are upholding the traditions of resistance narrated in this book.

The day will come when history will speak. But it will not be the history which will be taught in Brussels, Paris, Washington or the United Nations. It will be the history that will be taught in the countries which have won freedom from colonialism and its puppets. Africa will write its own history and in both north and south it will be a history of glory and dignity.

Patrice Lumumba

Contents

Preface

That there has always been a need for a book on the history of the ANC by an ANC member has long been recognized. This book is in partial fulfillment of that demand. This is not to suggest that there has been any paucity of books on the subject, but these have been mostly written by people looking in from the outside. Some of these authors have become experts on the subject, but one of the problems is that not all their theories are acceptable or friendly to us. This is a different book.

There are other reasons which led me to write this book. The innumerable discussions I held with the rank and file of the ANC on this topic led me to the inescapable, unavoidable and inevitable conclusion that one was needed. One of the young comrades once told me, "My life starts with the Soweto uprisings. What happened before that is a dark chapter to me." There was a need, I thought, to throw light on this dark chapter.

This brings me to the question of the methodology, sources and language in the book. I have attempted to show the roots of the ANC which run deep in the history of our people. There were problems which confronted me in this regard. The theme of the book is not the history of South African resistance, but the history of the ANC that is part of that resistance. But it is impossible to deal with the history of the ANC without dealing with the resistance prior to the formation of the ANC. Where does one start? How far can one deal with organizations which existed independently of the ANC? What about their impact and influence on the ANC and vice versa? Does this not detract ʿrom the main theme of the book? Connected with this was a problem of length. This explains why some incidents in the book are touched upon at times by way of passing reference. Indeed, in some cases this book takes the form of chapters in the history of the ANC. This was a difficult dilemma to solve.

I decided not to include coverage of early African resistance to colonial rule although this also needs to be written about. But one or two important points need to be said about this period. Above all, South Africa was not "discovered" by Jan van Riebeeck. Black people lived in the region long before Europe came to know about it. They resisted the imposition of colonial rule in many different ways, the first recorded war of resistance starting in May 1659, seven years after the occupation of the western Cape. But in the end the superior weaponry of the colonialists assured their dominance. Despite the valiant resistance of the indigenous people, by the 1880s practically all the independent African kingdoms had been conquered. This connects with another problem in South African historiography: did colonial wars result in racism or were they a product of racism? The interconnection between racism and colonialism is dealt with in this book. Whilst writing it I had in mind the Bulgarian saying, "The living close the eyes of the dead. The dead open the eyes of the living."

The chronology of the text was another problem. Although the chapters follow a strict chronology - by historical periods - within the chapters the chronology takes a different form. I have decided to deal with the epoch in each chapter by separating the events on a non-chronological basis, e.g. Africans, Indians, Coloureds, workers and so on within the epoch. The consequence of this is that the chronology shifts back from the end of the epoch to the beginning as each new category of events is dealt with. This approach or treatment of events might seem to obscure the broad sweep of historical events and developments which have their making among the categories of people and organizations at any one time, with each organization influencing and being influenced by others and its experiences rubbing off on, or being disregarded or overturned by others.

A history of a movement should take in account the interaction and inner relation of events which occur in parallel even if not in direct association. Some could argue that my approach might disrupt the patterns of assessment, remove events from their context, or allow societal factors to get lost. But in a book of this nature - a popular book - it is not easy to give a general picture of the growth, development and interaction of historical forces without losing some of the details which a non-historian might need. I decided to break periods and events down into thematic sections. There was also the need to prove historically the contribution of the Indian and Coloured communities to the history of the struggle. So as not to be misinterpreted, I am far from saying that the history of the liberation struggle in South Africa is a black man's history. A section of the white working class did play a role at the beginning of this century.

In this book I have attempted to explain where we come from as an introduction to the main theme which is the history and policy of the ANC and, what is more, our goal, perspective and future and consciousness. I did strive to destroy enemy values and ideology with the

PREFACE

aim of explaining the values of our ideology in a form acceptable and understandable to the people. After all, history and history-writing are not neutral but partisan and this explains why this book is, in the best sense of the term, less academic, less of a research work and more of a narrative, bearing in mind, of course, that being academic does not necessarily mean being scientific.

I have attempted to present the reader with ideas and reasons; I have attempted to formulate, explain and spread the ideas of the ANC - its teachings, theoretical propositions, political theories and lessons. I have attempted to inform, comment, evaluate and analyse the information that was available to me. In a sense, this book is also an attempt to transform theoretical knowledge into mass consciousness. My approach is influenced by and based on the conviction that history can only be relevant when it helps us to understand the present so as to master the future. There is a connection between the past, present and future, and the history of the ANC demonstrates that vividly.

Something should be said about the language in the book. To illustrate this let us take the 1969 Morogoro Conference of the ANC. I studied all the documents presented to and speeches made at the conference. This has been my approach through the book. That is why the language in the book is the language of the ANC. Some people may differ with me on this approach. It could be said that the arguments are then only self-serving justifications made by the actors themselves, not historical explanations of the processes that produced policies. Are the explanations of the actors acceptable, valid or are they not *post-facto* rationalizations? Is it not the task of a historian to interpret, instead of merely quoting the explanations of the motives given by the participants in events? A synthesis of the two approaches seemed to me the solution to avoid the problem of projecting a subjective or detached history of the ANC.

Although in this book I do not deal directly with enemy structures, philosophy, ideology and practical politics, I do deal with these questions in so far as they relate to and affect the liberation struggle. However, my approach is different from that of the idealists who maintain that racism is a "human feeling" which should be divorced from the politics and economics of apartheid. The ANC is not nebulous on the issue of racism. It analyses the economic roots of racism, its class character, its social effects and how to uproot it.

In this book I have paid attention to both the leaders of the ANC and the masses. This is because I believe any dichotomy between the leaders and the masses in the ANC is artificial. This is not to suggest

ix

that tensions and even conflicts between the two have not emerged in the past or present. But to denounce the founding fathers as "elitist" and "reformist" is tantamount to doing our history an injustice. Mokgethi Motlhabi in his book, *The Theory and Practice of Black Resistance to Apartheid,* goes so far as to maintain that the early ANC was;

> "a Congress of defeated people . . . Throughout the early years, therefore, the strategy of the ANC was based on beggar-tactics, making the early history of the movement that of obsequious representations and cap-in-hand deputations . . . Since 1882 until this time the Black struggle had . . . experienced nothing but failure in its aims. Yet the ANC had not once attempted to revise its approach.[1]

This is not how I understand the writing of history. Wishful thinking cannot replace the hard facts of life.

Those Africans who managed under difficult conditions to get a university (or any other form of) education were, and are, a pride to our people. By their very existence as a social stratum, without doing anything except working in their professional occupations, they helped to shatter the racist myth of the inherent or biological inferiority of Africans. Some went beyond that and formed the ANC and fought for the improvement of the lot of Africans. What I am saying is that there is no historical justification for an artificial demarcation between the ANC of today and the "early ANC". There was, and still is, development, change and continuity. To illustrate this point let me cite the example of the second ANC National Consultative Conference, held in Zambia in 1985. The doors of the ANC were opened to all South African revolutionaries irrespective of race, colour or creed. The ANC assumed the responsibility of being the leader not only of the Africans, but also of all forces in our society who are nationally oppressed, economically exploited and socially discriminated against. The question of national liberation and social emancipation of all South Africans, irrespective of race and colour became - in a quite clearer way than before - the two sides of the same coin. Thus, the ANC became a truly national liberation organization of all like-minded people - united in their hatred of colonialism, racism, exploitation and national degradation, sharing a common goal - and whose activities consist in propagating its ideas amongst the people and fighting in a constituency which it itself defines. President O.R. Tambo has been central in all these innovations and developments.

Talking about the contemporary history of the ANC, it is important to mention that there is a proliferation of theories which have nothing to do with reality. In his book, *Black Politics in South Africa Since 1945*, Tom Lodge talks of the "solidly middle class respectability of the Tambo leadership" and goes on to state (without providing any facts for his assertion) that "the current enthusiasm for the Freedom Charter" and the apparent downgrading of the more radical "Strategy and Tactics" adopted at Morogoro may also be indicative of a realistic perception of the danger of alienating the steadily growing black middle class."[2] While in this book I do not directly respond to all these theories (although in some cases I do) I have attempted to stick to one goal - putting the record straight.

This brings me to the question of the Pan African Congress (PAC). Does the story of the PAC belong to the history of the ANC? Yes, because it shows the contradications inherent in African nationalism. No, because its emergence was against the laws of social development which reflected themselves in the history of the ANC. I could not deal with this phenomenon at length, as it would only help to disrupt the flow of the narrative and detract from the main issue without contributing anything. In practical politics the ANC is becoming tired of carrying the PAC on its back, more so because it is said dead wood is very heavy. I see no reason in carrying that weight in this book.

The undocumented nature of this history in the post-1960 period is explained by the illegality of the ANC. This might give a false impression that at this time legal work was more substantial and had greater popular response and appeal than illegal work. This seems to reinforce and emphasize the relatively widespread belief in the ANC that the history of our struggle will be written at home. There is no reason to query that. We must liberate our country so that we can write our history. But this does not mean that we should "wait" for liberation before we start writing that history. Our endeavours today can only be a pointer - or a little more than that - to what has to be done. There are a number of grey areas in the research on the history of the ANC. We, ourselves are not unanimous on these questions, and I believe they will only finally be resolved when we write our history in a free and liberated South Africa. But we must start now. This book serves to do just that.

This book was written in the midst of a busy schedule. Our priority and preoccupation is the struggle for the liberation of our people and although writing this book is part of that struggle, it was definitely not my priority. I hope this book will help stimulate (or be part of the ongoing) debate and discussion.

I have said that the language used in this book is that of the ANC. But terminology which today is no longer acceptable or in use is also to be found in this book, either in quoted speeches or in articles or books of the time. I could do nothing about that. From 1912 to 1925 the ANC called itself the South African Native National Congress. But in this book I have consistently used the designation African National Congress. This is not a matter of political or policy decision - it is merely a question of convenience.

Hilary Rabkin, Beryl Baker and Jackie Hoogendyk typed the manuscript, while the comments made by Jack Simons were very valuable. Lionel "Rusty" Bernstein, Pallo Jordan and Jane Katjavivi, in different ways, contributed to the final shape of the book. There are other comrades who also helped me with their criticisms of and comments on the manuscript. But this is my book. It is not an "official history" of the ANC and definitely not the last word on the subject. This is not because I have any reason to think that the ANC will or might disown any of my views. I just want to emphasize that the opinions in this book are those of the author, not of the ANC. It is true that I, myself, am a product of the ANC and I have learnt a lot from my comrades in the ANC, but these are my ideas. It is important to emphasize this because some of my comrades will differ with me on a number of questions, including points of emphasis. But that is natural.

The idea of publishing this book in Zimbabwe was incidental. In general terms one can say the victory of the Zimbabwean people's struggle in 1980 made this possible, and in that broad sense this book is a product of the struggles of the people of Southern Africa: it is part of their struggles; it tells their story - a painful but inspiring story.

Whilst I was writing this book I kept on thinking about my family - whom I left in 1963 - especially my late brother, Mbuyiselo, and my sister, Vuyiswa, whom we called "Nokri" - whose sacrifices in sending me to school laid a basis for the ultimate writing of this book.

To all I say, "Thank you. Ningadinwa na ngomso - I will expect you to do the same tomorrow."

Francis Meli
London

A Note on Class and Colour in South Africa

The Dutch East India Company, founded in 1602, was largely responsible for making the Netherlands one of Europe's leading mercantile nations in the post-Renaissance period. During the 1600s, the Dutch merchants drove the Portuguese first out of the Indonesian archipelago in a number of fierce sea battles, gaining control over these waters by 1641. By dint of their naval power and the unbridled corruption of local officials, they soon gained a foothold in Malaya and later Ceylon (now Sri Lanka) "at the expense of the Portuguese". They suppressed the indigenous spice traders of the East and seized control of all Indonesian external trade.

Indonesian opposition to the Dutch centred on the Sultanate of Bantam, the largest on the island of Java. Under the leadership of an Islamic scholar and mystic, Sheik Yusuf, who was employed as a grand vizier and tutor in the royal court of Bantam, the patriots of Bantam began a war of resistance to Dutch colonialism in 1650. They succeeded in driving the Dutch merchants out of their ports and were gradually re-establishing control over their oil trade routes when the Dutch merchants began a concerted campaign to isolate Bantam from her neighbours. By picking off the sultanates one by one, the Dutch built up a formidable alliance of puppet states. By 1680, they felt strong enough to try and impose dependence on Bantam. Rather than accept the Dutch terms Sheik Yusuf, with a number of Bantam patriots, took to the hills and waged a guerrilla struggle against the Dutch puppet placed on the throne of Bantam. Three years of bitter fighting ensued until the Dutch managed to trick Sheik Yusuf into coming down from the hills to discuss peace terms. He was arrested on 14 December, 1683 and taken to Batavia, the Dutch stronghold in Indonesia, whence he was transported first to Ceylon, then to the Cape Province in South Africa as a prisoner of the Dutch. His followers were rounded up and shipped to the Cape Province as slaves. Their descendants formed the core of what later became known as the Cape Malay community.

The defeat of the Indonesian resistance fighters placed the Netherlands in undisputed control over trade between Europe and the Far East. The Cape acquired its strategic importance for the Dutch East India Company in this context. Van Riebeeck's task was both to establish a refreshment station and to secure the entrance to the Indian Ocean against foreign competitors. As in other colonies, the Dutch East India Company practised the mercantile system in its relations with the colonists at the Cape. The settlers were forbidden to engage in any form of local manufacturing, on the economic principle that such manufacturers would compete with the Netherlands' emergent factories. In 1657 the Netherlands released some of its servants in the Cape to become "free burghers", market gardeners, to supply its ships with fresh meat and vegetables. To work the settlers' farms, slaves were imported in 1658. The first slaves came from Madagascar (now Malagasy), Mozambique, Angola and Ceylon. Later, Indonesian prisoners of war were sold into slavery at the Cape. Slave labourers performed most of the menial and hard work in the Cape Colony until slavery was abolished by the British in 1834. They were the domestic workers in the settler homes, the agricultural workers who tilled the soil, the stevedores who handled the cargoes in the harbour; some were seamstresses, artisans and skilled craftsmen. By the end of the seventeenth century, South African colonial society in the western Cape looked something like this:

- The top layer was a small class of rich white landowners, who ran the farms that produced for the export market. Amongst them could be found all the leading officials of the Dutch East India Company who used their positions to seize the best farmlands and enrich themselves.
- On the tier below them were the urban "free burghers", usually absentee landowners, who preferred to live in towns where they ran inns, guest houses and taverns to service passing sailors.
- Beneath them were the "boeren", or farmers, struggling with a few slaves to make ends meet on the inhospitable sandy soil.
- Below them were the so-called "knechts", made up of retired sailors, soldiers and artisans. They worked for wages as overseers and slave drivers on the farms of the rich landowners.
- The whole structure was held up by the labour of slaves, who did most of the productive work in the colony and constituted the lowest rung of the Cape colonial society. Side by side with the slaves were the growing number of labour tenants, the indigenous Khoi-Khoi, nominally free, but held in bondage by hunger and terror. As a general rule, all the blacks in the colony were either slaves or labour tenants, and practically all the whites were freemen.

These are the roots of class and colour in South Africa, something which left an indelible imprint on the future of the country under white rule.

The slaves of the Cape Dutch colony could be classed in two basic categories: those owned by the Dutch East India Company and those owned by private individuals. Company slaves were invariably the most exploited. They worked as stevedores, millers and agricultural workers on the Dutch East India Company's property, and were often hired out to private individuals for a fee. Privately owned slaves could be found working as cooks, nannies, carpenters, agricultural workers, fishermen and sometimes even as entertainers in the homes of rich whites. To keep the slaves under their control the slave owners encouraged distinctions based on racial origin. Asian slaves were favoured as domestics and artisans, while arduous work was the province of the African slaves.

The Cape, however, did not prove a very profitable venture for the Dutch East India Company - compared with the Far East, the pickings were slender indeed. Unlike the American and Caribbean colonies, the Cape never became the home of the lucrative plantation economies. With the slow but steady growth of their community, white settlers began to evolve interests apart from those of the Dutch East India Company. They clamoured against the restrictions imposed on their trading activities and engaged in incessant smuggling to bypass these regulations. The conflict reached its climax on the eve of the first British occupation of 1795, when two inland settlements, Swellendam and Graaff Reinet, seceded from the Netherlands. The rebellion was quickly crushed by the British in the following year.

British occupation of the Cape reflected the change in fortunes of the European maritime states. Britain had overtaken the Netherlands as the leading trading nation and was already well on her way to becoming "the workshop of the world". Factory-based production with power-driven machines had replaced the small workshops of the earlier era. The Netherlands was beginning to decline and the Dutch East India Company itself went bankrupt four years later. British occupation broke the "stifling stranglehold" of Dutch mercantilism on the Cape, opening up the territory for further "economic development".

The first British occupation found the western Cape a "cosmopolitan society", drawing its population from various parts of Africa, Asia and Europe. Slavery was the dominant mode of production in and around Table Bay. The Cape Colony produced wheat, mutton, wine and vegetables for export, but depended on Europe for all its manufactured goods including "necessities of frontier life" such as gunpowder, iron and steel products, textiles and luxury goods. Its main asset was the technological achievement of Europe, whose outpost on the southern tip of Africa it was.

Cape colonial society was also riven with internal conflicts arising from its inequitable nature. The dominant strand of internal conflict was that between the slaves and the slave owners. Contrary to the myth of an idyllic paternalism propagated by the apologists of the system, slavery at the Cape was characterized by the grossest forms of brutality and intense class conflicts. As a form of undisguised exploitation, slavery could only be maintained by force. Tortures such as flogging, branding, mutilation and the thumbscrew were common forms of enforcement. In extreme cases, death by breaking on the wheel, flogging, hanging or immolation were not unknown.

The slaves, in turn, fought back with everything at their disposal. One of the forms of resistance was escape or fleeing: the slaves, collectively or individually tried to break out of the system by escaping and/or returning to their homelands. Escape plots were common amongst the newly landed slaves and were characteristic of the early days of slavery at the Cape. Most of the recorded cases refer to the 1770s. The Khoi-Khoi living "beyond the boundaries" of the colony received escapees, as did the westward Xhosa. Hundreds of escaped slaves swelled the ranks of the Griqua and Koranna in the north-western Cape, bringing to their host communities the skills they had mastered during servitude. The slaves also resorted to individual attacks by way of reprisal for brutality. Acts of sabotage and arson were not infrequent means of hitting back at the perpetrators of their misery.

Radical forms of resistance only began to emerge towards the last days of slavery at the Cape. This was the time when anti-slavery agitation in Britain and other slave-holding countries became more vocal. News of the successful slave revolt in Haiti in 1804 also reached the stevedores at the harbour.

When the slave trade was abolished in the British empire in 1834, everyone knew that the abolition of slavery itself was imminent. Slave revolts took place but they were doomed to failure. Slavery was finally abolished in 1834 by an Act of the British Parliament. The terms under which it took place favoured the slave owners, all of whom received compensation for the loss of their property. The slaves, who had fed, clothed and sustained these drones were condemned to two years of "apprenticeship" after abolition, so that slave owners could adjust to the change.

Britain had "returned the Cape to the Dutch" in 1803, then retaken it three years later. Before the second British occupation, the "cosmopolitan society" that had grown up in the Cape had been "pressed into a common mould" by the religious and political intolerance of the Dutch East India Company. Non-Dutch settlers had been forced to abandon their own languages and culture and a large measure of social uniformity had been imposed on the white community by the church and state. The slaves and the Khoi-Khoi had their distinctive cultures crushed and were adopting the local creolized Dutch (later known as Afrikaans) as their language. Culturally, the Cape Colony was a backwater, with no newspaper, a small but little-used library and a few church schools run by the Dutch Reformed Church. These schools did little more than prepare children for confirmation. The pastimes of the settlers were card-playing, hunting and dancing. Until this time the Dutch produced no poetry, no music, no drama. The only art form that thrived was architecture.

British domination catalysed a number of socio-cultural changes. The absolution of the mercantile system and the introduction of the high wool-bearing Merino sheep helped change the economic fortunes of the Cape. The growth of wool farming and the wool trade provided the stimulus for the development of a finance market, so that by 1831 a number of small local banks had been set up. In 1861 they were unified under the rubric of the Standard Bank of South Africa, with 29 district branches directly linked to the finance capital of the world, London. In the port cities, Cape Town and Port Elizabeth, small pockets of local industry were beginning to emerge.

From amongst the 1820 British settlers, a handful of talented men like Thomas Pringle started the first newspaper, laying the basis for a tradition of South African journalism. It is from this community that the first seeds of liberalism germinated.

Above all, however, the British colonial state in South Africa was used as the battering ram of the process of primitive capital accumulation. It systematically seized African land and turned the erstwhile peasants into a readily exploitable landless proleteriat for the benefit of the settler farmers. Legislation, like the Caledon Code of 1809, press-ganged the nominally free Khoi-Khoi into the service of the settler farmers and Ordinance 49 of 1828 extended the same provisions to the Africans. Taxation, restrictions of free movement and traders collaborated, often unconsciously, to undermine the economic base of African society.

Along the frontiers between black and white, a multifaceted process of "interaction" unfolded, involving commerce, labour and a large measure of cultural interplay. Despite its own limitations, the settler colony was part of a vigorous empire in the ascendant. Its onslaught against African society was total and many-pronged. Each prong reinforced the others.

The African societies, in contrast - the Xhosa, Zulu, Tswana, Sotho, Pedi, Shangaan, Venda, Ndebele, San and Khoi suffered under a number of grave disadvantages. They were technologically unsophisticated and this held up the pace of internal change at a time when Europe was plunging headlong into the machine age. African kingdoms were virtually self-contained units, offering few opportunities for wider co-operation and co-ordinated defence. This enabled the colonialists to deal with each unit on a piecemeal basis. The technical superiority of the settler community was its advantage. They could produce faster and more abundantly. Africans were forced to turn to European traders to meet their needs, in the process marginalizing their own crafts and skills by disuse, which resulted in the dislocation of the traditional equilibrium between agriculture and crafts.

The missionary and the trader were the principle agents of these transformations. However, the Africans' need to adapt to the European presence was no less important a factor. As the process continued, previously homogeneous communities became divided, undermining the cohesion of African society. The interplay of these factors rendered African societies more vulnerable to the disintegrative forces of colonialism. Military force, applied as an ultimate sanction, pauperized them by the seizure of the basic form of productive property - the land.

British colonialism gradually prepared the social and economic conditions for the windfall of 1866 - the discovery of diamonds near Kimberley. The opening of the mines, first at Kimberley in 1867, then the gold mines on the Witwatersrand in 1885, marked the watershed of South African economic development. It firmly implanted the capitalist mode of production in our country, for the first time involving large numbers of the indigenous people in the modern economy. The massive importation of capital, capital goods and skilled immigrants, dramatically changed the demographic configuration of the country and catapulted South Africa into the centre of inter-imperialist rivalry. Taxation, the means traditionally used by the colonial state to prize the African peasant from the land, was streamlined.

It was the economic and cultural interaction between black and white, which took place along the frontiers, that led to the steady integration of the Africans into the settler-controlled modern economy. Conquest speeded up the process by imposing taxes that induced African peasants to become involved in the cash economy. In and around the mission stations another form of integration was unfolding With encouragement from Sir George Grey, the missionaries had expanded their operations by building schools where African converts learnt and mastered European agricultural techniques, skills and literacy. From among these converts emerged a stratum of landowning African farmers, living outside the traditional societies. This Westernized elite, "the school people", was distinct and distinguishable from the "unschooled" Africans. Producing for their own consumption and selling their surplus on the market, these farmers were both highly productive and efficient. In Natal, groups of African converts sometimes clubbed together to buy or lease land which they farmed co-operatively. Even in the Boer Republics of the Transvaal and the Orange Free State they turned the squatter system practised by the Boers to their advantage. It is from amongst this group that the first sprinkling of African professionals and intellectuals came.

But it was the mining revolution which drew Africans into the modern economy. Before 1870, what was to become the city of Kimberley was practically bare veld. By the following year, its population, housed in tents, shanties and other rudimentary shelters, had risen to 50 000. Africans came from the area now forming South Africa as well as from beyond. In 1873, the Cape and Natal governments were able to raise capital to begin railway construction, connecting Wellington (the railhead of the Cape at the time), Durban, East London and Port

Elizabeth with the diamond fields. Smaller concentrations of Africans also began appearing at the port cities and on railway construction sites. Captured African resisters, convicts and workmen built the breakwater at Cape Town harbour, cut the passes that connected Wellington to the Karoo and helped build the line between East London and Queenstown. Kimberley, however, had the largest concentration of Africans so integrated. The urban areas became the fastest growing centres of African proleterianization and were to become the most decisive as industrialization developed.

At the end of the century, South Africa went through the Anglo-Boer War (1899-1902), a war which has been dubbed an "anti-imperalist struggle" but was so "only in an extremely technical and qualified sense" because for the Africans in the Transvaal:

> The characterisation of Kruger's campaign as a progressive anti-colonial war must have sounded very odd indeed, for they were living in a semi-feudal state whose rigidly enforced constitution, after acknowledging its authority from the Almighty (who is also, by the way, the acknowledged inspirer of the current South African Act) proclaimed that there shall be no equality between black and white in church and state.[1]

The Anglo-Boer War ended in the imposition of British domination over the whole of South Africa. In many respects, the war was a political act waged to bring the political institutions into line with the economic realities of domination by British mining and finance capital. The terms agreed at Vereeniging in 1902 opened the way to a rapprochement between Boer and Briton on the basis of common interest in the super-exploitation of black labour. This reconciliation was given palpable expression in the R3 million pledge towards the rehabilitation of the former Boer Republics.

On of the unintended side-effects of the Anglo-Boer War had been the closure of the mines and the consequent dispersal of the African mine workers. The mining companies clamoured for more workers but were unable to attract them because of the low wages paid. As a result indentured Chinese labourers were recruited from Hong Kong in 1903, to fill the gap left by insufficient African labour recruits. More "efficient" means had been devised to "free" African peasants from the soil. It was in part to meet this crisis that the new tax was instituted in 1905.

Before the colonialists came to our country, our people were already evolving a civilization which was defying tribal exclusiveness. The common territory occupied was determining common loyalty. This process is more noticeable among the Zulu and Sotho people. There was intermarriage, trade and contact. This is not to suggest that there were no conflicts, succession disputes or that "blood relations" had completely disappeared. But there was a process in motion.

The invasion of our country by the colonialists set the clock back. The real problem that confronted our people was that two different and antagonistic social systems confronted each other: there was the emergent capitalist system (colonialism) on the one hand, and the pre-capitalist African societies on the other. But it should be said that the Africans who resisted colonialism were not fighting for the preservation of the already crumbling tribal system. They were fighting for the defence of hard-earned achievements of our people. Indeed, Africans were forward-looking because they fought for a noble cause: namely, that technical superiority should not be misused for the exploitation of people and their destruction, but should be used for human progress.

Colonialism committed many crimes in South Africa. The colonialists' search for land, cattle, raw materials, markets and labour power (which they now monopolize) led them to commit (and they are still committing) almost irreparable damage and unpardonable crimes against our people. The genocidal wars that they waged destroyed productive forces, including innumerable human lives, smashed flourishing social systems, ruined material and spiritual cultures and crushed the self-confidence of the African people in South Africa and their philosophy of life. They obliterated the nascent will and embryonic national consciousness of the people; they introduced new ways of thinking, alien norms of behaviour and foreign cultural values. The aim was simple: to inculcate among the African people a feeling of inferiority towards and rejection of their own heritage and potential. In their devastating wars the colonialists demolished everything and left nothing but ruins.

In the process of mental enslavement, the missionaries played a significant part. They introduced formal education, a missionary undertaking whose aim was the evangelization of our people. The African had to read the Bible, even memorize it, but not interpret it. Education in these institutions was bookish in the extreme. Again the aim was simple: the ideological and political centre was to be the church rather than African institutions. At the turn of the century, there was "dual power" in the rural areas of South Africa - the power of the chiefs and that of the church. There were also other forces, such as the trader, the colonial government and white community, which militated against African resistance.

The progressive African chiefs who then opposed colonialism were the respected and recognized spokesmen and leaders of their people. They were freedom fighters and did not permit themselves to be absorbed by the colonial administration, as our present-day chiefs have done.

This brings me to another specificity of South African reality. Colonialism and capitalism in South Africa had a strange marriage. Capitalism in South Africa, like in all colonies, was not a result of internal developments or a bourgeois revolution against feudalism, as was the case in Europe. This explains its deformity and distortion. This explains the peculiar nature of colonialism in South Africa. The liberation movement calls it colonialism of a special type. In 1910, when white South Africa became independent of Britain, the colonial power was no longer based in London but in Pretoria. This explains why our struggle is different from other struggles which were conducted on the continent. It also explains the different context of the struggle of the Namibian people who are fighting against a colonial power which is across the border.

*Josiah T. Gumede,
ANC President-General,
in the Soviet Union
December 1927*

*Josiah T. Gumede at Congress against
Colonial Oppression and
Imperialism Brussels 1927*

The Revd J.L. Dube,
first President of the ANC

Sol Plaatje,
first Secretary-General
of the ANC

ANC delegation to London, 1914, (from left to right): Dr W. Rubusana, T. Mapikela, the Revd J.L. Dube, S. Msane and Sol Plaatje

*Walter Sisulu
burning his pass*

*Dr Dadoo,
President of the
SA Indian Congress,
with Dr Moroka,
President
of the ANC, 1952*

Oliver Tambo and Nelson Mandela, Addis Ababa, 1962

The peasants' revolt, Pondoland, 1960

bert Resha, Nelson Mandela and Houari Boumedienne, Algiers, 1962

James la Guma

A spirited UDF meeting

Youths demonstrate at the execution of ANC combatants

Lilian Ngoyi

Beyers Naude

Oliver Tambo

Alfred Nzo

Resettlement at Katlehong

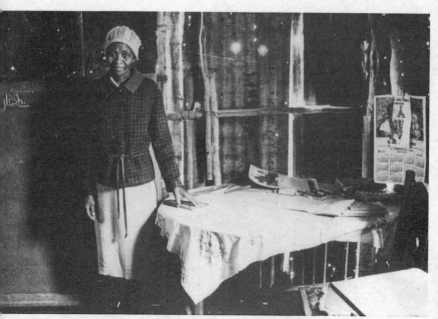

The teacher at Rooigrond Resettlement Area School

1
Sources of Inspiration

Towards the end of the nineteenth century, new social forces began to emerge in South Africa. These were African ministers of religion, school teachers, magistrates' clerks, interpreters, small traders, peasants, farmers and workers. Together with some of the traditional rulers - the chiefs - they opened up a new chapter in South African history.

The social structure of African society was by this time changing, and this had repercussions on traditional forms of organization, thinking and ideology. This was a period of widespread political expectation. An African nationalism which cut across (but did not replace) ethnic identity began to emerge. "Tribal" organization of society was being undermined and weakened by colonialism and new movements which were uniting the people began to emerge.

An examination of this period shows quite clearly that the history of South Africa developed unevenly. But one theme was common: the will to survive and defeat the forces of colonialism. This was the root of African nationalism. It was expressed and reflected in the thinking, philosophies, political behaviour and teachings of individuals, and I shall look at some examples of these individuals in their historical context. My concern, however, is not so much the biographical data - important as that is - but the social forces that made these individuals act in the way they did.

The emergence of the African working class

The discovery of diamonds and gold in the last third of the nineteenth century was a significant event which led to the emergence of a new social force in African society - the working class.

Africans had been "living and working in Cape Town as early as the 1830s" [1], and from the 1850s, there were Africans employed in road-making and on the harbours in the Cape. But the discovery of diamonds in 1867 transformed Kimberley into a burgeoning mine. Then in 1886 gold was discovered on the Witwatersrand. There emerged an environment in which, during subsequent years, African nationalism was to grow most rapidly. The new mining and later industrial sites drew in migrant peasants and held them as urban proletarians. This coming together of people from different ethnic backgrounds into a single black brotherhood was a new phenomenon, as Lionel Forman remarks:

> Here was the nucleus of a true African proletariat, whose future would be in the cities, and whose only way of keeping lawfully alive would be by the sale of its labour. Here was the nucleus of a new class, whose ties with the tribal society would become of the very slenderest; whose economic - and inevitably political - weapon would be that of the workers of all lands, the strike. [2]

Though by 1872, according to a contemporary press report, there were already an estimated 20 000 African workers at Kimberley, the operative word was "nucleus." These workers were able, even at that early stage, to regard themselves not so much as Zulu, Xhosa, Sotho, Tswana and so on but as Africans. This does not mean that the ethnic element disappeared or was forgotten. But it does mean that it was of secondary importance; these men saw themselves as drawn into a single fraternity by their economic interest and this led to a consciousness that all Africans had a common political destiny. This was a prerequisite for an all-embracing African nationalism. It was due to the fact that the emergence of the African working class in South Africa tended to enhance not so much class as national consciousness; the economic grievances that might have led to class struggles, including trade-union action, produced instead a strong current of national feeling among Africans. [3]

But the weapon of the working class - the strike - soon became their form of struggle:

> It is remarkable how soon these men were using the universal weapon of the working class - the strike. In December 1882, before there is any record of a strike by white workers in South Africa, one hundred Africans at a Kimberley mine stopped work for two days and brought the mine to a halt, when wages were reduced from 25s to 20s per week . . . By 1884 there were at Kimberley no fewer than four different Non-European Benefit Societies, the predecessors of a trade union movement. [4]

Some of these workers did not come to Kimberley because of starvation or the oppressive colonial system. They had other motives. Gwayi Tyamzashe, a Lovedale graduate, who in 1873 became the first African to complete theological studies in South Africa, came to Kimberley to preach the gospel to the diamond diggers in 1872, and became a writer. An eye-witness also reported that:

Those coming from far up in the interior come with the sole purpose of securing guns. [They stay] no longer here than is necessary to get some £6 or £7 for the guns. Hence you will see hundreds of them leaving the fields and as many arriving from the North almost every day. [5]

In other words, coming to work on the diamond fields was also regarded as a means to pursue the anti-colonial armed resistance in defence of land, cattle and independence.

The process of proletarianization of Africans was also conditioned by essentially coercive or extra-economic factors; the continued existence of the pre-capitalist sector; and the institutionalization of migrant labour, low wages and many other disabilities. The Africans' position was determined by the profit motive of the mining capitalists and also by the greed of white miners. Two main extra-economic methods, namely, the legislative power of the state and the monopolistic recruiting organizations, were employed to ensure the exploitation of minerals by cheap African labour. The tax and pass laws brought African labour to the mines and controlled it once it was there. The pass laws were introduced under direct pressure from the Chamber of Mines in 1896. They stipulated, among other things, that African miners must wear a metal plate or a "badge" on the arm. This system was later amended and Africans were made to carry passes, documents used to control their movements and where they could live and work.

The Glen Grey Act was another instrument in this process of enslavement. It introduced a tax which, in the words of the mineowner, Cape politician and arch-imperialist, Cecil Rhodes, "removed Natives from the life of sloth and laziness, teaching them the dignity of labour, and made them contribute to the prosperity of the state and made them give some return for our wise and good government." [6]

In the 1890s a powerful and well-organized white capitalist class emerged with ownership of gold and diamond mines in the hands of a few groups of capitalists. Control was centralized. Not only that, it was consolidated by the establishment of the Chamber of Mines in 1887 and two recruiting organizations: the Native Recruiting Corporation, which recruited labour from within South Africa, Bechuanaland (now Botswana), Basutoland (now Lesotho) and Swaziland; and the Witwatersrand Native Labour Association (WNLA) which recruited elsewhere in Africa. [7]

This institutionalized migrant labour ensured a cheap, rightless, voteless and unorganized labour force. It became a justification for pathetically low wages; it hindered the class mobilization of African migrants and especially, the emergence of trade unions; it prevented

3

the workers from developing skills in the performance and control of their work and inhibited the effective formation of a class of African workers.

But the situation was not completely bleak: the young African workers developed initiatives and actions that were suited to the environment and their situation as migrants. In the period 1901-02, there were strikes and what they called "desertions" (on a mass scale) at the Consolidated Main Reef, Geldenhuis, Langlaagte, and Durban Roodepoort Mines as well as at the Vereeniging Coal Mines. It is important to state that the term desertion as applied by the management had negative overtones in that it implied a dereliction of duty. It was part of the management's excuse to avoid any critical examination of the conditions of employment and reasons which caused workers to leave in large numbers and it justified the use of every possible punitive measure against workers. [8]

The problems that faced the African miners were made even worse by the Anglo-Boer War. During this war, 20 000 or more workers were commandeered by the Boer governments of the Transvaal and Orange Free State, either to work without pay for the Boer commandos or in other occupations related to the war effort. [9] Wages were reduced by the Chamber of Mines from 50 shillings, (their level before the Anglo-Boer War) to 30-35 shillings per month. By 1900 a maximum monthly wage of only 20 shillings was introduced. Not only that, a curfew was put into operation: all assemblies of Africans were prohibited; frequent police raids were made into the compounds where workers had to live, to maintain control "over the labour force and to discourage any protests by workers".

Hardships accumulated: 8 000 African workers were conscripted to build a new railway for transporting coal along the Witwatersrand Gold Reef at 10 pence, that is less than a shilling a day; 4 000 men were drafted to form a cheap labour force for the army in the war and the rest were retained by the mines for maintenance work at one shilling a day. Martial-law restrictions were placed on the movement of Africans. It was impossible to return home; they were therefore compelled to remain on the mines long after their contracts had expired.

In addition, working in the mines could, literally, be deadly. The death rate rose steeply from 92 in May 1902 to 247 in November of the same year. Between these months the average monthly death rate per thousand workers was 48,5 and in July 1903, it had reached 112,54. [10] That is why it was important for miners to choose a workplace where conditions were relatively better. "In an environment where death rates were sometimes one in ten, the choice of mine could be a matter of life or death." [11]

Moreover, even before they started work, the miners often arrived in a poor physical state, having travelled long distances on foot or in closed railway coaches with no sanitary facilities - classified as goods rather than passengers. One in eight recruits was found physically unfit to begin work.

It was under these conditions that protests by black workers took place. There were many forms of protest, including refusing to begin work on arrival at the mines, which was, in itself, a means of expressing dissatisfaction with the rates of pay and conditions of work. Another major grievance was that the recruiting agencies often brought the miners to work under false pretences. Even the chiefs were involved at times on the side of the people:

> As early as 8 January [1902], Asaph Moruthani, the secretary to the Pedi Chief, Sekukuni II, who had been sent to accompany the work party to the gold fields and report on their conditions of service, complained that the men had been deceived concerning their ultimate destination. Sekukuni had originally refused to supply workers to private industry, but on the assurance of the local administration that the men were required for government work, he had permitted them to leave.[12]

The workers also demanded equal remuneration and the right to look for work instead of working for a contractor. Compound managers turned workers' discontent into open anger. They rejected out of hand applications by workers for temporary passes to leave the compound, even to visit a store situated within a few hundred metres of the mine - a store with food supplies that were vital for supplementing their diet. Another complaint was ill-treatment: miners were thrashed in the compound and down the mine with a cat-o'-nine tails. They were thrashed on the testicles, and shut up like dogs. Complaints were made to the magistrates about "ill treatment at the hands of the resident engineer who, they reported, regularly sjambokked workers and had them thrown among burning embers."[13]

In 1905 alone, more than 3 585 complaints were made at pass offices along the Gold Reef. These had some measure of success, for example in recovering wages due to workers, correcting some abuses and settling cases of contracts being "extended" without permission of the workers. The courts proved, however, to be lenient towards any white miners convicted of assaulting black ones - a clear example of the state's collaborative violence against black miners.

The group withdrawal of labour - so-called "desertion" - was another form of struggle. Miners would break down the gates of the compounds, some carrying knobkerries, bottles and stones, and would march to town to lay their grievances before the magistrate. At times this included demanding the dismissal of the compound manager.

Initial resistance was often started by potential recruits in the rural areas. The workers either developed their own routes to the Gold Reef avoiding the WNLA tentacles, or would make use of the system. They would take advantage of the facilities and transport provided by labour agents, study the complicated pass system and even forge passes or buy forged ones, and would then leave the mines to look for work in towns. In 1907, the Chairman of Rand Mines described the miners' form of strike as follows:

> The native method of striking is very simple. It must be remembered that he is not a permanent workman. He is always going home, and if he is not satisfied with the conditions of employment, he simply does not come out again. The conditions of South Africa make it perfectly possible for him to do this.[14]

These strikes and acts of protest were not only confined to the mining industry. Nevertheless, they were small in scale, took place at different times, in a variety of districts, and were not co-ordinated. Their significance lies in the fact that they were the earliest organized protests by black workers, the first generation of black wage-earners.

What about working-class consciousness at this stage? The characteristic feature of these strikes, walk-outs and withdrawals of labour was that they involved workers from different ethnic groups who confronted the mineowners and administration separately and at different times. Ethnicity did play a role; it was both a divisive and binding force in the protests. Groups of migrant workers originating from a particular area or ethnic group would often withdraw their labour at a particular time. But this should not be misconstrued to mean that "consciousness" had not yet begun to transcend ethnic divisions. It does mean that class consciousness was not seen as a rejection of ethnicity.

The association of resistance with ethnic identity rather than overall worker consciousness testifies to the fact that then the migrant was not a fully fledged worker but a worker-in-the-making. In these circumstances workers would form groups, usually ethnically based, in their compounds to protect themselves from the compound police, possibly from other groups and most of all from the coercive measures of management. These groups provided a measure of security for individual members faced with the daily struggle for survival in the compound and underground. It is true that the management enforced "tribalism" in a variety of ways by dividing workers along ethnic lines, but this tended to cohesion and invigorated worker solidarity, defence and resistance: "Many of the work stoppages or strikes on the Reef in the early part of the decade appeared to coalesce along ethnic lines."[15] This development of ethnic solidarity should, however, be viewed as a

6

particular form of response rather than a transference of tribal values.

Though these work stoppages, confrontations and worker actions during the first decade of the twentieth century were limited in scope and number, they did indicate the potential that existed for the articulation of worker grievances and the organization of effective resistance. There is clear evidence of an emerging and growing working-class consciousness. African miners were far from being passive; they were quick to identify the strengths and weaknesses of the exploitative system to which they were exposed and to adjust their actions accordingly. Within the confines of a highly repressive system, African miners made a positive attempt to alleviate their lot and to minimize their oppression.

Religious influences: the early Christian converts and independent churches

The introduction of Christianity in South Africa was a complicated process which affected many aspects of African society. In analysing this process we shall have to start with the early beginnings, before Christianity took on a mass character in South Africa; before Africans formed their own independent churches with new concepts and values.

In September 1799, when the Revd Johannes Theodosius van der Kemp, from the London Missionary Society, arrived on the banks of Keiskamahoek River in the Cape his mission was clear: to evangelize the Africans. We should remember that this was a period of tense conflict and bloody wars between the colonialists and the indigenous African population. In 1811 Dr van der Kemp was succeeded by the Revd James Read. His first African convert was Ntsikana, son of Gaba, who was converted "some time in 1815".[16] This brought Ntsikana into conflict with some of his contemporaries, notably Makhanda (or Nxele, the Left-Handed as he was popularly known) whose religion was based more on African concepts of the spirits and was geared towards confrontation with colonialism rather than reconciliation. But the real significance of Ntsikana's conversion lies in the fact that it was the beginning of colonial cultural aggression. The Christian missions saw their role as part of the "civilizing process" of European domination and preached an acceptance of colonialism. Nevertheless, though Ntsikana accepted Christianity, he foresaw the damage it might do to African societies, and warned people of this. That was his prophecy, his greatness, for which he will ever be remembered by the African people.

7

John Knox Bokwe, has written that old Soga, the father of Tiyo Soga, was the first to embrace Ntsikana's new teaching and to accept Christianity.[17] According to Bokwe, Soga's family and relatives formed the first nucleus of a Christian congregation when European missionaries arrived to settle at the Emgwali (Stutterheim) mission station, from where they spread out to form other stations.

Tiyo Soga (1829-71) died at an early age. But his short life was full of incidents and rich in experience. He was the first ordained African minister of the United Presbyterian Church in Scotland where he studied, in 1856. The problem, according to his biographer, was that he was a "victim of cultural conquest":[18] he was attached to royalty, especially British royalty. Tiyo Soga

> was always loyal to authority, even colonial authority, which he saw as a means of disseminating Christianity and civilization among the blacks. This subservience to authority, so noticeable in his negotiations with government about the establishment of the mission station at Mgwali, was partly attributable to his Calvinistic background.[19]

This put him in a very difficult position, between the missionaries who were generally opposed by the Africans because they were regarded as agents of the colonial government, and the rest of the Africans - his people.

But this was only one aspect of Tiyo Soga's character. He was also a prolific writer of hymns and articles in newspapers, and a translator of books into Xhosa. Tiyo Soga was Africa-conscious - proud of the continent and people of Africa - and, at the same time, black-conscious. This was partly due to the fact that he himself experienced racism in South Africa and Scotland (where he studied) and, to make things worse, he married a Scotswoman. This is why he told his sons:

> You will ever cherish the memory of your mother as that of an upright conscientious thrifty Christian Scotswoman. You will ever be thankful for your connection by this tie to the white race. But if you do not wish to feel the taunt of men, which you sometimes may well feel - take your place in the world as coloured, not as white men; as Kafirs, not as Englishmen . . . For your own sakes, never appear ashamed that your father was a Kafir, and that you inherit some African blood.[20]

Soga's words were taken heed of by his sons, but in fairness to Tiyo Soga, we must point out that the word "Kafir" or "Kaffir", which is of non-African origin, did not have the derogatory connotation attached to it today. All the same, Tiyo Soga was a "man of two worlds, who ultimately decided to throw in his lot with the blacks."[21] His life reflects a certain trend, or for that matter a certain stage, in the history of black Christianity in South Africa.

Nehemia Tile was to play a more significant religious and political role in South Africa's history. A dominant figure in the early history of the church in South Africa, Nehemiah Tile established the Thembu church in 1883, "the earliest fully established independent church in the sub-continent".[22] This developed into a significant movement of political protest, a response of the Africans to the process of expansion of colonialism in that area.

Nehemiah Tile's origins are somewhat obscure. In the early 1870s he worked in Thembuland as a Wesleyan evangelist, helping the Revd Peter Hargreaves, a pioneer missionary, whose Clarkebury circuit fell within the Queenstown missionary district. Recognizing Tile's potential, the Wesleyan church sent him to Healdtown College, where he joined a handful of Africans studying theology and came under the influence of such leading African Wesleyans as Richard Kawa and James Dwane.

From 1879, Tile served as a probationer minister, moving from one area to another in Thembuland. He increasingly came into conflict with his superior, the Revd Theophilus Chubb, the superintendent of the Clarkebury education institution, and he left the Wesleyan church. Two reasons seem to have immediately provoked this stand, namely discrimination in the church and the general political activity in Thembu social life. The Wesleyan church could not accept Tile's involvement in Thembu politics, alleging that Tile had stirred up hostility to the magistrates in Thembuland; had addressed a public meeting on the Sabbath; had not kept Chubb informed of his political work; and had donated an ox at the circumcision of Dalindyebo, the son of the Thembu paramount chief, Ngangelizwe.

The Cape Native Affairs Department also put pressure on Tile. The Transkeian rebellion of 1880-81, the influx of the Trekboers from what was then called the Cape Colony (a portion of the eastern Cape) into Emigrant Thembuland in 1882-83 and the War of Dispossession of 1887 demonstrated not only the reality of white intrusion but also the hardships of armed resistance.

The formation of the Thembu church signified a continuation of Tile's protest and combined religious and political aims. It enabled Tile to articulate and provide channels for the expression of the deep-felt grievances of the people. "Tile now spearheaded another, more subtle, form of opposition."[23] In August 1883 he organized a meeting at Ngangelizwe's great place, which adopted a petition to the Cape government signed by the paramount chief and his three sons, requesting that all but one of the magistrates be removed from Thembuland. In December, another petition followed, signed by more chiefs and members of Ngangelizwe's family. The authorities feared Tile's influence on Ngangelizwe and in April 1884, Elliot, the Chief Magistrate, wrote that Ngangelizwe was "entirely in the hands of Tile." [24] By May 1884, Tile's demands had grown: no hut tax, for this would merely support the magistrates. He took his campaign into the colonial press and sent statements and articles in support of Ngangelizwe's petition to the *Cape Mercury* and the *Cape Argus*. De Wet, the new secretary for Native Affairs, visited Mtata in September 1884 and was confronted by Tile, who was the chief spokesman for Ngangelizwe and the Thembu, at a mass meeting.

Because of his politico-religious activities, Tile was arrested and put in jail. He was charged with "incitement" and denounced as an "agitator". This did not intimidate him, however. On the contrary, it seemed to inspire him and his colleagues.

The Revd Dr Bengt Sundkler, who is generally taken to be the authority on independent churches in South Africa, seems to know very little about Nehemiah Tile. [25] It is therefore important to point out the significance of Tile and his movement. Tile's secession was a pointer to a new direction, an alternative, which would lead to the establishment of an independent African church. It was a forerunner of a protest movement founded by the Revd Moses Mangena Mokone in 1894. The Thembu church was the predecessor of the Ethiopian church. Tile's support derived from the fact that the Wesleyan church, the oldest and most influential mission in Thembuland, had become associated with the imposition of colonialism and Tile, expressing the deep-rooted feelings of his people, resented this. Tile understood that black Christianity, if it was to be a force of resistance with a lengthy existence, had to form an alliance with the paramount chief, endowing him with a religious sanctity and enhancing his traditional role, helping to buttress his authority which was being weakened and eroded by missionary activity and the political and economic penetration into the area by the colonialists. [26] He understood the connection between colonialism and missionary activity.

Tile had radical views on relations between black and white in South Africa, in which ethnic considerations among Africans took second place to a common destiny of blacks. The Thembu church was African-run, rejecting white racist and paternalistic control and asserting African independence of action. Though it used Wesleyan forms of worship, which were modified in that prayers were said for the paramount chief, his heir and rule, Tile did alter the wording of a traditional prayer in order to remove any implication that the Thembu were in a state of political subordination. The church itself became more than just a place of religious worship: it signified a political protest movement seeking to escape the reality of colonial rule. In the Thembu church where all men and women were equal and black, there

10

was no white racist control.

Whereas in the past white pressure led Africans to offer resistance by appealing to the ancestral spirits, the new church signified the usage of a new tool in the struggle for freedom: the use of a Christian framework to express African equality in the age of white domination. Tile broke with the church with which he was associated, formed a new church and worked with the traditional political leadership which he assisted in resisting colonialism. C. Saunders, whose invaluable research on Tile has helped us to understand the man, comments:

> The head of the Thembu church set his political sights on a return to the days of independent chiefly rule, instead of looking forward to participation in a common society, with the Transkeian territories part of a multi-racial Cape. In doing so he was moving in a direction opposite not only to that of the bulk of the new African elite that emerged in the Eastern Cape and east of the Kei from the late 1870s, but also to the dominant tradition of twentieth century African nationalism.[27]

Edward Roux also states that "some of the independent African churches that were purely tribalistic affairs or confined to particular areas."[28] But the younger generation of black South Africans, who are the heirs to this great heritage of militant tradition of resistance of the nineteenth century, and are indebted to their forefathers for this legacy, view the matter somewhat differently. It is their considered opinion that when the Africans fought in the last century they were not fighting for "a return to the past" or for the "preservation" of their social system. On the contrary, they fought for its *defence* and *development,* they fought and died for the defence of hard-earned achievements, for a noble cause: namely that education, Christianity, and technical superiority should not be misused for the exploitation and destruction of people, but should be used for progress. In short, their ancestors were forward-looking. As for the accusation that some of these organizations were "tribally" or "tribalistically" inclined, the answer is simple. The poverty and pass laws have tended to confine Africans in one area or region. Organization had to start from somewhere and if by sheer accident of history the people spoke the same language and had the same culture, that is not necessarily "tribalism".

Nehemiah Tile died shortly before Christmas in 1891, but his church lived on, although subjected to many pressures. Tengo Jabavu, a staunch Wesleyan, strongly opposed to the Thembu church, attacked it in the columns of his newspaper, *Imvo Zabantsundu.* By 1895, King Dalindyebo, Ngangelizwe's son and successor, had severed all links with the church, and its minister (Tile's successors), who had neither theological training nor government recognition, became frustrated.

If an impression is created that the movement for black church in-

11

dependence from missionary control was confined to the Cape, that has to be corrected. In Natal, in 1846, the first African convert in that part of our country, Umbulazi, was baptized by Dr Newton Adams of the American Missionary board. In 1885, at Taung, then in Bechuanaland, the London Missionary Society encountered some problems. Chief Kgantlapane took an active part in the founding of the Native Independent Congregational church and appointed ministers of his own choice to lead this church. Four years later in 1889, a "young and over-zealous" missionary of the Berlin Mission to the Bapedi in the Transvaal, J.A. Winter, anxious to give the African church leaders more responsibility, formed another independent church - the Lutheran Bapedi church-- and Khanyane Napo, an evangelist of the Anglican church in Pretoria, formed the African church.[29]

These attempts were isolated and sporadic, but "when these ideas spread to the Witwatersrand, the whole movement took a new momentum."[30] Thousands of African workers went to work in the gold mines. Some were Christian workers, mostly Wesleyans: "In 1885, there were in Johannesburg no less than sixty-five such voluntary preachers of the Wesleyan church, coming from various parts of the country".[31]

One of these was a Wesleyan minister, Moses Mangena Mokone. He was born in the Transvaal in 1851 and in 1870 went to Natal and worked there for 10 shillings a month on the sugar plantations. He then went to Durban, where he worked as a domestic servant and attended night school. In 1874, he was baptized by the Wesleyans and took up preaching. Mokone resigned from the Wesleyan church in 1892. He was later followed by the Revds Marcus Gabashane, J.G. Xaba, P.S. Kuze, J.M. Dwane, Abraham Mngqibisa, J.Z. Tantsi and Samson Mtintso. Mokone opposed what he regarded as racial segregation within the church, whereby there were separate conferences for white and African ministers, whites being allowed to attend the black meetings, if they so desired, while blacks were excluded from white meetings. Together with other ministers, evangelists, teachers, and ordinary adherents of the Wesleyan church, Mokone formed the Ethiopian church.

Mokone's church had wide horizons and was not limited to any ethnic group. The name for the church came from an interpretation of the scriptures, and this in itself was a new departure since Africans were taught to memorize parts of the Bible, not interpret it. Psalm 68, verse 31 says that "Ethiopia shall soon stretch out her hands unto God." Mokone took this to mean that Africans had the right to independent church organizations under African leadership.

The root causes of Ethiopianism were:

(a) the colour line between black and white, especially within the church;

(b) the land question: "some of the African land syndicates before 1913 were composed of Ethiopian leaders". [32]

(c) African unemployment: "many of the outbursts of the independent church movements occurred during this period of bitterness caused by unemployment". [33]

Other Ethiopian church leaders were Khanyane Napo, S. Brander, Jonas Goduka (Tile's successor as head of the Thembu church) and James Dwane. Dwane was born in 1848. Ordained in 1881 as a Wesleyan minister, he was a gifted speaker, with great ability and a powerful personality. He was sent to England in 1894-95 to represent his church and to solicit financial support. As soon as he returned to South Africa, he quarrelled with his mission authorities about the disposal of the money. He left the mission church to join forces in 1896 with Mokone and became a leader of the new movement. In 1898 and 1899, Dwane travelled to the US and in 1900 founded his "Order of Ethiopia Church". The Abyssinian victory over the colonialists at Adowa in 1896 had a great impact on the leaders of Ethiopianism in South Africa. Dwane even wrote to King Menelik of Ethiopia "asking him to take oversight of the religious conditions in Egypt and the Sudan and that he, Dwane, had tried to collect funds for this purpose among the Negroes of America". [34]

Charlotte Maxeke was instrumental in introducing the African Methodist Episcopal (AME) church, an offshoot of the black American AME church, to South Africa. [35] She wrote to the Revd M.M. Mokone, telling him about the AME church. On the Revd Mokone's initiative, the fourth annual conference of the Ethiopian church, in 1896, decided to merge the Ethiopian church with the AME.

Who was Charlotte Maxeke? Charlotte Makgomo Manye was born on 7 April 1874. As a young girl she had a lovely deep voice, sang in concerts in many places and joined a group of singers organized by a Mr Bam that later toured England where she sang before Queen Victoria. Two years later, the group travelled to Canada and the United States, where she was offered an opportunity for university training. She studied at Wilberforce University in Cleveland, Ohio, which was run by the AME church.

While still at Wilberforce, Charlotte Manye met and married the Revd Marshall Maxeke, who was a student there. She also made friends with some of the future leaders of the black community in the United States. One of them was Dr W.E.B. Du Bois, a leading Afro-American, African statesman and academic who, years later, remembered of her:

> I have known Charlotte Manye Maxeke since 1894, when I went to Wilberforce University as a teacher. She was one of the three or four students from South Africa, and was the only woman. She was especially the friend of Nina Gomer, the student who afterwards became my wife. We were interested in Charlotte Manye because of her clear mind, her fund of subtle humour and the straight-forward honesty of her character . . . she did her work with a slow, quiet determination that augured well for her future. Since then, and at long intervals, I have had the opportunity of following her work through the glimpses which I have had from far off South Africa. I regard Mrs Maxeke as a pioneer in one of the greatest of human causes, working in extraordinarily difficult circumstances to lead a people, in the face of prejudice, not only against her race but against her sex. To fight not simply the natural and inherent difficulties of education and social uplift, but to fight with little money and little outside aid was indeed a tremendous task. I think that what Mrs Maxeke has accomplished should encourage all men, especially those of African descent. And in addition to that, it should inspire the white residents of South Africa and of America to revise their hastily-made judgements concerning the possibilities of the Negro race. [36]

The Revds Samuel Jacobus Brander, Joshua Mphothleng Mphela, and Steven Nguato of the Ethiopian Catholic church in Zion appeared before the South African Native Affairs Commission on 4 October 1904 and explained the reasons for their breakaway from the "Church of England" to form the AME, affiliated to the AME of America. They did so because the black Americans "had education and other things better than we had. We considered that it would be better for us to join them, so that they could help us, being Coloured people themselves".[37] The AME in the US promised to pay for a school to be built and staffed in the Transvaal but the South African branch found that they had to do everything themselves "and at the same time collect our yearly income, and also take collections for Easter Day, contingent moneys, and all that money had to be forwarded to America".[38] This eventually caused a rift between the black American AME church and the independent churches in South Africa.

These religious expressions were a reflection of deep underlying economic and political questions. They represented a struggle not only against cultural conquest through religion and education, but also against the wide political domination and economic penetration of colonialism. The independent churches were symptoms of an African revolt against the colonialists' missionary crusade, an expression of distrust, resistance and opposition, a sign of the vitality of the religious and cultural heritage of the Africans.

The African press

Interestingly, it was the missionaries who played a pioneering role in the establishment of a black press in South Africa.

The British and Foreign Bible Society, which started during the Napoleonic wars, set as its aim the provision of the Scriptures in "every language". They created a system of spelling and of writing languages never before set down, established rules of typography and helped to train compositors and printers. At Genadendaal, the Moravian mission station in the western Cape; and at the Wesleyan mission in the eastern Cape, the printing of African languages was introduced with the same aim in mind - the preaching of the gospel and promotion of literacy through the provision of religious literature in African languages.

In the eastern Cape a paper called *Umshumayeli Wendaba* (Preacher of the News) was published from July 1837 to 1841. The second periodical to appear, *Isibuto Samava* (Collection of Opinions) began in January 1843 and continued till July 1884. Then followed *Ikwezi* (Morning Star) from August 1884 to December 1845 at Tyume mission station. It was on 14 August 1850 that *Isitunywa Senyanga* (The Monthly Messenger) was printed in King William's Town, published by the Wesleyan Mission Press, with a circulation average of 800. This was followed by *Indaba* (News), a monthly brought out by the Lovedale mission press from August 1862 until January 1865.[39] It was edited by the Revd Bryce Ross, had a circulation of 500-600 copies, with two-thirds of its contents in Xhosa and the rest in English. Dr James Stewart, head of Lovedale, the Presbyterian mission college, then replaced *Indaba* with *The Kaffir Express* (with the Xhosa section called *Isigidimi Sama Xosa*). This continued until 1876 when the English section was renamed *The Christian Express*.

The Revd Soga was a regular contributor to the *The Kaffir Express* in the 1860s "but his premature death put an end to this promising development".[40] After 1870, the paper was edited by John Knox Bokwe, who was then 15 years old. A former clerk at Lovedale, Bokwe became a Presbyterian minister, a writer of stories, religious books, hymns and even plays. In 1876, the African section of *The Kaffir Express* was edited and managed by the Revd Elijah Makiwane. Born in 1850 in Sheshegu, the Revd Makiwane came to Lovedale in 1865 and qualified in theology. In 1875, a year before he took over *Isigidimi*, he was ordained in the United Free Church of Scotland. John Tengo Jabavu joined *Isigidimi* and became its editor in 1881 up to 1884. *Isigidimi* continued until December 1888, when William Wellington Gqoba (Jabavu's successor) died. Since 1922, *The Christian Express* has become known as *The South African Outlook*, a missionary journal.

In Natal, work in this field was done by the American missionaries, Alden, Grout, Lindley, Tyler and others who introduced printing equipment and started one of the first periodicals at Esidumbini mission station.

The Tswana newspapers, according to Eric Rosenthal, "were the first real newspapers ever issued for the Bantu people".[41] This refers to *Molekudi wa Bechuana*, which appeared from 1856-57 and whose editor was the Revd Ludorf at the Wesleyan mission at Thaba 'Nchu. It carried religious articles, but sections in it were on current politics and social events. It appeared monthly and "one of the very few surviving copies was in the hands of the well-known journalist Solomon T. Plaatje".[42]

Between 1883 and 1898, the London Missionary Society at Kuruman published a monthly, *Mahoko a Bechwana* (Batswana News). It was printed at the Moffat Institute and the editors were the Revds John Brown, A.J. Gould and R. Price. It grew into an attractive magazine. Plaatje says about it:

> During the first week of each month the native peasants in Bechuanaland and elsewhere, used to look forward to its arrival as eagerly as the white up-country farmers now await the arrival of the daily papers. How little did the writer dream when frequently called upon as a boy to read the news to groups of men sewing karosses under the shady trees outside the cattle fold, that journalism would afterwards mean his bread and cheese."[43]

Following the example of the London Missionary Society, the Lutheran Mission supported a monthly magazine, *Moshupa Tsela* (The Guide), at Bethanie in the Transvaal, edited by the Revds Behreus and Meyer and later by the Revd Tonsing.

A key development in these missionary undertakings was the emergence not only of African contributors to the press but also that of African journalists, managers and editors. One of these was Silas Molema. Born in 1850 and educated at Healdtown, Molema later returned to Mafeking and in 1878 set up a school. Plaatje remembered that, "The school was often interrupted by the several quarrels with the Boers as the teacher, being a sub-chief, always went on active service at the head of his regiment."[44] This school - the first in the area which was not a missionary institute - was housed in a chapel Molema's father had built. Molema taught until 1888 when the Wesleyans took charge and appointed him as headmaster.

On the 27 April 1901, Molema established a Tswana/English weekly, *Koranta ea Becoana* (The Tswana Gazette) at Mafeking. Plaatje assisted him in this. At first, the paper was owned by G.N.H. Whales, the editor of the local *Mafeking Mail,* and was printed on the *Mail's* press.

On 5 September 1901 - by which time 12 issues of *Koranta* had appeared - a new agreement was reached, and for a consideration of £25, Molema purchased copyright from Whales and effectively assumed control of the paper.[45] Molema did not stop at that however. He decided to order a printing press so that *Koranta* could be independent of the *Mail's* press. It was later called the Bechuana Printing Works. *Koranta* was the first Tswana newspaper to be run by Africans. It provided a vehicle for their education and representation. Plaatje became its editor. Its popularity rose and many people appreciated Plaatje's endeavours. It continued until 1908.

At Pietersburg, Transvaal, Simon Majakathata Phamotse started the *Native Eye* at the beginning of this century and in 1910, Daniel Simon Letanka launched *Motsoalle* (The Friend). The name dissatisfied Letanka however, and he therefore changed it to *Moronioa* (The Messenger).

In Natal, we had the example of Mark Radebe, a versatile press pioneer. Born at Pietermaritzburg and educated at Lovedale, Radebe first worked as a shop assistant with a firm in Durban and later began his own newspaper, *Ipepa lo Hlanga* (The Paper of the Nation) in 1900. This was basically a non-missionary paper sponsored largely by the founders of the Natal Native Congress.

In 1902, the Revd John Langalibalele Dube, also known as Mafukuzela, entered journalism with the Zulu/English *Ilanga lase Natal,* which replaced *Ipepa lo Hlanga.* (I shall discuss the ideas and activities of Dube later.) In Pretoria in 1912, Sefako Mapoch Makgatho[46] (later to be President-General of the ANC), together with Alfred Mangena (a co-founder of the ANC) edited *The Native Advocate.*

The appearance of John Tengo Jabavu on the political scene in South Africa was a new development in the history of the black press. Here was a black man whose paper was not influenced by missionaries but by white politicians. Born in 1859 at Tyatyora near Fort Beaufort, Jabavu began life by herding his father's cattle; went to the Healdtown Wesleyan mission school; became a teacher and "at this stage of his career felt the lure of journalism".[47] In 1876, he decided to be an apprentice in a printing works at Somerset East where he also obtained a chance to continue his studies. Originally, he wanted to learn the technical side of his trade but he was then tempted to write. Jabavu's first journalist ventures were some articles written under a pen-name for the *Cape Argus*. Then, while still in his early twenties, he decided to publish a newspaper himself. He planned everything: the name, political stance, printing, languages - partly in Xhosa and partly in English. "He had everything in readiness except the money to start the venture".[48] Two white Cape liberals - Sir James Rose-Innes and Mr Weir - came to "his rescue", and *Imvo Zabantsundu* (African Opinions) was launched on 3 November 1884. Rosenthal comments:

Subscribers came in shoals and the demand for the *Imvo* increased rapidly - as did the printer's bill! The Natives received the paper with acclamation, reading it themselves and reading it aloud to others. To them it seemed to usher in a new era. It was a long step forward and was much appreciated.[49]

According to a contemporary of Jabavu's, Plaatje, *Imvo* "had a kind of monopoly of African journalism and deserved wide reputation."[50] But soon *Imvo* experienced problems: a bank overdraft and subscriptions in arrears. Again the Cape liberals came to Jabavu's "rescue", appointed an accountant and bookkeeper and "financial stability was restored."[51] In 1876, however, *Izwi Labantu* (The Voice of the People) "was started in East London by the Revd Walter Rubusana and other members of the Cape African elite who were in disagreement with Jabavu's strategy in politics. *Izwi Labantu* was founded as a counterpoise to *Imvo Zabantsundu*; the dissatisfaction of many Cape Africans with the role played by Jabavu in Cape politics especially during the 1890s gave urgency to the need for a rival organ".[52]

Imvo "could hardly hold its ground against the new rival".[53] The editor of *Izwi Labantu* was A.K. Soga.

Plaatje records that *Imvo* began to sink into difficulties and had to cast about for a financial rescuer and "prominent supporters of the Government came to rescue it; three out of ten members of the first Union Cabinet became shareholders in the sinking *Imvo*."[54] The editor became a "manager" in a paper which was becoming African only in appearance and Jabavu was not doing full justice to his employers because he did not tell them the whole truth about African opinion. Plaatje commented on this as follows:

God forbid that we should ever find that our mind had become the property of some one other than ourselves, but should such a misfortune ever overtake us, we should at least strive to serve our new proprietor diligently, and whenever our people are unanimously opposed to a policy we should consider it a part of our duty to tell him so; but that is not Mr Jabavu's way of serving a master.[55]

Africans in the British Cape Colony enjoyed some civil liberties in comparison with those elsewhere in South Africa; they were not specifically excluded from voting. Those eligible to vote were former citizens of the Batavian Republic, natural born and naturalized British subjects, or those who could fulfil a £25 property or £50-a-year wage qualification. This low property or wage requirement was designed to enable large numbers of Afrikaners in the Cape to vote, and also made some Coloureds and Africans eligible. The Cape liberals - within the English-speaking community - supported the retention of this "non-racial" franchise because it favoured them: most Coloured and African voters voted for the English rather than the Afrikaner candidates. The Afrikaners and some English-speaking people pressed, however, for the Africans to be disenfranchised. When conflict between the English and Afrikaners was minimal, agreement on disenfranchising the Africans was possible; but whenever conflict worsened, English politicians again defended the "non-racial" franchise.

Jabavu's political approach was much conditioned by the white Cape liberals who supported him. He seems to have accepted the white categorization of Africans as "civilized" (Christianized) or "un-civilized" (heathen). Thus he accepted the limited African voting rights in the Cape (which only affected some 10 per cent of the entire voting population). Roux has described this as "what we might call Bantu political liberalism".[56]

Jabavu belonged to that first generation of African leaders to mount a sustained campaign to arouse political awareness and national con-sciousness among the Africans in the Cape, and proved the significant role that could be played by the press in this process. L.D. Ngcongco states, however, that Jabavu's efforts fell "outside the context of nationalism . . . In the final analysis the failure of Tengo Jabavu as a political leader was the failure of liberalism in Cape politics."[57]

It would be wrong to regard Jabavu's political history and career as all negative, however. He helped to form the Native Electoral Associa-tion in 1884 and campaigned vigorously against the disenfranchisement of Africans in the eastern Cape in 1887. From 1908 until its opening in 1916, he campaigned for the founding of the University College of Fort Hare, for African students. In 1909 he was on the delegation that went to Britain to discuss the pending unification of the four provinces of South Africa, and in 1911 he attended the Universal Races Congress in London, where he met such famous pan-African leaders as Dr du Bois.

When Africans planned and formed the ANC in 1912, however, "Jabavu was conspicuous by his absence . . . Likewise, when the newly formed Congress attacked the Natives Land Act of 1913 *Imvo* was the only organ that saw any merit in it.[58] According to Ngcongco, Jabavu's "failures were more striking than his successes. Many will accordingly remember him not for what he did, but for what he could not do."[59]

Jabavu also came into conflict with the Revd Walter Rubusana. Born in 1858, Rubusana was educated at Lovedale and in 1884 was or-dained a minister of the London Missionary Society. He went to the US to study and was awarded the honorary degree of Doctor of

Philisophy by the black college, McKinley University, for his *History of South Africa from the Native Standpoint.* He also helped standardize the revised version of the Xhosa Bible. In 1910 Rubusana was elected as the first and only African member of the Cape Province Parliament, despite Jabavu's opposition. Then when he stood for election on 14 March 1914 as a provincial councillor for a seat in the Transkei (after the Union was formed), Jabavu stood against him. The results were tragic: Payne, the white candidate, received 1 004 votes (practically all the white votes and a few African ones); Rubusana got 852; and Jabavu 294!

These individual endeavours and, at times, isolated attempts to develop the black press culminated in the formation of *Abantu-Batho* (The People) in 1912. It was established with capital of £3 000, most of which was supplied by the Queen Regent of Swaziland, Nabotsibeni. *Abantu-Batho,* produced in Johannesburg and whose managing director was Pixley ka (son of) Isaka Seme, differed from the existing black papers in that it was launched by people who had founded a national organization. It became the mouthpiece and later official organ of the newly founded African National Congress. It was national in character; hence the "bilingualism" in its name (Zulu-Xhosa/Sotho-Tswana) and articles were written in all major African languages in South Africa: Sesotho, Setswana, Sixhosa, Sizulu and English. Other African papers such as *Motsoalle* and *Umlomo wa Bantu* were incorporated. The first editor was C. Kunene, formerly a schoolmaster at Edendale, Natal and later on the staff of *Ikwezi:* "For five years - till his death in 1916 - Kunene ran the paper with considerable success."[60]

Abantu-Batho was at one stage the most widely read paper among the Africans. It attracted to itself many outstanding African journalists. Among those who were editors of the paper and/or regular contributors to its columns were T.D. Mweli Skota, Saul Msane, Robert Grendon, R.I.V. Selope Thema, and D.S. Letanka. Of these Letanka had the longest period of service on the paper, being assistant editor and editor at various times in the period 1912-31.[61]

The political, educative and mobilizing influence of *Abantu-Batho* can be gauged - among other things - by the impact it had on ordinary Africans. Let us take the example of Selope Thema as an illustration. Born in Mafarane in the northern Transvaal on 10 February 1896, Selope Thema went to study in Lovedale in the eastern Cape. He was much influenced by S.M. Makgatho, who came to Pietersburg in 1912, while Provincial President of the Transvaal ANC. Early in 1915, Thema found his way to Johannesburg "after having organized a strong branch of the Congress which was destined to play a prominent part in the years that followed".[62]

In Johannesburg, he immediately came into contact with the ANC headquarters - his long cherished wish - and came to know the editor of *Abantu-Batho*. Thema confesses in his unpublished autobiography, that *Abantu-Batho* "helped me in my journalistic endeavour and made it possible for me to express my views on questions that affected Africans."[63] What was appealing to the Africans in the columns of *Abantu-Batho* was the message of unity and the vision of freedom which came out every week.

Abantu-Batho was really the first African paper with the clear purpose of developing the political awareness and national consciousness of the Africans. The historical significance of this development is that it established African political opinion as an autonomous factor in its own right - a task which was to be taken more seriously by the ANC in the succeeding years.

Political organization

Amongst Africans

Forman states that the developments in the years 1881-84 are an illustration of the fact that history takes jumps forward - that a change in the economy leads to the emergence of entirely new social phenomena.[64] These economic changes - that is the discovery of diamonds and gold with the resultant emergence of the African working class - were accompanied by another process: the articulation of the aspirations of the Africans by non-working class forces.

As early as 1882, the Africans in the Cape formed a political organization, Imbumba yama Afrika (Union of Africans) which advocated African unity (as opposed to religious denominational diversity) and planned representations to white authorities. In December 1883, S.N. Mvambo, writing from Peddie, declared:

> Anyone looking at things as they are, could even go so far as to say it was a great mistake to bring so much church denominations to the black people. For the black man makes the fatal mistake of thinking that if he is an Anglican he has nothing to do with anything suggested by a Wesleyan, and the Wesleyan also thinks so, and so does the Presbyterian. Imbumba must make sure that all these three are represented at the conference, for we must be united on political matters. In fighting for national rights, we must fight together. Although they look as if they belong to various churches, the white people are solidly united when it comes to matters of this nature. We Blacks think that these churches are hostile to one another, and in that we lose our political rights.[65]

This statement of purpose, aims and objects of Imbumba was neces-

21

sary to counteract not only denominational divisions but also white unity at a political level - "for we must be united on political matters" - and this unity was supposed to form a basis for struggle - "in fighting for national rights, we must fight together." This statement was a call for a search for black identity.

In 1884, two additional organizations were formed in the Cape, namely the Native Education Association and the Native Electoral Association, which were concerned mainly with electoral politics.

But it was during the Anglo-Boer War and immediately after the Peace of Vereeniging in May 1902, that concrete steps were taken by the Africans to form a movement which would devise some method of presenting grievances and complaints of the Africans to the government. This growing awareness and consciousness of a need for a political organization of Africans on a broader basis led Martin Lutuli, Saul Msane and Josiah Gumede to meet Harriette Colenso[66] "to discuss the formation of an African political organization. In July 1900, the Natal Native Congress was formed. Its first secretary was H.C. Matiwane and the Chairman was Martin Lutuli, an uncle of Chief Albert Lutuli. Mark Radebe was a co-founder. Lutuli was chairman for three years, after which he was replaced by Skweleti Nyongwana and Lutuli became vice-chairman. The Natal Native Congress had a secretary at Verulam; local committees managed local affairs and members of the Congress were Christians only. But the object and intention was to represent the whole African community in Natal.

In the years 1903-05, the South African Native Commission - established to formulate a policy on African affairs - travelled throughout the four colonies (the Cape, Orange River Colony, Natal and Transvaal) to take evidence from both Africans and whites. These testimonies are interesting in that the different representatives of African organizations were afforded the opportunity to express their grievances and complaints; to explain the policies of their organizations and to suggest solutions to the problems facing the country. Let us look at a few examples.

On 28 May 1904, Lutuli gave testimony on behalf of the Natal Native Congress before the commission. He explained that the Natal Native Congress was the voice of the Africans in Natal, who came together to talk about their problems and if they had any complaints they presented them to the government:

If we want to talk to the Government, one man cannot talk alone, we must come together and decide things, and hear the opinion of others on a certain thing. Then if it is necessary for it to go to the Government, we appoint some delegates from that meeting to talk with the Government on that subject.[67]

Lutuli had no confidence in the Secretary for Native Affairs because he represented other parties; was not sent by Africans; and had to follow the line of those who sent him to Parliament.

In the eastern Cape, in 1902, Africans close to the East London newspaper *Izwi Labantu* and therefore opposed to Jabavu's preoccupation with white politics, founded the South African Native Congress. The tasks of this organization were to co-ordinate African activities in the Cape Colony, particularly in connection with electoral politics. The political orientation of the South African Native Congress is clear from a statement of its executive to the Native Affairs Commission in 1903 on "Questions Affecting the Natives and Coloured People Resident in British South Africa".[68] In a rather moderate tone, the document discusses problems of education: "the disparity between the grants allowed per pupil to white and black" and the question of the exploitation of the teachers - "the salaries paid to teachers are scandalously illiberal, forcing many to adopt other means to obtain a livelihood".[69] The document also discusses such questions as administration of justice, civil service, franchise, the labour question and so on.

Of particular interest is the testimony of the Revds E.T. Mpela and B. Kumalo, J. Twayi, Al Jordaan, J. Mocher, J. Lavers and Petre Thaslane, of the Native Vigilance Association of the Orange River Colony on 23 September 1904. What is striking (but not surprising if one takes into account the multi-ethnic composition of the province) is the "non-tribal" composition of the leadership of this organization, that is judging by the delegation. They belonged to Sotho, Xhosa, Zulu and other ethnic groups and included ministers of religion, a brickmaker, cartage contractors, a mason and a dray-cart driver.

The Revd B. Kumalo, spokesman of the delegation of the Native Vigilance Association of the Orange River Colony argued with the chairman of the Native Affairs Commission about the Christian (and therefore "civilized") Africans and the "heathen" (and therefore "backward") Africans. Kumalo said: "We consider that the most of the people here in the Orange River Colony are civilized." Asked about the number of the Christians in the Orange River Colony, he replied: "I do not consider that Christianity forms what we call civilization only." The chairman of the Commission, becoming frustrated and confused, asked about how many could read and write and the answer was simple: "Even that I do not consider as civilization". At which point, the chairman, completely baffled, asked: "What is civilization?" and the Revd Kumalo replied, coolly, "Civilization is the state of living and of progressiveness, even whether you write or cannot write; if you live in a state of progressiveness, that is civilization." The chairman then asked: "Is that in the dictionary?" The Revd Kumalo replied: "I did not look at the dictionary; but I consider in my explanation of the thing, that that is the position. Of course, the knowledge of writing and reading must come in sometimes to cause civilization but that is not the most essential factor."[70]

Even religious groups could not escape the inquisition. The Revds Samuel Jacobus Brander and Joshua Mphothleng Mphela and Steven Nguato of the Ethiopian Catholic Church in Zion, appeared before the same commission. The racist chairman must have been surprised and embarrassed by the answers of the Revd Brander, the African convert:

Chairman: "Would you like the white man to marry the Native
                  woman?"
Revd Brander: "I should think so."
Chairman: "And the Native man to marry the white woman?"
Revd Brander: "I should think so." [71]

Various testimonies and petitions to King Edward VII give a clear picture of African problems and grievances. These include statements from the Native United Political Associations of the Transvaal Colony (25 April 1905), the Orange River Colony Native Congress (June 1906), the Natal Native Congress (October 1908), and from the "aboriginal natives of South Africa, resident in the Transvaal" (22 October 1908) as well as the resolutions of the South African Native Congress (10 April 1906) and the petition to the Secretary of State for the Colonies from the Natal Native Congress (October 1908). They show
(a)   an acute awareness of the magnitude of African disabilities and
       a sharp antagonism to any continuation of the political system of
       the Boer Republic;[72]
(b)   the degree to which the new organization accepted the promises
       and language (if not the ideology implicit in it) of the teachings
       of the Christian missionaries and the British system of
       government.

There is a strong element of elitism inherent in the utterances of these early African radicals. The division of Africans into "heathens" and Christians and by implication into the "backward" and "civilized" was accepted, and consequently "qualified", "civilised" Africans were expected to have the same rights as white voters. There was soon a noticeable shift of emphasis in the language used, however. Whereas in the earlier statements the hope and concern for a gradual (but irreversible) advance of all Africans was accompanied by a pride in being "loyal and civilized British subjects", the language in later years changes. We even see a petition of 22 October 1908 from the "aboriginal natives of South Africa, resident in the Transvaal" (not from "civilized loyal British subjects") who claimed "representation in the Parliament of a United South Africa".

The developments taking place in South Africa were also reflected and found expression in the speeches and writings of Africans from South Africa studying abroad. Pixley ka Isaka Seme is perhaps the best example. On 5 April 1906, he won the first prize of the Curtis Medal Orations at Columbia University where he studied. In this speech Seme chose to speak on what was then an "obscure" topic; "The Regeneration of Africa". He started off by stating a seemingly obvious fact: "I am an African, and I set my pride in my race over against a hostile public opinion."[73] In this sentence he articulated the continental approach which has characterized the thinking of all progressive-minded African leaders and which found its full expression in the formation of the OAU in 1963. He also expressed an anti-racism which was anti-colonial in essence, and asserted his national pride and identity. Seme went further:

> The African already recognises his anomalous position and desires a change. The brighter day is rising upon Africa ... Yes, the regeneration of Africa belongs to this new and powerful period. By this term regeneration I wish to be understood to mean the entrance into a new life embracing the diverse phases of a higher, complex existence. The basic factor which assures their regeneration resides in the awakened race consciousness ... The African people, although not a strictly homogeneous race, possess a common fundamental sentiment which is everywhere manifest, crystallising itself into one common controlling idea. Conflicts and strife are rapidly disappearing before perception of the true intertribal relation, which relation should subsist among a people with a common identity.[74]

In beautiful words, indeed poetic language, Seme described this "new spirit" which acts as a "leavening ferment" and therefore shall raise "the anxious and aspiring masses to the level of their ancient glory"; an ancestral greatness which constitutes the Africans' greatest source of inspiration. Seme noted the Africans' refusal "to camp forever on the borders of the industrial world"; the unquenchable thirst for knowledge which forced Africans to send their children to Europe, "who return to their country like arrows, to drive darkness from the land". And with a sense of prophecy, "The regeneration of Africa means a new and unique civilization is soon to be added to the world."

I have quoted at length from Seme's speech because it expresses the mood and thinking of a new generation of African intellectuals at the beginning of this century. Moreover, the words uttered by Seme have inspired many progressive-minded Africans on the African continent and are still valid and relevant today. President Kwame Nkrumah quoted Seme's speech in full when he opened the First International Congress of Africanists in Accra, Ghana, on 2 December 1962.

It is interesting to note the American influences on the thinking of the men who later became the founding fathers of the African National Congress. Sundkler remarks:

a surprising number of Ethiopian leaders have for a shorter or longer time studied in America. A Natal Native Affairs Commission of 1906-07 found that up to that time, at least a hundred and fifty Africans from South Africa, some of them with definite Ethiopian affiliations, had gone to America for studies.[75]

Peter Walshe states that between 1896 and 1924, twenty-two South Africans attended the Lincoln University alone.[76]

While such social awareness and political consciousness was manifesting itself among the African students abroad, political developments in South Africa were moving towards the formation of a political movement of Africans. The Revd James Calata, former Secretary-General of the ANC and President of the Cape ANC made a presidential address in New Brighton, Port Elizabeth on 4 July 1938, in which he referred to a large conference, "ingqungquthela", which met in Queenstown in 1908.[77] It was followed in October 1908 by a petition organized by the Transvaal Native Unions, with 3 764 signatures, and asking for a common-roll franchise throughout South Africa plus separate representation for the mass of Africans unable to qualify for this.[78] In February 1909, the Orange River Colony held its congress and in March further congresses were held in the Cape, Natal and Transvaal.

The draft South Africa Act published in February 1909, which was a draft of the constitution of the country, was discussed at these meetings, and resolutions deprecating the colour bar and the failure to extend the African franchise from the Cape to the north were passed. It was from these regional conferences that 60 elected delegates came to Bloemfontein to attend the South African Native Convention on 24-26 March 1909. The South African Native Convention comprised delegates from the Cape Colony, Natal, Transvaal, Orange River Colony and Bechuanaland. The leader of the Cape delegation for the South African Native Congress, the Revd Walter Rubusana, was elected President of the Convention. They discussed those clauses of the Draft Act relating to Africans and Coloured people. They arrived, as far as the Draft Act was concerned, at the following decision:

The franchise has been enjoyed for more than 50 years by the native and coloured races of the Cape Colony, but is not extended to the native and coloured races of the Orange River Colony, the Transvaal and the Colony of Natal, and this Convention seriously deprecates the absence, in the said Draft Act of the principle of equal rights for all the races in the South African colonies.[79]

The Convention emphatically rejected clauses 25, 33 and 44 of the Draft South African Act which defended the colour bar and clause 55 entrenching the Cape vote was left unaltered. The aim of the Convention was to democratize the Draft Act and save it from racism. They hoped to extend the African vote in the Cape to the other provinces. They were also against the incorporation of the High Commission Territories; Bechuanaland, Basutoland (now Lesotho) and Swaziland, into the Union of South Africa.

These resolutions were delivered to the governors and prime ministers of the four colonies (the Cape, Orange River Colony, Natal and Transvaal), to the Rt Hon. Sir John H. de Villiers and to Lord Selborne, the British High Commissioner, for transfer to the British Secretary of State for the Colonies. A deputation was also sent to Britain, comprising the Revd W. Rubusana, President of the Native Convention; T.M. Mapikela of the Orange River Colony and D. Dwanya of the Cape; Tengo Jabavu of the Cape Convention; and W.P. Schreiner was also invited to join them. The Transvaal Native Congress appointed Alfred Mangena who was studying in London as their representative and instructed him "to work in co-operation with the other delegates".[80] Pixley ka Isaka Seme, who was at this time in Oxford, made contact with the delegation and discussed the formation of an African organization with them. However they failed tó get the colour bar clauses removed from the constitution although the High Commission Territories were not incorporated into South Africa.

The Coloured community

The Coloured community was more proletarianized than the African people, hence the early signs of a Coloured class-cum-national consciousness. In December 1884, there was a move by the Coloureds to commemorate the jubilee of slave emancipation. A meeting called for "a more general and closer union among the Coloured classes, who have hitherto been separated by unimportant distinctions"[81] and urged that the establishment of a newspaper "suited to the Coloured classes" be considered.[82]

Independent Coloured political activity goes back to the 1880s. At that time, the Coloured people enjoyed "full political rights" in the Cape, but Britain was already considering forcing "confederation" on the various South African communities. The end of the Anglo-Boer War brought new ideas and new threats. As a result, in the opening months of 1902, a group of Coloured leaders formed the African People's Organization, a Coloured organization, in Cape Town. The president was W. Collins and the secretary, P. Eckstein. The Coloureds were alert to the possibility that Britain would be happy to sell their rights as the price of unity and therefore, as an "anonymous Coloured historian" put it, "The more intelligent of the Coloured people saw that in such an event it would be necessary to safeguard their interests, or there soon would be no interests to safeguard."[83]

The formation of the African People's Organization (APO) on a national level signified not only the first step in this direction, but also that it was the first nationwide political organization to demand full equality for all South Africans.[84]

Soon there were branches in Johannesburg, Graaff Reinet, Cradock, Paarl and several towns in the western Cape. The second APO conference, which was held in Graaff Reinet in April 1904 and had 30-40 delegates from branches all over the country, elected Matt. J. Fredericks as secretary. Fredericks was the first Coloured political leader of importance. There was dissension in this APO conference (largely personal disputes) but to save the situation and the organization, Fredericks "effected a coup and assumed complete control". This was, however, a progressive "coup" because "as a result the APO came out of its crisis stronger than before."[85]

It was at this time that Fredericks and others asked Dr A. Abdurahman, a member of the Cape Town Municipal Council, to assume the presidency, and at a conference at Somerset East at Easter 1905, Abdurahman was elected President. Forman remarks:

Abdurahman - for all his faults - is undoubtedly one of the giants in the history of the liberation movement. After Gandhi, he stands out among the men of the early years of this country. It is utterly shameful that no one has yet written his biography.[86]

The movement expanded with new energy and vitality infused into it by Abdurahman and the membership roll showed a large increase. Its methods of struggle were petitions and deputations.

All the Non-European organizations persevered with the deputation type of struggle until as late as 1920. It is not correct to sneer at these deputations. In the circumstances of the times, they marked a stage of development of militant approach, they were supported by the most advanced political leaders and strongly opposed by the government and its stooges.[87]

There was another dimension in Coloured political life: the issue of African-Coloured political unity. In 1907, APO accepted an invitation to attend a joint conference of Africans and Coloureds at Queenstown in November to agree on a common attitude to the Cape elections of 1908. This was of great significance as the first serious attempt to fuse the Africans and Coloureds into one political whole. At the Conference

28

there were 120 delegates.

Everything indicates that the political organization of APO reached "a level of organizational stability and efficiency which has never been reached by any of the liberatory organizations which followed with the possible exception of the Communist Party".[88] The APO official organ "unimaginatively entitled the APO was published fortnightly from 24 May 1909 and had 16 glossy pages, containing well-written articles, well-argued discussion, and comprehensive coverage of branch activities. APO branches met regularly and sent in full reports to the newspaper. The organization was functioning "amazingly well" and had stable, nationwide support".

At least in its earlier years, APO was decidedly sympathetic to socialism - its 1908 conference met in the Socialist Hall in Buitenkant Street, Cape Town; it supported A.W. Noon, a Cape Town Municipal councillor, "a true friend of all workers of every class and creed and colour . . . with declared socialist views".[89] And in Kimberley APO played a conspicuous part in the return of the militant white socialist J.F. Trembath to the municipal council. But this APO-socialist friendship did not last long. It came to an abrupt end in 1910, when the Labour Party betrayed socialism by adopting a white labour policy. As a result, relations between the socialist movement and this black organization moved from friendship to active hostility.

Trembath supported the Labour policy. He stood for parliament as a member of the Labour Party, and was defeated largely as a result of APO opposition. To demonstrate the reactionary nature of the Labour Party, let us quote from its official organ *The Worker*:

APO, the mouthpiece of black, brown, snuff and butter [should have] the seat of its pants kicked through the top of its pepper-corned head . . . After a nigger has absorbed the poison into his head, he will reckon that the white woman is his game . . . The APO editor . . . should get 25 of the best [lashes]. [90]

On the other hand, APO had a relatively advanced attitude to the class struggle. During the strike of white railway workers APO said of those who scabbed:

It is impossible to conceive a more reprehensible and disreputable manner of obtaining work than by . . . blacklegism . . . Let it be hoped that in seeking work, men will never forget their moral obligations to their fellow-men, be they white or black. [91]

On the occasion of the approval by Britain in 1909 of the Colour Bar Act of the Union, APO editorialized:

The struggle has not ended. It has just begun. We, the Coloured and Native peoples of South Africa, have a tremendous fight before us. We have the war of wars to wage ... No longer must we look to our flabby friends in Great Britain.

Our political destiny is in our hands, and we must be prepared to face the fight with grim determination to succeed ... How are we to set about [it]? In our opinion there is but one way and that is the economic method. Undoubtedly the Coloured and Native races of South Africa hold the strongest weapon ever placed in the hands of any class. The very stability, the prosperity, even the continuance for but a few days of the economic existence of South Africa depends on the labour market; and we are the labour market ...

It may ere long come about that the necessity will be imposed on us, not in any isolated sphere of labour or in any particular district, but in every sphere and throughout the whole subcontinent to refuse to bolster up the economic fabric of the people who refuse us political freedom. That would bring the selfish white politicians to their knees.

The editorial goes further to predict:

It would even go far to show the white manual workers the value of combination which is the only weapon whereby they will free themselves from the shackles of that cursed wage system, which is sapping the independence of the people, weakening the national love of honour, and increasing the severity and extent of poverty for the production of a few sordid millionaires.[92]

Forman is of the opinion that these words were written "almost certainly" by Dr Abdurahman and because they are as true today as they were then, they show how far ahead of his time Dr Abdurahman, in his early years, was.

The Indian community

The first batch of Indian immigrants arrived in South Africa in 1860, bringing with them a wide variety of backgrounds, culture, languages and customs. They came as indentured labourers and worked on the sugar plantations in Natal. The living and working conditions were akin to slavery, working from sunrise to sunset for a pittance. Indian workers were insulted and exploited, flogged, and deprived of wages and rations. As time went on, they refused to renew their indentures and therefore became "free men"; found employment as market gardeners, mineworkers, railway and council workers, small traders, hawkers, hotel and domestic workers. It is from these indentured labourers that Indian workers emerged who later played an important role in the Indian national movement.

The humiliations and insults to Indians' dignity soon developed into sharp economic, cultural and other differences; they were segregated into specially designated areas and, in 1891 were summarily expelled from the Orange Free State. The letter of the Ordinance introduced in 1890 and adopted by the Provincial Administration after Union in 1910, reads as follows: "No Arab, Chinaman, coolie or other Asiatic coloured person, except a Cape Malay, may settle or remain in the Free State for longer than two months without Government permission".[93]

According to Ruth Tomaselli,[94] a Transvaal law passed in 1885 forced the Indians to live in segregated areas and to pay £25 in order to enable them to trade; this fee was "beyond the means of most indentured Indians". The Gold Law in 1898, which curtailed appointments on any land proclaimed for mining, meant that the only available employment for indentured Indians was at the lowest economic levels.

It is these laws which led to the formation of the Natal Indian Congress by Gandhi and others in 1894. The Indians in Natal were subjected to the same form of attack which stimulated the Africans to unite. Natal's constitution of 1856, like that of the Cape, had no colour bar. But within a year of the grant of responsible government in 1893, the Natal government set about disenfranchising the Indians. Again, just as in the Cape, it was necessary to word the Act so that it could be argued in Britain that there was no actual race discrimination. This was done by excluding from the vote, any person, "irrespective of colour", who was a native of a country which did not itself enjoy parliamentary institutions. The only people affected were, of course, the Indians. In 1894, parliament unanimously passed this law.

Mohandas Karamchad Gandhi, a young advocate recently qualified in Britain, was sent from India to South Africa to appear in a civil case in 1892. Gandhi helped to create and build the Natal Indian Congress in 1894, and the Transvaal British Indian Association and the weekly journal, *Indian Opinion* in 1903. Though Gandhi did not see the need to form an alliance with the Africans, especially during the Bambata rebellion of 1906, he did mobilize the Indians in 1906 and 1913.

In 1906, the Transvaal government attempted to force the Indians to carry passes and Gandhi launched the first "passive" resistance campaign, a form of struggle which was to become the symbol of Gandhism, influencing the character of the South African liberation movement and shaking British colonialism in India. Maureen Tayal writes:

In September 1906, the first passive resistance pledge was taken by some 3,000 Indians at a mass meeting in Johannesburg. The meeting was by far the largest Indian political demonstration that had ever taken place in Transvaal, the pledge the first act of political defiance against the government. Both were the product of a swift massive organisational effort such as had never been undertaken before. The resisters pledged themselves to go to jail rather than take out registration certifi-

31

cates under the terms of a newly introduced ordinance meant, in the first instance, to determine who had the right to reside in the Transvaal, after which no further Asian immigration would be permitted. A deputation of resisters sailed to London to put their case to the imperial government. [95]

By June 1909, the statistics of the people arrested varied from 2 124 to over 2 500 and, said Tayal, "it was impossible to confirm either of these figures without access to police records for the period which, I was informed by the chief archivist in the Pretoria Archives in September 1976, have been destroyed". [96]

The 1913 resistance was directed against a £3 annual poll tax imposed on all those indentured after 1895. The first mass strike of Indian workers brought 60 000 Indian workers and farm labourers throughout Natal out on strike. The racist authorities opened fire, and killed and wounded a number of Indian strikers.

To generalize what has been discussed above, we can say that there were different trends and tendencies in South Africa at the end of the nineteenth century. The history of resistance was uneven, starting with the Africans of the Cape, engulfing all the oppressed nationalities - Coloureds and Indians - and running parallel, that is each community rebelling against the specific injustices that affected it. We see both resistance and collaboration expressing themselves. The politico-religious movements, which took the form of the religion of the oppressed, were the ideological expression of the progressive tendencies of the anti-colonial resistance. The African people at this time were living in a period of high political expectation. This was the period when Enoch Mankayi Sontonga composed what later became the African national anthem - *Nkosi Sikelel 'i Afrika* in 1897.

Born in Lovedale, Cape Province, in 1860, Sontonga left school at an early age and went to live in Johannesburg. A devout Christian, endowed with a wonderful voice and fond of music, Sontonga wrote the music and words to the song. He made good use of his talent in the church. *Nkosi Sikelela* was publicly sung for the first time in 1899 at the ordination of the Revd M. Boweni, a Methodist priest: "The occasion was one of wide joy but the composition was inspired by a somewhat melancholy strain." This could not be otherwise because the Africans were far from happy during the days of the Anglo-Boer War.

Sontonga died in 1904 but African teachers and poets such as J.L. Dube (later ANC President-General), R.T. Caluza, and S.E.K. Mqhayi popularized it. The song was originally intended as a hymn but it began to be sung in schools and churches in all provinces and developed an adaptation acknowledging the unity of our people. It was sung on 8 January 1912 when the ANC was formed and in 1925, the ANC adopted it as its national anthem. Today it is sung beyond the borders of South Africa. In adapted forms it is the national anthem of Tanzania, Zambia and Zimbabwe, and of the South West African People's Organization (SWAPO) of Namibia.

The character of these forces allowed for the realization of relative unity in joint resistance against the conquerors. By "character" I mean the simple fact that it was a question of personal abilities and not royal descent that enabled this new generation of leaders to rise from lower social sections to be leaders in the struggle for freedom. I use the term "relative unity" advisedly because some of the African papers were "openly critical" of the AME church, for example.

This was the golden age of the black press in South Africa. The vision, determination and commitment of those pioneers in the African newspaper world can be appreciated properly if one takes into account the fact that then there was no national African organization; the readership and circulation and therefore revenues were limited by the low level of African literacy.

The weakening of African traditional organization of society by colonialism led to the emergence of movements that sought to unify Africans. This became effective at the end of the last century - when armed resistance was coming to its close and therefore the fate of the Africans was seemingly sealed. The compromise between cultural traditions and Christian religion, together with a vision of the future, ensured mass influence. Ethiopianism - a link between the traditional and the new social forces which were beginning to emerge in the mines, plantations, seaports, compounds, mission stations and so on - became important since missions became a direct weapon of colonial expansion; missionaries became agents of colonialism irrespective of their subjective will. Religious nationalism corresponded with the new conditions.

A knowledge of this background is important for understanding the depths from which the black protest movement emerged and the historical roots of the ANC. Andre Odendaal, in his book *Vukani Bantu! The Beginnings of Black Protest Politics in South Africa to 1912* also discusses the emergence of black political organization during this period, influenced in particular by protest against the Act of Union which defined the nature of South Africa as it is today. The stage was set for a new political force that could voice African grievances and campaign for change - the ANC.

2
The Formation of the African National Congress (ANC)

I have already stated that resistance started with colonialism itself. This resistance took many forms depending on the relationship of forces, the weapons available to and used by the oppressed, the nature of oppression, the specific grievances, the possibility of victory and the preparedness of the oppressed to confront the colonizers. By the turn of the century, the Africans had many grievances. I cannot exhaust them all, and shall mention just some.

The South African Act of Union which was passed by the British House of Commons in 1909 and ratified by the South African Parliament on 31 May 1910 - the anniversary date of the Treaty of Vereeniging (31 May 1902) signed after the Anglo-Boer War - was based on a colour-bar clause that precluded all blacks from being eligible to become members of parliament. But even before then, Africans suffered untold disabilities.

When translated into practice, the Act of Union meant the repression of all blacks in every conceivable form; it was used to curtail African freedom of movement; to deny blacks the rights of trading in their (or any other) areas; to cripple their education and generally to deny them basic human rights and chances of equality of opportunity in economic development, cultural welfare and social advance.

Other laws were quickly passed to consolidate white power and perpetuate the colonial relations between the white minority and the black majority. These included:

- the Dutch Reformed Church Act, 1911, excluding blacks from membership;
- the Native Labour Regulation Act, 1911, for the benefit of mineowners;
- the Immigrants Restriction Act, 1911, imprisoning Indians in their province of domicile;

34

- the Mines and Works Act, 1911, used to protect whites behind colour bars;
- the Defence Act, 1912, providing for an all-white citizenship force and so on.

There were also many other grievances. Professor D.D.T. Jabavu,[1] son of Tengo Javabu, states that an African was required to carry as many as 12 different "legal" documents to avoid being imprisoned when challenged by the police - the pass system. According to the pass laws Africans could be arrested and removed from one place to another for any reason at any time. This pass system was closely connected with direct taxation. Under poll-tax law, Africans were forced to pay a tax altogether disproportionate to their earnings, which not only made inroads into the earnings of most Africans but constituted one of the most heart-rending grievances among Africans. Boys under 18 were taxed because magistrates were allowed to estimate a boy's age from his appearance. Taxation was also used as a means of compelling people to labour in the service of the whites. Not only that: many white farmers paid wages in kind only and some paid the £1 poll tax, and then bound the Africans for a year at a time to work on their farms. The poll tax receipt was made into a kind of pass, so that when an African failed to produce it to a policeman, he was prosecuted on a criminal charge and was liable to imprisonment. They even taxed blankets - 25 per cent on imported blankets - an indispensable article of apparel among rural Africans.

Old-age pensions were paid every month to old white people but not to Africans. On the contrary, elderly Africans were compelled to pay the "universal" native poll-tax till death if, in the judgement of the magistrates, they had cattle. There were other forms of discrimination such as the curfew regulations which stipulated that it was a criminal offence for an African man (and in some provinces women as well) to be in town, outside the location, without a night pass after 9 pm; excessive rents; lack of adequate transport facilities to and from work and high costs of existing transport; indifference of town councils and appalling or non-existent medical services. The injustice in law courts was legalized. The Masters and Servants Law enabled the white farmers to repudiate a contract entered into with an African servant and then turn round and imprison that servant, if he refused to continue to serve. The law also instituted punishment by flogging.

This is just the tip of the iceberg, but it serves to drive the point home, namely that African complaints about discrimination and injustice were based on real suffering.

8 January 1912

Faced with these problems and the fact that their interests had been totally disregarded in the absence of a political organization of their own which could voice their grievances and aspirations, the new African intellectuals - some of whom had just come back from Europe and America - worked and educated the people on their rights, duties and obligations to the state and to themselves, individually as well as collectively, and to promote mutual help, feelings of brotherhood and a spirit of togetherness among them.

Pixley ka Isaka Seme was vocal on the question of African unity. Writing in October 1911, he said he was "requested by several Natives, Leaders and Chiefs, to write a full and concise statement" on the proposed South African Native Congress but, he continued, "I feel, however, that I shall better meet their desire as well as more properly treat this subject if I disregard the pretentious title and write on the simple subject of Native Union, for after all, this is what the Congress shall be."[2]

Seme wanted to emphasize the question of unity - a unity that cut across but did not replace ethnic characteristics. After explaining what he thought such a congress should do he emphasized the urgency of forming one:

> Again, it is conclusively urgent that this Congress should meet this year, because a matter which is so vitally important to our progress and welfare should not be unnecessarily postponed by reason of personal differences and selfishness of our leaders.

Then he came to his central theme:

> The demon of racialism, the aberrations of the Xhosa-Fingo feud, the animosity that exists between the Zulus and the Tongaas, between the Basutos and every other Native must be buried and forgotten; it has shed among us sufficient blood! We are one people. These divisions, these jealousies, are the cause of all our woes and of all our backwardness and ignorance today. [3]

Seme and the African intellectuals from abroad were not, however, the originators of the idea of forming a congress to represent Africans. Regional congresses had grown up in all four provinces of the country since the turn of the century. These had made attempts to unite Africans before Seme made his call or even before he came back from abroad. Brian Willan states:

> Towards the end of 1908, a number of meetings were convened in different parts of the country and they invariably passed resolutions against the colour-bar clauses in the draft South African Act (which had emerged from the discussions held by

whites), protesting against the failure of the white policy-makers to extend the Cape franchise to the northern colonies. This movement of protest culminated in a South African Native Convention, held in Bloemfontein from 24 to 26 March, 1909. [4]

It was at the Bloemfontein convention that the decision was taken to send a deputation to England to express African opposition to the Draft Act of Union. It was the most representative gathering ever to have been convened by Africans and it further resolved that "a permanent organization (of the same name) should be formed".[5] A year later, in March 1910, the convention held its second annual meeting, also in Bloemfontein.

It is against this background that one has to understand the remarks of Willan, the biographer of Sol Plaatje:

An awareness of the importance of achieving unity of this kind was not, of course, new, and even before the Act of Union some experience in trying to reconcile the immense political and regional differences that existed had been gained in organisations like the South African Native Press Association, in which Plaatje had played a leading part in 1903 and 1904, in the Native Convention held in Bloemfontein in 1909, and then in the formation of a permanent - if not altogether representative - organisation of the same name, which maintained a somewhat discreet existence throughout 1910 and 1911; in this, too, Plaatje played a part, occupying the position of Assistant Secretary.

It was from the experience of the South African Native Convention that Congress actually emerged, and it is clear that a great deal of discussion and deliberation, in which Plaatje was much involved, had taken place before Pixley Seme, a lawyer trained at Columbia University, U.S.A., and Jesus College, Oxford, who had recently returned to South Africa, was able to issue his now famous clarion call for unity at the end of 1911. Plaatje had been amongst those who attended a special meeting of the executive committee of the convention, held in Johannesburg early in August 1911, which provided Seme with the first opportunity to expand upon his ideas about the need for a more vigorous, more representative, above all a more united political organisation . . .

Plaatje claimed to have made possible the establishment of Congress by persuading the leaders of the two main Transvaal African organisations already in existence, the Transvaal Native Congress and the Transvaal Native Political Organisation, to set aside their differences and rivalries and cooperate in setting up a single, national body.[6]

My intention is not to prove whether it was Plaatje or Seme who initiated the formation of the South African Native National Congress which later became the ANC - in any case there were other people involved in the process - but to state the simple fact that the formation of the ANC was a result of the people's experience and the leaders were responding to the people's demands.

On 8 January 1912 Africans gathered from all four provinces of South Africa and Béchuanaland. Some came formally dressed in suits, frock coats, top hats and carrying umbrellas. They met in Bloemfontein. Once again, it was Seme who gave the keynote address:

> Chiefs of royal blood and gentlemen of our race, we have gathered here to consider and discuss a theme which my colleagues and I have decided to place before you. We have discovered that in the land of their birth, Africans are treated as hewers of wood and drawers of water. The white people of this country have formed what is known as the Union of South Africa - a union which we have no voice in the making of the laws and no part in their administration. We have called you therefore to this Conference so that we can together devise ways and means of forming our national union for the purpose of creating national unity and defending our rights and privileges. [7]

After the opening speeches the gathering sang Tiyo Soga's *Lizalis idinga Lakho, Thixo Nkosi Yenyaniso (Fulfil thy Promise, God, Thou Lord of Truth)*. Seme formally moved that the South African Native National Congress be established. The motion was then put to a vote, and passed unanimously with loud cheers, all delegates standing.

The inaugural conference decided that two houses, the Upper and Lower House, should be established. Seven paramount chiefs, appointed as Honorary Presidents, made up the Upper House. These were:

- Dalindyebo of the Thembus;
- Montsioa of the Barolong;
- Lewanika of Barotseland (part of Zambia);
- Letsie II of Basutoland;
- Khama of Bechuanaland;
- Marclane of Pondoland; and
- Moepi of the Bakgatla.

Dinizulu, the Zulu chief who was deposed and exiled to the Transvaal by the British was later also included.

The National Executive Committee (of the Lower House) consisted of:

- The Revd John L. Dube, President-General;
- Solomon T. Plaatje, Secretary-General;
- Pixley ka Isaka Seme, Treasurer-General;
- Thomas Mapikela, Speaker;
- Montsioa (of the Barolong), Recording Secretary;
- The Revd Mqoboli of the Wesleyan Church was Chaplain-in-Chief with the Revd H.R. Ngcayiya as his assistant;
- The Revd Walter Rubusana, Meshack Pelem, Sam Makgatho and Alfred Mangena were elected Vice-Presidents.

The first National Executive of the ANC is interesting in many respects: it consisted of four ministers of religion, lawyers, an editor, a building contractor, a teacher and estate agent, an interpreter and Native Labour Agent (who recruited African mineworkers). These were people who had gone to mission schools; five of them had also studied abroad. They were prominent in local political organizations, in the African press, and church circles; some had already become national figures. They were relatively young - in their twenties and early thirties. The four provinces were well represented on the Executive.

A word on the inclusion of the chiefs. They were honoured, in accordance with African tradition, by being involved in this new organization as Honorary Presidents in the Upper House. They "represented" the rural masses who were the majority of the people at the time and the section most affected by land robbery. There was a need for an alliance between the peasants and the young intelligentsia since the working class was still in the process of formation. These chiefs were recognized spokesmen of their people; they had fought against colonialism and some of them were victimized, deposed or banished. It is said that in 1912 Dube addressed a group of Africans in Zululand to explain the new movement and to appeal for unity. A member of the audience shouted, "I thank Bambata. I thank Bambata very much. Would this spirit might continue! I do not mean the Bambata of the bush who perished at Nkandhla, but I mean this new spirit which we have just heard explained."[8]

The name of the new organization was, however, a bone of contention. Plaatje strongly believed that the Congress should have an African name and he was strongly supported in this by Joshua Molema. But the meeting decided by a majority to adopt the recommendation that the new organization should be known as the South African Native National Congress. Plaatje clearly felt strongly about the issue, because, on his insistence, the Executive Committee were authorized to remain behind to "complete the unfinished job and review the constitution".[9] Once again he urged that the Congress's name be changed and he read a letter from Cleopas Kunene (later to be editor of the Congress's official organ, *Abantu-Batho*) who proposed the name "Imbizo Yabantu". Plaatje was again defeated, however and Section 1 of the constitution affirmed that "The name of this organization should be the South African Native National Congress."[10]

At this inaugural conference 11 papers were read, the topics ranging from African marriage and divorce; African beer; schools and churches to African labour, and the land question.

Nkosi Sikelela was sung on 8 January. Then at the conclusion of the proceedings John Knox Bokwe's *Give a Thought to Africa* was sung and the delegates returned home to report back to their respective organizations and communities.

It has been said that this conference signified the birthday not only of the ANC but also of the nation - the ANC was assigned the task of being a midwife in the process of national rebirth and regeneration.[11] This meant the creation of a loyalty of a new type - a non-tribal loyalty - which was inherently anti-colonial and, by implication, anti-missionary. This was an act of national salvation, a continuation - under new historical conditions - of the anti-colonial struggle of our people which began with colonialism itself.

What about the founding fathers of the Congress? Dr A.B. Xuma has gone on record as saying that they "displayed great vision and laid a broad foundation on which to build the superstructure for African freedom and liberty in the land of their forefathers".[12] He went on to say that they proclaimed through the organization they set up and efforts they made, that only through unity and concerted action of all, can justice and freedom be achieved. These men made sacrifices and suffered privations in the cause of African freedom; some of them went to jail, but they remained popular, loyal and true to the cause of their people. They pointed the way for us; they showed that freedom is precious and a heavy price must be paid to obtain it.

These men led a full and varied life. Some of them had immense talent and ability - men who rose by their own efforts to become, during their lifetime, some of the best known black South Africans of their generation. They were in the forefront of their people for the greater part of their adult life. They contributed to our political history, history of the press and literature, especially literature in African languages.

When one considers the difficulties, discouragement and financial hardship they faced throughout their adult lives, the achievements of these men are clear. They worked with determination to serve the interests of their people in conditions and circumstances that were extremely hard. This, however, gave a sense of unity and purpose to their many-sided lives and careers. They also had their limitations, however - their beliefs and approach were conditioned by the times in which they operated, and were soon to be overtaken by political events and socio-economic changes in South Africa. *One of their greatest contributions to our struggle nevertheless remains: by forming the ANC, they established African political opinion as an autonomous factor in its own right in South Africa.*

The early years (1912-19)

The Native Land Act of 1913 under which the white population of one and a half million was allotted more than 90 per cent of the total land, while the African population of five and a half million got less than 10 per cent, was one of the most burning issues for the new Congress. In the 70 + years that have followed, nothing has changed substantially in this unjust division except that the population statistics have risen drastically - out of a population of 30 million there are more than 25 million blacks who possess a mere 13 per cent of the land.

Before 1913, with the exception of the Orange Free State, Africans could purchase and lease land outside the reserves upon the same basis as whites. White farmers were, by 1912, becoming alarmed at the increasing acquisition of farms by Africans, especially in the Transvaal. A further problem was that of the so-called squatters. These were Africans who secured land from white owners in return for rent paid usually either in services, cash or kind. The Land Act of 1913 was meant to stop this development. It denied Africans the right to own land, except in the reserves, sited on areas too small for their proposed population, where the soil was infertile or eroded, or in areas infested with mosquitoes and therefore where malaria is rife.

This legalized land robbery forced many Africans to the towns, beginning the urbanization and continuing the proletarianization of Africans. The struggle against the Land Act was a struggle for the return of the land robbed by colonialists from the Africans. In other words, the Land Act had the double function of suppressing the emerging African peasantry which was becoming a threat to the white farmer and also creating a mass of cheap labour in the rural areas.

Solomon Plaatje in his book *Native Life in South Africa*, first published in 1916 makes a devastating critique of the Act. He travelled through the Orange Free State, Transvaal and the Cape studying the effects of the Land Act and wrote, "Awakening on Friday morning, June 20, 1913, the South African native found himself, not actually a slave, but a pariah in the land of his birth."[13] He described the plight of one evicted family, the Kgobadis, whose goats were dying one by one "as fast as they were born and left by the roadside for the jackals and vultures to feast upon". He continued:

> This visitation was not confined to Kgobadi's stock. Mrs Kgobadi carried a sick baby when the eviction took place, and she had to transfer her darling from the cottage to the jolting oxwagon in which they left the farm. Two days out the little one began to sink as a result of privation and exposure on the road, and the night before we met them its little soul was released from its earthly bonds. The death of the child added a fresh perplexity to the stricken parents. They had no right or title to the farm

land through which they trekked: they must keep to the public roads - the only places in the country open to the outcasts if they are possessed of travelling permit. The deceased child had to be buried, but where, when, and how?

This young wandering family decided to dig a grave under the cover of darkness of that night, when no one was looking, and in that crude manner the dead child was interred - and interred amid fear and trembling, as well as the throbs of a torturing anguish, in a stolen grave, lest the proprietor of the spot, or any of his servants, should surprise them in the act. Even criminals dropping straight from the gallows have an undisputed claim to six feet of ground on which to rest their criminal remains, but under the cruel operation of the Natives' Land Act little children, whose only crime is that God did not make them white, are sometimes denied that right in their ancestral home.[14]

This case alone underlines the brutality with which the Land Act was enforced.

The ANC mounted a campaign against the Land Act. Resolutions, telegraphic and other representations were made. In March 1913, the Annual Conference of the ANC appointed a deputation to present African objections to the Act to the government. This deputation consisted of J.L. Dube; Dr. W.B. Rubusana; Mangena; the Revd L. Dlepu; W.Z. Fenyang; S. Msane; L.T. Mvabaza; D. Letanka and Sol T. Plaatje, although he was unable to proceed to Cape Town.

On 5 July 1913, the ANC called a meeting specifically to receive the report of the delegates to Cape Town and further to consider what other actions might be taken. Africans from as far south as East London and King William's Town and from as far north as the Zoutpansberg in the northern Transvaal and also from Natal and Bechuanaland met in Johannesburg: "They had gathered to discuss the situation arising from the serious conditions created by the Native Land Act."[15] On the platform were John Dube, R.S. Msimang and Plaatje. Dr Rubusana gave the report. He told the audience about the delegation's four interviews with members of Parliament: every effort had failed.

Mission to London

Rubusana had earlier (in May 1913) written a letter to Lord Gladstone, the British Governor-General of South Africa, asking him not to agree to the Bill until he had heard the African view. Two months later, in July, J. Dube, as ANC President-General, also wrote to Lord Gladstone, asking for an interview so that he could explain the nature of the damage to Africans that the Act would cause. Lord Gladstone would not, however, see them. It was therefore decided that the next step in the ANC's campaign would be to appeal to the British Government "and also to take steps to appraise the British public of the mode of government carried on in British South Africa under the Union Jack, and to invoke their assistance to abrogate the obnoxious law that had brought the Congress together".[16]

Why did people think that Britain and the British public might help? It was argued that if South Africa were really British, then any suffering taking place in the country must be the concern of His Majesty the King and the British public. But were our predecessors not aware that the Union Act was a creation of Britain? The ANC deputation were embarking on a journey consisting of 1 600 kilometres (1 000 miles) by rail - from Johannesburg to Cape Town - and 9 600 kilometres (6 000 miles) by sea from Cape Town to London. This was no easy matter, as Plaatje pointed out:

> When the Europeans of South Africa went to England to ask the Imperial Government for a constitution, their delegates were easily sent because the native taxpayers, although with hardly any hope of benefitting by the gift - which amounted to a curtailment of their rights - were compelled to contribute to the travelling and other expenses of their envoys; but in the Natives' own case no such funds are at his disposal, even though his taxes had been used by a Parliament in which he is unrepresented as a rod for his back. [17]

Something had to be done to meet this critical situation. S. Msane was deputed to tour the country and ask for funds from the Africans. In Johannesburg a committee was formed to superintend this effort and to take charge of the funds which might be raised. Its members were W.F. Jemsana (Chairman), E.M. Cele (Treasurer) D.S. Letanka, R.W. Msimang, H.D. Mkize, B.G. Phooko, D.D. Tywakadi, D. Moeletsi, M.D. Ndabezita, H. Selby Msimang (Honorary Secretary), and S. Msane (Organizer).

At the same time, a deputation was sent to Pretoria to present the government with three resolutions passed by the third ANC Conference:

(a) Condolences were sent to the government on the death of J.W. Sauer, Minister of Justice and Native Affairs, who died just as the ANC was about to meet.

(b) The Africans dissociated themselves entirely from the armed clashes between the white workers and the government on the Witwatersrand and elsewhere and preferred to seek redress for their grievances through constitutional means. This was a reference to the general strike by white workers, which took place in 1913-14. The government proclaimed martial law and mobilized 70 000 armed men to crush the strike. Hundreds of strikers, trade union

43

leaders and Labour Party leaders were arrested; some went to jail singing the *Red Flag*. A number of trade union leaders were deported to Britain under the hurriedly introduced Indemnity and Undesirables Special Deportation Bill.[18]

(c) Since the representations to the authorities had failed, the Africans had now decided to raise funds for the purpose and convey their appeal to Britain and the British public.

Safe conduct was also requested for Msane to tour the African villages. The members of this deputation were Chief Karl Kekane and S.M. Makgatho (Transvaal); E. Mamba (Transkei); S. Msane and the Revd Twala (Natal); Sol T. Plaatje (Cape); and J.M. Nyokong (Orange Free State).

S.F. Malan, Minister of Native Affairs, "confessed to a feeling of relief at the moderation of their tone".[19] General Botha, the Prime Minister, was against the idea of an African delegation going to England. Plaatje reports:

> General Botha's efforts against the deputation, without offering any homes to the evicted Natives, was probably the best stimulus towards the deputation fund. The premier visited a northern tribe some time after and was said to have warned the Chief and his people against the pretensions of the Native Congress. When Mr Dube called there a few days later, they handed him £200 towards the deputation fund, which they had collected since General Botha's visit. Mr Saul Msane similarly raised £360 for the fund in the Eastern Transvaal where the Premier warned the Natives against the deputation without offering them any relief.[20]

At this juncture we need to address ourselves to the often-repeated thesis that the ANC at this time and later was reformist. Perhaps the best way to answer this is to pose concrete questions. Why did the ANC approach the government before consulting with the masses regarding a deputation to London? Why did the ANC send a delegation at all, especially after the first one in 1909 failed? Why did they give condolences to the government when the Minister of Justice and Native Affairs, Sauer, died? And why did the ANC Conference adopt a resolution which stated that "the Natives disassociated themselves entirely from the industrial strikes on the Witwatersrand and elsewhere and preferred to seek redress for their grievances through constitutional rather than by violent means?"

It would be wrong to deduce from this that the ANC at this time was simply reformist and end there. Some obvious reasons for their approach come to mind:

(1) Deputations and appeals were part of traditional African political custom.

(2) In 1915, the enemy was different from our enemy today. Our

forefathers were different from us. The conflicts between British and Boer, and therefore between English-speaking and Afrikaans-speaking whites, were sharper than they are today and this gave rise to a hope - realistic or not - that Britain might concede to the pleas of the Africans;

(3) The social composition of the ANC and its leadership, which consisted mainly of ministers of religion and lawyers and was definitely not working class, was another reason. The African working class was still very weak at that time and so the ANC lacked the necessary strength to challenge white power directly; it had to use other tactics.

(4) The betrayal of the interests of the working class by the white union leaders and later by the mass of white workers. Their neglect of the plight and aspirations of Africans in their demands generated a feeling of mistrust by Africans as to the real intentions of white workers who emphasized the "class struggle" and were unwilling to understand the question of national oppression of the Africans and other blacks.

As a result of the white miners' strike, the ANC was refused permission to hold a meeting in Johannesburg but it was held in Kimberley on 27 February 1914. Those present included John Dube (ANC President-General), Makgatho (Vice-President), Prince Malunge ka Mbandeni of Swaziland, Chiefs Molotlegi and Maniogale from the Transvaal, Chief Moiloa of the Tswana, E.M. Cele of Natal, Meshack Pelem from the Cape, J.M. Nyokong and S. Litheko of the Orange Free State and others. I. Joshua (Chairman of APO - a Coloured organization - see Chapter 1) Lakey, September and other APO committee members were also at the meeting. A public reception in the City Hall was attended by hundreds of Coloured people cheering the musicians of their African brothers. APO sent a speaker, H. Van Rooyen, to welcome the delegates on its behalf and Joseph Kokozela also welcomed the delegates to Kimberley on behalf of the Kimberley and Beaconsfield branches of the ANC.

The meeting chose members of the deputation that finally went to London (they were democratically elected through the ballot). These were J. Dube, Dr Rubusana, Sol T. Plaatje, Saul Msane and T.M. Mapikela.

Dube and Rubusana sailed on a mailship bound for England on 16 May 1914 and Plaatje, Mapikela and Msane sailed the following day. Upon their arrival in Britain the deputation contacted the Anti-Slavery and Aborigines' Protection Society which offered to assist them. But this Society had its own aims and its own very definite ideas. J.H. Harris, the Society's Organizing Secretary, explained to Lord Harcourt,

Secretary of State for the Colonies, that the Society's policy was to use its "influence in the direction of securing a modification of their [the ANC's] original programme and an abstention from public agitation pending the exhaustion of every constitutional means open to them.[21] Harris therefore persuaded the delegates to replace the demand for the repeal of the Native Land Act with proposals instead for the modification and suspension of part of the Act. The Society arranged an interview for the delegates with Lord Harcourt on condition that they confined themselves to the points laid out by him and Harris.

The ANC delegation had to wait for weeks before being granted an interview with Lord Harcourt because he was "awaiting instructions from General Botha before deciding when, where and how to meet the deputation of the Native Congress".[22] They finally met him at the end of June. Harris, who wished to be present, could not come because the Colonial Office saw no need for that. Free from Harris' influence and supervision the ANC delegation expressed its views in much stronger and forthright terms than Harris had prescribed. Lord Harcourt was not impressed:

> Mr Harcourt made no notes and asked no questions at the interview accorded to our deputation. He listened to how desperately we resisted the passing of the law; how the Government ignored all our representations, and those of all the churches and missionary bodies on our behalf; how we twice applied to Lord Gladstone for opportunities to inform him of the ruin which is wrought by the law among our people; how Lord Gladstone wrote in each instance saying it was "not within his constitutional functions" to see us. To all this Mr Harcourt replied with another assurance of General Botha that "we have not exhausted all South African remedies before coming to England".[23]

Back in South Africa, the ANC had called a special meeting in Bloemfontein:

> First to express its disappointment at the cold reception given to the native deputation by the Imperial Government; and secondly, to express its thanks to the British public for the kind reception given to the deputation; and, thirdly, to devise ways and means for the députation to tour the United Kingdom on a mission, revealing to the British people the manner in which the Colonial Government discharges its trust to the coloured people.[24]

But the ANC could not forge ahead with its plans because of the outbreak of the First World War and instead resolved "itself at once into a patriotic demonstration, decided to hang up native grievances against the South African Parliament till a better time and to tender the authorities every assistance".[25] The outbreak of the war exacerbated the differences of opinion already developing amongst the delegates in London. This explains why "the members of the native deputation to

England were longing to catch the first steamer back to South Africa to join their countrymen and proceed to the front".[26]

Other factors also influenced the delegation's decision to return. Most critical were the differences between delegates. Indeed, Dube had already left London. Plaatje remained to continue the campaign single-handed. He wanted to complete and publish his book about the Land Act, which he had started writing on the journey and wanted printed "immediately after landing in England". He also had another reason for wanting to complete the book: his anger at the way in which the Anti-Slavery and Aborigines' Protection Society had sought to control and therefore undermine the deputation's campaign in England. The Society in turn attempted to suppress the book and Harris verbally attacked Plaatje personally.

The problems that faced Plaatje in Britain are reflected in the book. They were:

a) the intransigence of the British Government and its officials;

b) the hostility of the Anti-Slavery and Aborigines' Protection Society, a Society supposedly devoted to the interests of "native races" of the empire, but which pursued a vicious attack on one of the leading representatives of South Africa's black population.

The theme of Plaatje's book is that the Land Act is a "tyrannical enactment" that represented the triumph of "Boer principles" over British notions of "fair play and justice". The Africans - "loyal British subjects" - were being "crushed by the Boers". "Dutch inhumanity" was his favourite phrase and it was contrasted with "British justice", hence the pride in being "loyal British subjects" or "loyalty to the King".

In fairness to Plaatje, this feeling of "loyalty" to Britain was fairly widespread at the time. A.C. Jordan explained this when writing about S.E.K. Mqhayi, the Xhosa poet:

Mqhayi possessed this quality, hence his being known as *Imbongi ye Sizwe Jikelele,* which title was conferred upon him by a Zulu in Johannesburg. But Mqhayi had a double loyalty. As a Xhosa he was loyal to the Xhosa chiefs and their ancestors, and as a British subject he had to be loyal to the British King. A poem written during the Boer War in the *Izwi Laba Ntu* of March 13, 1900, shows how very sincerely Mqhayi had accepted British guardianship. Each stanza has a refrain, "Singama Britani" (We are Britons!). Nurtured in Christianity and in the policy of the "Old Cape Liberals", he believed that the conquest of Southern Africa by the British was the working out of a Divine Purpose. After the defeat in 1879, he makes the Zulus say in the poem *Isandlwana,* "Wozani, ma Britani, sigezan izingozi" (Come, ye Britons, let's bathe one another's wounds!). Then the Zulus go on to tell the British that their own defeat was the working out of God's purpose, so that from the British, the Zulus might receive a new life, a new birth, a new learning, and see the Love of the Son of the Great-Great, and fight His battles ...

47

In the elegy written on the disaster of the Mendi, though bemoaning the loss of the flower of Africa, he reminds his people that some such worthy sacrifice had to be made if they truly loved Britain; he reminds them how God sacrificed His own Son, the Messiah. Again the working-out of a Divine Purpose! If the ties with Britain are to break, as they threaten to do, this sacrifice must be.[27]

Plaatje and his contemporaries saw their approach as a tactic. They had strong views on the oppression of their people, but perhaps the problem was that of correctly identifying the enemy. In those days, Africans thought that the Boers were the only enemy (and Plaatje knew them from the Orange Free State, his place of birth). They identified the clash of interests between Boer and Briton and thought these conflicts could be used to their advantage and that the task was therefore, to win the British over to their side by showing African "loyalty" to the king. The interconnection between colonialism and imperialism was not properly understood.

Plaatje spent two and a half years in England addressing meetings all over the country - over 300 meetings, sometimes at the rate of one every two or three days. He reached a wide audience and the publication of his book in May 1916 helped him in his endeavours. He finally returned home in 1917.

The First World War and its aftermath

In the years 1914-16, the ANC had largely refrained from any criticism of the South African government as a demonstration of their "loyalty to the King and Empire" in the war against Germany. But in October 1916, at a meeting in Pietermaritzburg, the ANC became critical of the Report of the Beaumont Commission. This was in connection, again, with the Land Act. It was, however, at the annual conference of the ANC in Bloemfontein in May-June 1917 that Plaatje made what the *Rand Daily Mail* called "a vicious attack on the Government which practically sounded the tocsin of a black v. white propaganda".[28]

The question of the ANC delegation to England was reviewed. It was felt that Dube had made some compromises by his apparent acceptance of the principle - if not the practice - of segregation, and he was ousted from the presidency of the ANC. Selope Thema had acted as Secretary-General during Plaatje's absence but "out of loyalty to his president ... decided to step down". Plaatje was offered the presidency but he turned it down, although he did agree to serve as Senior Vice-President. For three weeks, the ANC was without a president until S.M. Makgatho was appointed President-General on 23 June 1917.

The outbreak of the First World War posed serious political questions for the ANC. The war was fought for more colonies. But not only that. It was fought with the help of the colonies. It is one of those bitter ironies of the First World War that the colonial people had to pay such a high price for their own enslavement. Through deceit, bribery and corruption, the Africans were made to believe that colonialists were going to grant them freedom after the war.

South Africa was very much involved in the war. On behalf of Britain and its allies, South African armed forces attacked and defeated German forces in Namibia (then German South West Africa) in 1915 and then took over control of the territory. The ANC protested against the incorporation of Namibia into South Africa - a burning issue even today. A South African brigade under a British military man, Larkin, and 364 airforce from the Royal Flying Corps were sent to France as South Africa's "contribution". Out of the 60 000 white South African soldiers who participated in the war 19 556 were reported "fallen", "missing" or "wounded".[29] These figures are misleading because they do not included the casualties of the war against the Germans in Namibia and against Lettow-Vorbeck in East Africa. Moreover, the number of Africans who went to Europe and were killed remains a mystery up to today. We are, however, in a position to use our imaginations if we take into consideration that:

> No official statistics are given of the number of Native and Coloured workers likewise killed and wounded, but unofficial reports reveal even greater losses on their part. Besides, the Native and Coloured toilers received the most brutal, inhuman and slave treatment in "the labour conscript armies", which numbered 23 000 in South West Africa, 17 000 in East Africa and 21 000 in Europe. [30]

Towards the end of the war, says Walshe, 865 Africans lost their lives, including 600 who drowned on 21 February 1917, when the warship *Mendi* struck a rock near the Isle of Wight in the British Channel and sank. [31]

These factors explain the militant positions taken by the ANC by the end of the war, especially at the annual conference in Bloemfontein in May-June 1917 when Plaatje, in the presence of the Deputy-Mayor of Bloemfontein, town officials and representatives from the Labour Party made what the South African Press called a "poisonous attack" on the government, a speech which received what amounted to a standing ovation. [32]

The influence of the crisis of capitalism following the First World War, the Great Socialist October Revolution in Russia and the subsequent world-wide revolutionary upsurge had a significant impact on South Africa. It was at this time that a wave of strikes took place, such as when 100 000 African mineworkers went on strike for higher wages in March 1918, or the campaign of the ANC against the pass laws in the Orange Free State and Transvaal in 1919 and the protest demonstration in which more than 700 ANC members and sympathisers were arrested. The 1920 strike of 71 000 African mineworkers on the Witwatersrand was a success in that the mineowners found themselves forced to make a 25 per cent increase in the wages of African workers. It is not accidental that the Industrial and Commercial Workers' Union of Africa was formed by Clements Kadalie in 1919 during this period of strike fever (see chapter 3). The Africans learnt and saw the importance of the weapon of the strike. One consequence of these strikes was an increase in membership of the ANC.

Protests against passes for African women

Whilst the ANC was dealing with issues arising from the Union Act and the Land Act and problems connected with consolidating the movement and working out an overall strategy, a new issue arose - African women in the Orange Free State were being forced either to buy passes every month or go to prison. In both instances they were exposed to the indecent provision of the law which allowed male constables to insult them.

There was a new element to those pass laws. In the past, the pass regulations had never been enforced against clergymen's wives or against the "families of respectable" Africans, but now a wife of a minister had to produce a pass on demand and like every other black woman she had to pay a shilling for a fresh pass at the end of the month. The result, as Plaatje says, was that a family consisting of, say, a mother and five daughters paid the municipality six shillings every month "whether as a penalty for the colour of their skins or a penalty for their sex it is not clear which".[33]

Africans made all possible constitutional appeals against these outrages, but without success. A deputation of women from Bloemfontein - Mrs A.S. Gabashane, Mrs Kotsi and Mrs Louw - went to Cape Town to air their grievances about passes to H. Burton, Minister of Native Affairs and also sent a petition to Lady Gladstone. Having exhausted all these constitutional measures without success and witnessing the spread of further problems for African women and children under the terms of the Native Land Act, they decided to "throw off their shawls" and to take the law into their hands:

A crowd of six hundred women, in July 1913, marched to the Municipal Offices at Bloemfontein and asked to see the Mayor. He was not in, so they called for the Town Clerk. The Deputy Mayor came out, and they deposited before him a bag containing their passes of the previous month and politely signified their intention not to buy any more passes.[34]

At Jaggersfontein a similar demonstration was led by a Mozambican woman. The women were arrested, but refused to pay the fines imposed on them. The authorities were scarcely prepared for such a sudden influx, and there was not sufficient accommodation for the fifty-two women prisoners, who were conveyed on donkey carts to the adjoining village of Fauresmith.

In Winburg as well there was similar resistance. Eight hundred women singing hymns marched to the town hall and addressed the authorities. They were tired of making friendly appeals which bore no fruit and they resolved to carry no passes, much less to pay a shilling each per month for passes: "they all resolutely refused to pay their fines, and there was a rumour that the Central Government had been appealed to for funds and for material to fit out a new jail to cope with the difficulty."[35]

Brutal methods were used to deal with the women protesters, "The first batch of prisoners from Bloemfontein were conveyed south to Edenburg; and as further batches came down from Bloemfontein they had to be retransferred north to Kroonstad."[36]

Plaatje visited the prison in Kroonstad in August 1913 accompanied by the wife of the Revd A.P. Pitso of Kroonstad and Mrs Petrus. He was shocked to see the conditions of the women:

A severe shock burst upon us, inside the prison walls, when the matron withdrew the barriers and the emaciated figures of ladies and young girls of our acquaintance filed out and greeted us. It was an exceptionally cold week and our hearts bled to see young women of Bloemfontein, who had spent all their lives in the capital and never knew what it was to walk without socks, walking the chilly cemented floors and the cold and sharp pebbles without boots. Their own boots and shoes had been taken off, they told us, and they were, throughout the winter, forced to perform hard labour bare footed.[37]

Plaatje and the members of his delegation reacted to this scene and their hearts were filled with pity and sympathy, but there was a sense of pride and confidence which expressed itself in mutual solidarity:

Tears rolled down our cheeks as we saw the cracks on their bare feet, the swelling and chilblains which made them look like sheep suffering from foot and mouth disease ... To our surprise, however, they vowed never to buy passes, even if they had to come back.

The typical attitude of white racists towards this inhumanity was that "instead of being sent to prison with hard labour, these mad caps should be flogged". Plaatje, then Secretary-General of the ANC, telegraphed General Botha "and pointed out to him that over two hundred Coloured women were at that time languishing in jail for resenting a crime committed upon them". Botha did not respond.

In 1918 an African women's organization, the Bantu Women's League, was formed; T.D. Mweli Skota, in his African Yearly Register (1931), called it a branch of the African National Congress. Founder and spearhead of this movement was Charlotte Maxeke. She achieved political prominence as a leader of women demonstrators against proposals to extend the pass system to women. She became President of this League "for many years". As such, she led a delegation to the Prime Minister to discuss the question of the passes for women in the Orange Free State. The League which had branches almost all over the country, demonstrated widely against passes for women.[38]

New directions and constitutional changes

The leadership of the ANC was also preoccupied with drafting its own constitution, rules and regulations. There was a need for comprehensive machinery by which to manage and direct national affairs; for the management of officers in the discharge of their duties; control of the collection and expenditure of funds; and for regulations setting out the conduct of the organization and co-ordination between branches, provincial congresses and the mother body.

At the inaugural meeting in Bloemfontein on 8 January 1912, a list of "21 objects" was drawn up, including the need:

To encourage mutual understanding and to bring together into common action as one political people all tribes and clans of various tribes or races and by means of combined effort and united political organisation to defend their freedom, rights and privileges; to educate Parliament and Provincial Councils, municipalities, other bodies and the public generally regarding the requirements and aspirations of the African and to enlist the sympathy and support of Europeans; to educate African people on their rights, duties and obligations to the state and to themselves and to promote mutual help; to record all grievances and wants of the African people and to seek by constitutional means the redress thereof, to agitate and advocate by just means for the removal of the colour bar in political, education and industrial fields and for equitable representation of Africans in Parliament or in those bodies that are vested with legislative matters affecting the coloured races; to be the medium of representative opinion and to formulate a standard policy on Native Affairs for the benefit and guidance of the Union Government and Parliament; to discourage and contend against racialism and tribal feuds or to secure the elimination of racialism and tribal feuds, jealousy and petty quarrels by economic combination, education, goodwill and by other means; to establish or to assist the establishment of National

Colleges or Public Institutions free from denominationalism or state control; to encourage inculcation and practices of habits of industry; thrift and cleanliness among the people and to propagate the gospel of the dignity of labour.[39]

I have quoted these demands verbatim and at length. They show the enormity of the tasks facing the ANC at the time.

They also show clearly the thinking of ANC leaders and indicate their shortcomings. The most obvious weakness is the fact that there is no mention of equality and national liberation of the Africans - a demand which has become central and a hallmark of our movement today. But if one considers that even in Europe in 1912 the working class, which had more than 50 years of experience in class struggle, was still finding its way, one understands the shortcomings of the ANC at that time. In fact its very existence under the colonial conditions of Africa was a revolutionary step.

The Extraordinary Meeting of the Executive Committee of the ANC held at Bloemfontein on 1 August 1914 "considered, amended, read and confirmed and declared" the draft constitution of both Houses to be the constitution of the ANC.[40] But already a year thereafter, on 3 August 1915, at the Fourth Annual Meeting of the ANC, held at Kroonstad, Orange Free State, dissatisfaction with the constitution was expressed and a resolution was adopted for the revision of the constitution.

The members of the select committee entrusted with this task were:

- Natal: J.T. Gumede (Pietermaritzburg) and W.W. Ndhlovu (Vryheid);
- Cape: E.P.B. Koti (Queenstown) and E. Tshongwana (Lusikisiki);
- Orange Free State: J.B. Twayi; T.M. Mapikela (Bloemfontein) and the Revd A.P. Pitso (Kroonstad);
- Transvaal: D.S. Letanka (Johannesburg) and S.M. Makgatho (Pretoria);
- Swaziland: B. Nxumalo (Bremersdorp).
- R.W. Msimang was Chairman of the Committee.[41]

The committee met at Pietermaritzburg in October 1916. Most of the discussion was through correspondence as travelling was expensive. It was not until 2 August 1918 that the select committee made its report to the Executive Committee in Bloemfontein who read and discussed the revised constitution "clause by clause", made certain alterations and amendments, then agreed upon and formally adopted it.

The constitution is lengthy, bulky and detailed. Jack Simons has discussed this in relation to the question of membership. He says it:

provided for three kinds of individual members, all required to belong to the aboriginal races of Africa. This proviso was interpreted to include Coloureds on the

53

assumption that the ancestors of at least one parent were aborigines. Ordinary membership was open to men over the age of 18 years; honorary membership could be conferred on persons who had rendered outstanding service to the people; while auxiliary membership, without voting rights, existed for members of the Bantu Women's National League, who provided shelter and food for the delegates. [42]

One fact which needs to be mentioned is that the ANC is referred to in the constitution as a "Pan-African Association".[43] This is of great significance because it shows that as early as 1919, the African National Congress enshrined in its constitution the lofty ideals of African unity which are now embodied in the Charter of the Organization for African Unity (OAU). The ANC was perhaps the first organization to do so. Even Dr du Bois, the father of Pan-Africanism - which in the parlance of today would be African unity - has this to say about the first Pan-African Congress in Paris which he initiated and founded in 1919, "I was without credential or influence, but the idea took on."[44]

In 1919, for the third time, Africans sent a delegation to appeal to the British Government. The delegates were H.R. Ngcayiya, Selope Thema, L.T. Mvabaza, J.T. Gumede and Sol T. Plaatje. In Britain they met many public and political figures, including Lloyd George, the British Prime Minister, on 21 November 1919 - "In many ways it was surprising that this took place at all."[45] The ANC delegation enumerated the daily humiliations and arrests, the pass laws, other discriminatory legislation and the unbearable living conditions Africans suffered because being voteless meant that they were helpless. They put their case so powerfully and eloquently that Lloyd George confessed:

> You have said enough to convince me that it is certainly a case which ought to be taken into the consideration of the South African Government and I shall certainly take the earliest opportunity of presenting the whole of the facts to General Smuts. [46]

Lloyd George did pursue the matter with General Smuts but Smuts would not be moved even when Lloyd George talked of the threat of "Bolshevism" and "Garveyism" to the "whole existing structure of society". (The anti-colonial philosophy of Marcus Garvey, a Jamaican who preached "Africa for the Africans" mobilized blacks throughout the world. His philosophy influenced some sections within the ANC).

It was the socialist movement and the British working class that gave the ANC delegation a warm welcome and reception. The ANC delegation used this opportunity to produce pamphlets on issues such as the legal disabilities suffered by Africans in South Africa; they embarked on speaking tours under the auspices of the Independent Labour Party and interviews with them appeared in left-wing newspapers, including one by Fenner Brockway.

The sending of ANC delegations abroad helped the ANC leadership to realize that the future well-being of our people would have to be fought within South Africa and that new strategies would have to be devised to come to terms with the realities of the South African situation - an important realization. With the inspiration of some of the members of the delegation, especially Plaatje, their sympathisers in Britain decided to form "a committee to watch over Native interest".[47] These were the early beginnings of what decades later developed into the Anti Apartheid Movements of Britain, Western Europe and all over the world. The other point the ANC delegation realized was the extent and depth of collaboration between the British Government, the hard-headed officials of the Colonial Office, and the South African authorities. This must have been traumatic to people who regarded themselves as "loyal to the Empire", as British subjects or in the words of Mqhayi "Singama Britani" (we are Britons).

It was these experiences that made the ANC forge links with the Pan-African movement, make direct contact with its leader, Du Bois, who was very close to Plaatje, and even attempt to implement the ideals of Pan-Africanism. In fact, even the idea of the existence of the ANC as a permanent organization was closer to Du Bois' ideas rather than to those of Booker Washington, who advocated that justice for black Americans would come through economic self-improvement rather than political self-assertion.

These attempts of the ANC to link our struggle with the rest of the black world and the colonial world, were motivated by a need for a collective and international condemnation of colonialism and racism. This open association with the colonized and oppressed people throughout the world was indeed a shift in ANC policy - a shift in so far as it meant that our movement no longer depended on deputations to London.

The activities of the ANC leaders of the time - and Plaatje, the *morulaganyi* (editor), needs special mention in this regard - show that the founding fathers of the ANC went beyond just making general allegations of hardships without producing any specific cases that can bear examination. They wrote books and pamphlets containing instances of actual cases of hardship, visited the affected areas and families and took sworn statements from the sufferers. Plaatje translated some of Shakespeare's works into Setswana, fought for a new Tswana orthography and translated Tswana idioms and proverbs into English. This was all part and parcel of an effort to establish African political opinion as an autonomous factor in its own right in South African history. The sending of delegations to the South African government authorities and to Britain, the remoulding of the ANC and revision of the constitution were all aspects of this noble effort - an effort which has paid dividends over the years.

African nationalism and socialism

The first association of white workers in the form of a trade union was formed in Cape Town by white craftsmen employed by the woodwork industry in 1881 - the Amalgamated Society of Carpenters and Joiners, whose headquarters were in England. Unions were formed on the diamond mines in Kimberley in 1884; the Amalgamated Society of Engineers was formed in 1886; and the South African Typographical Union in 1889. Then unions emerged on the gold and coal mines of the Transvaal.

These trade unions were British in origin and were formed as branches of British organizations. This is significant in order to explain their structure and character. In Britain, until the London Strike of 1899, unskilled workers were not included in trade unions. South African white trade unionism reflected the pre-1889 British system. This nineteenth century notion of British trade unionism fitted perfectly into the racial classification and division of workers in South Africa. Therefore, from the beginning the interests of black and white workers clashed. The white workers who aimed at the control and maintenance of the position of skilled work were interested also in advancing and protecting their own positions, defending and maintaining the differential wage structures and their industrial status, that is, obtaining increased pay and common concessions such as paid leave and recognition of their unions.

This racism among the white workers became clearer when Chinese labour was introduced into the gold mining industry in 1904-09. This had become necessary after African workers were dispersed during the Anglo-Boer War of 1899-1902. The British authorities decided to import indentured unskilled labour from Asia and the Labour Importation Ordinance (Ordinance 17 of 1904) of the Transvaal permitted both the importation of Chinese workers and discrimination against them.

It was at this time that the Federation of Trades was established and recognized by both the South African government (1913) and the Chamber of Mines (1915). The labour unrest amongst white miners (1907 and 1914), which was allegedly caused by "competition" between white and black miners, resulted in the establishment of the South African Industrial Federation (SAIF) in 1914. This federation protected the interests of the white miners and these were the workers who formed the bulk of the group which supported the South African Labour Party established in 1909.[48]

56

The emergence of the South African Labour Party dates back to the 1890s when "militant working class ideas, and rudimentary socialist ones had already begun to make their appearance in South Africa . . . but many years were to pass before any names were to stand out bold for their contribution to the liberation movement".[49] In 1902, a branch of the British Social Democratic Federation was established in the Cape. Similar groups emerged in Johannesburg in the same year. These socialists were internationalists: the Cape Social Democrats organized a public meeting in solidarity with the 1905 Russian Revolution.

In May 1904, Wilfred Harrison (later to be a founder member of the South African Communist Party) announced in Cape Town the aims of the Social Democratic Federation: the abolition of capitalism and landlordism; the socialization of all means of production, distribution and exchange, that is the ownership and control of all means of production. South Africa's first socialist paper *The Cape Socialist*, was issued in 1904.

These groups were separate labour organizations united into the South African Labour Party in 1909. In 1913, the Labour Party affiliated to the Second International and had good relations with the International Socialist Bureau. It supported the Stuttgart anti-war resolution of the socialist parties. South Africa had been represented at the Stuttgart Congress of 1907.

Soon thereafter, problems emerged leading to tensions, sharp differences and tremendous diversity within the party, and ending in open conflict. The immediate cause was the First World War of 1914-18. Until 1915, the policy of the Labour Party towards the war was one of compromise between the pro-war and anti-war factions. But by October 1915, the right wing led by E. Cresswell had already asserted itself. There arose the necessity for the left to regroup and expose these manoeuvres, and they formed themselves into the War on War League within the Labour Party. The League soon developed into the International League of the South African Labour Party, but it was not long before the right wing expelled its members from the Labour Party. The left-wingers then formed the International Socialist League of South Africa (ISL) under the leadership of D.I. Jones, S.P. Bunting and W.H. "Bill" Andrews.

The League published a weekly, *The International*, which first appeared on 10 September 1915.

The emphasis on internationalism in South Africa at this early period was of great significance not only for anti-war propaganda (anti-militarism) but for the orientation of the white labour movement towards the emergent, racially discriminated against and nationally oppressed black workers. This view was expressed eloquently by D.I. Jones in an editorial in *The International* on "The Parting of the Ways" in which he justified their decision to organize themselves:

An internationalism which does not concede the fullest rights which the native working class is capable of claiming will be a sham. One of the justifications for our withdrawal from the labour party is that it gives us untrammelled freedom to deal, regardless of political fortunes, with the great and fascinating problem of the native. If the League deals resolutely in consonance with socialist principles with the native question, it will succeed in shaking South African capitalism to its foundations. Then and not till then, shall we be able to talk about the South African proletariat in our international relations. Not till we free the native can we hope to free the white. [50]

This foresight of Jones - "not till we free the native can we hope to free the white" - was a manifestation of the ability of these new white radicals to grasp at that early stage the fundamental problem facing the white labour movement. There was, however, also a problem with these far-sighted white radicals. "Not till we free the native" also implied that the Africans would be freed by the white, socialist working-class movement. However, these errors of interpretation can be explained by the poor state of organization of the Africans, especially the working class, the lack of experience of the white socialists (who were largely immigrants to South Africa) and their inadequate theoretical grounding.

Apart from the few radicals, white workers did not integrate Africans into the trade unions and did not assist Africans in forming their own African organizations. Instead they looked upon Africans as "dangerous competitors" - people who were offering labour at a cheaper rate than their own - and hence they adopted the vicious anti-African theories of the ruling class and sided with it against the liberation movements of the blacks and later their trade unions. In this context, white reaction to the 1918 strikes of African workers is instructive. The South African Industrial Federation, a white trade-union body headed by the notorious Archie Crawford, approached the racist white government and offered to raise "labour battalions" for use "in case of Native rising or rebellion". [51]

It should be remembered that one of the greatest fears of the regime of the time was the united action of militant white workers/socialists and Africans. This became clear during the strike of the white railway men in January 1914. Martial law was proclaimed, white trade unionists and Labour MPs were arrested and nine trade unionists were arrested in the middle of the night on the orders of General Smuts, Minister of Defence. They were put secretly and illegally aboard the steamship *"Umgeni"* and deported to England. *South Africa*, a newspaper owned by the mining magnate, Sir Abe Bailey, wrote in a characteristic style, "A number of anarchists in the subcontinent have been hunted down and trapped like vermin. Many of the social snakes of the country are now occupying prison cells, preparatory we sincerely trust, to banishment from the land." [52]

There is another important aspect to the question of internationalism - its relevance to the blacks. This becomes even more evident when we consider that the black working class was still in its infancy, the first generation of the founding fathers of the ANC were not integrated into industry, and thousands of rural Africans and their descendants were not part of a settled working-class community. African people were still in the main peasants, doing casual and temporary jobs to earn a little hard cash before returning to the land. The process of urbanization and proletarianization was taking place but the African working class was still in the process of formation - it was an emergent working class which needed guidance and internationalist solidarity.

February 1916, according to Forman, saw a landmark in the history of the liberation movement - "the first coming together in the Transvaal of the white socialists and the African National Congress". [53] This was a meeting called by the socialists to discuss the Land Act and Saul Msane of the ANC spoke at the meeting. In June 1916, an ANC leader, Robert Grendon, editor of the ANC organ *Abantu-Batho,* addressed a Johannesburg socialist meeting on "the link between black and white". A large number of Africans were present.

The Native Administration Bill was introduced in 1917 to place the Africans at the mercy of the Native Affairs Department with recourse to courts. These changes were to affect every aspect of African life. The International Socialist League called a protest meeting against this law in the Johannesburg Trades Hall in March - "a historic meeting, for it was the first political action taken by the socialists on a matter not directly linked with the white workers". [54]

The shift of the white socialists towards the blacks and the active participation of the ANC leaders in socialist meetings had fruitful results. In July 1917, in Johannesburg, the country's first African workers' organization was formed. This was the Industrial Workers of Africa (IWA) whose slogan was "Sifuna zonke" (We want everything). It was not long thereafter (to be precise, in December)) that a conference was called to discuss black unity. This conference, the first of its kind, was attended by representatives of the ANC (Transvaal), the APO and the IWA, comprising Africans, Coloureds, and a few white socialists. It appointed a non-racial committee of workers "to draw up a scheme for future co-operation". [55]

In February 1918, hardly two months after this conference, 30 000 - 40 000 African miners on the East Rand boycotted the mine concession stores. This was as a result of the doubling of prices during the war years while wages had remained the same: workers were protesting against the storekeepers and their rising prices. The IWA and ISL jointly issued a leaflet in Zulu and Sesotho to the boycotters. It was in this leaflet that, for the first time in Zulu and Sesotho, the famous call of Marx was reiterated: "Workers of all lands unite. You have nothing to lose but your chains. You have a world to win."[56] Another important strike broke out in 1918: 150 or so collectors of lavatory buckets were up in arms. This was before Johannesburg had waterborne sewage. The strikers were threatened: "If you attempt to escape and it is necessary you will be shot down. If you refuse to obey orders you will receive lashes", and they were arrested and sent back to work under police escort.[57]

The ANC called several protest meetings about the vicious treatment of strikers. Some of these meetings were called by the workers themselves and resolutions were taken: one of them demanded a pay increase of one shilling a day and another meeting called for a general strike. Various speakers including the socialist, T.P. Tinker, a foundation member of the IWA, addressed these meetings. In fact, the strike did spread beyond Johannesburg, to Durban. This, and the call for a general strike instilled fear in the government; soldiers were mobilized and marched through Johannesburg and the white unions were loyal to the government. But despite all this, the workers were released, thanks to the militancy of the black population and the white socialist supporters.

This "bucket" strike led to the arrest of five progressive leaders of the ANC - D.S. Letanka, L.J. Mvabaza, J.D. Ngojo, H. Kraai and A. Cetyiwe - and three ISL leaders - Bunting, Tinker and Hanscombe. Their trial was a forerunner of the 1956 Treason Trial as T.D. Mweli Skota in his *"Black Folks Who's Who"* implies, "For the first time in South Africa members of the European and Native races, in common cause united, were arrested and charged together because of their political activities."[58]

It is interesting to record in relation to this trial the case of Luke Massina, a police informer, who infiltrated the IWA and was paid £3 10 shillings for his work. Under cross-examination Massina repudiated his evidence and told the court that the evidence had been written out for him by the police: "All that evidence was false" Massina stated. This is one of the enemy's weaknesses - to get information about the liberation movement, they must use Africans who are either "neutralised" in the process or who become "converted" to the liberating and appealing ideas of the liberation movement.

The contacts between the ANC and the socialist movement during the war improved and strengthened each group and were of mutual benefit. They helped the theoretically advanced section of the socialist movement to appreciate, if not to understand, the struggles waged by the ANC. As an example, let us take the case of the stand of Plaatje, the Secretary-General of the ANC. When he attacked the white government, at the Annual Conference of the ANC at Bloemfontein in May-June 1917, the ISL commented, "It is gratifying to see a native leader standing up fearlessly without mincing words. It is a sign of awakening in the native workers generally." [59]

The pamphlets and leaflets which were distributed in the wake of the upsurge following the October Revolution in Russia, e.g. "The Bolsheviks are Coming", emphasized the question of black and white unity and went further to reiterate the message of Jones of 1915 - "while the black worker is oppressed the white worker cannot be free".

When the South African Communist Party was formed in 1921, a firm basis for the elaboration of relations between socialists and the ANC was laid. These early socialists were white, with the exception of T.W. Thibedi, an African who was a founder member of the SACP and a leading figure in the socialist/communist movement in the 1920s and 1930s. They were predominantly British immigrant workers (although amongst them there were Russian emigres) on the big industrial complexes around Johannesburg, and in Cape Town and Durban. Their political experience was mainly confined to that of the organizations they formed which were modelled along British lines, but they were grappling with a South African reality that was different from Britain. Not all the founders of the ISL were Marxists: they were Fabians, co-operators, syndicalists, anarchists and so on. Inspired by the October Revolution, they set themselves the task of seizing power but their vision was that this would be done by the white workers with the backing of the Africans, who were to be guaranteed the "fullest rights they are capable of exercising" - a controversial formulation!

These developments did have an impact on the young ANC. When it was formed, "tribal" differences and animosities were regarded by the ANC as the main problem to be tackled, but six years later the problem of class and ideological differences had emerged. Plaatje was an example of this process. Apologizing to the De Beers Company for not replying on time to a letter from them because he had to attend a meeting of the ANC Executive Committee on 2 August 1918, Plaatje wrote:

> I had to attend the Native Congress at Bloemfontein to prevent the spread among our people of the Johannesburg Socialist propaganda. I think you are aware of our difficulties in that connection since Mr Pickering, writing to me on an entirely different matter ended his letter thus: "For God's sake keep them (natives) off the labour agitators."

The ten Transvaal delegates came to Congress with a concord and determination that was perfectly astounding and foreign to our customary native demeanour at conferences. They spoke almost in unison, in short sentences nearly every one of which began and ended with the word "strike". It was not difficult to understand the course of their backing, for they even preceded the Congress and endeavoured to poison the minds of delegates from other parts. It was only late on the second day that we succeeded in satisfying the delegates, to report, on getting to their homes, that the Socialists' method of pitting up black and white will land our people in serious disaster, while the worst that could happen to the white men would be but a temporary inconvenience. When they took the train for Johannesburg, from Bloemfontein station, I am told one of them remarked that they would have "converted Congress had not De Beers given Plaatje a Hall". This seems intensely reassuring as indicating that Kimberley will be about the last place that these black Bolsheviks of Johannesburg will pay attention to, thus leaving us free to combat their activities in other parts of the Union".[60]

I have quoted this letter from Plaatje at length, because it demonstrates the fears of the mining companies and their attempts to influence sections of the ANC leadership. When Plaatje talks of the "black" Bolsheviks of Johannesburg in 1918 he is actually referring to that section of the ANC which was for militant action - strikes and demonstrations - which Plaatje, being a firm believer in "constitutional" forms of struggle and lobbying, distrusted. There was also the fear that the white power structure was all-powerful and, therefore, that any direct challenge to this enemy would have disastrous repercussions for the Africans. This all tends to prove that the ANC from its earliest days, has always consisted of people with different political views but who were united by their common hatred and rejection of national oppression. It also shows the difficult, delicate and thorny path the early socialists had to travel.

3
The ANC and Workers' Organizations (1919-28)

The rise and fall of the Industrial and Commercial Workers' Union (ICU)

The ICU, formed in 1919, was not without antecedents. One of them was the IWA, an African trade union formed in 1917 by the ISL. The IWA fought against the pass laws and for higher wages, and strove to heighten the consciousness of African workers. It was an expression of the class consciousness of black workers. It did not last long, however, because it did not incorporate all sections of the working class: it was not national at a time when a national or nation-wide organization was needed. When the ICU was formed, the IWA co-operated with it in organizing strikes and then later joined the ICU *en bloc*. What it stood for was not lost but grew through the ICU.

The ICU - which the African workers later called "I see you, white man" - was formed by Clements Kadalie on 17 January 1919. Who was Kadalie? He has given us his life story in his autobiography.[1] It is an unusual book in that he is very conscious of his own qualities, intelligence and importance. These are perhaps the reminiscences of an old man - his book was written a few years before his death in East London (Cape Province) in 1951 and it was first published in 1970. Before we deal with Kadalie's movement, impact, success and failures, however, let us know the man first.

Born at Chifira Village, near Bandawe mission station on the west shores of Lake Nyasa, where the first Scottish missionaries led by Robert Laws of Livingstonia, began their work in East Central Africa (then Nyasaland, now Malawi), Kadalie developed not only to be the father of African trade unionism in South Africa but also a major figure in its industrial history. His exact date of birth is not known "but it was recorded in the Mission Register that I was christened on Easter Day 1896".[2] He was the grandson of Chief Chimeyu - a paramount chief of the Ngoni, the "well-known Askari group in East Central Africa", the "descendants of the Zulu" - and the first son of Musa Kadalie. Chief Chimeyu's first meeting with a "muzungu" (a white man) was with Dr David Livingstone.

Kadalie went to school up to the equivalent of today's matriculation and later he enrolled with the Efficiency Institute in Cape Town, taking lessons in the art of public speaking, as he put it. He acted as the principal's private secretary and secretary of the Young Men's Christian Association (YMCA) and later as a head teacher in Nyasaland. He taught for a year in Nyasaland and then "left home early in 1915 in quest of a higher civilized life".[3] He travelled on foot to Portuguese East Africa (now Mozambique) and worked in the office on a cotton plantation. But he did not stay because "the cotton planter, who was an Englishman, was very cruel. He daily sjambokked [whipped] labourers for petty offences. At times he shot at the native labourers."[4] After a month Kadalie left for Southern Rhodesia (now Zimbabwe) where he worked on the Shamva mine as a clerk. Later he moved on to Salisbury (now Harare) and then to the Falcon mines in Umvuma, near Fort Victoria (now Masvingo). Here the compound manager was very cruel: "This man used to get up at about 4 a.m. daily in order to send out various shifts. Every morning he sjambokked the African miners, while his cruel dogs would come to his aid by biting his victims to death at times."

During the First World War, Kadalie tried to enlist in the army but his application was not taken up. In 1916 he therefore decided to leave Umvuma for Bulawayo. Early in 1918, he was in Kimberley in South Africa and soon thereafter reached Cape Town where he was welcomed at the station by his brother, Robert Victor Kadalie. In Cape Town he was employed in various jobs as a packer, messenger and "delivery boy", amongst other things.

This early history of Kadalie is important because it throws light on the background of one of the leaders of the first generation of African workers (perhaps it explains aspects of politics and behaviour) and this helps us to be more realistic in assessing the achievements, weaknesses and mistakes of that time. Here is a man who came from a relatively well-off family, acquired some missionary education, worked on the mines in Rhodesia and entered the South African labour force but not via the mines.

Though there were clear reasons for the foundation of the ICU, its actual formation was "accidental". Kadalie was reading the *Cape Argus* in Darling Street, Cape Town, to his friends, when a white constable pushed him off the pavement and assaulted him. A.F. Batty, a white politician, who later contested the Cape Town Harbour Constituency in a by-election as a Labour Party candidate, advised Kadalie to report the matter to the police. However, instead of listening to his case, the sergeant in charge started cross-examining Kadalie and then made an apology on behalf of the constable. He stated that the constable had assaulted Kadalie because of his mental weakness arising from overwork with the epidemic cases which were then raging in the city!

Kadalie was then enrolled as Batty's electoral agent. They discussed the advisability of forming a trade union and Batty advised Kadalie that he should "embark on trade union activities instead of politics".[5] So the ICU was born. The first meeting was held in Excelsior Hall, Buitengracht Street, on 17 January 1919; 24 members, mostly Coloureds, were enrolled that day and 24 shillings was contributed as entrance fee. A bank account was opened and it was resolved to hold weekly meetings.

Soon after its formation, on 17 December 1919, Kadalie brought African and Coloured dock-workers out on strike. This came about as a result of an appeal by the White Railway Workers' Union which asked the ICU for assistance in preventing the export of food. The ICU agreed to help, but added its own demand for an increase in wages for its members. The strike was successful but the white railwaymen then refused to support the demands of the ICU because, they alleged, it had gone beyond its original agreement. Thus the seeds of confusion and disagreement between black and white workers were sown right at the beginning of black trade unionism.

In 1920, the ICU became involved in the struggles of the working people in Port Elizabeth when it had to mourn its first African martyrs — 23 people killed and many more injured in a mass demonstration. During the First World War, the prices of foodstuffs and necessities in Port Elizabeth had increased by 105 per cent and the minimum wages of Africans was 4 shillings a day, leaving "the African real income below that of 1914".[6] This was the cause of the problem. The mass demonstration was for a wage of 10 shillings a day. The leader of Port Elizabeth, Masabalala, "a well educated African in the employ of Lennons (wholesale chemists) where he was liked and respected" and "a good speaker and popular at meetings, was arrested".[7] A commission of inquiry into these disturbances was appointed by the government and the ICU demanded that a black be included in the commission, "For the first time in the history of South Africa, a non-European, Dr A. Abdurahman, was appointed on the Commission of Inquiry."[8]

It was at this time that the ICU spread like a veld fire. From 1922 to 1924 Kadalie consolidated his position in the Cape Province; later, he began to advance into the country districts and the northern provinces, and this led to the rapid growth of the ICU. Its membership increased rapidly from 30 000 in 1924, to 39 000 in 1926 and by 1927 it had 100 000 members! This should be viewed against the background that in the years 1918-21 South Africa had 801 000 African workers (350 000 in mining and transport and 450 000 in agriculture) out of a total of 1 060 000 workers.[9] The reputation of the ICU also rose during this period. At an Easter meeting in 1925 the South African Association of Employees' Organizations (SAAEO), the forerunner of the SATUC, passed a resolution supporting the Bloemfontein demand of the ICU for a minimum wage: "this was the first public recognition of the existence of the ICU by the white workers organization".[10] Also in 1925 the then Prime Minister of South Africa, General J.B.M. Hertzog, confessed in the House of Assembly that: "Kadalie had been a very active agitator, and one of no mean culture, with the result that through his action and the actions of one or two others, there had been a scare for the last six or seven months throughout the Union".[11]

A key functionary of the ICU, who helped to build the organization in Natal, was Gilbert Coka. Born in January 1910, Coka was influenced by his father who was "an active steward in the Church and was also interested in the African National Congress affairs".[12] Later he came under the influence of people like A.W. Champion, D.L. Bopela, I.J. London and Sam Dunn, who went to Vryheid to address a meeting of the ICU. "The coming of the ICU leaders was a memorable event. It stirred the district for miles. Not since the news of King Dinizulu's death, had Vryheid seen such a huge multitude."[13]

The people's grievances, especially those in rural areas, were very concrete. Their landlords compelled them to work the year round without any pay; they demanded the services of all family members; they sjambokked and maltreated their tenants - cases of burning and shooting were frequent. Land tenure for the peasants was insecure; they could not build decent houses; they were liable to eviction from farms at any season and moment; they did not have the time to attend to the proper cultivation of their patches of near-barren land; they were compelled to dip their cattle frequently while their landlords seldom did so - failing to do so or being in arrears with their dipping fees meant that they could be criminally prosecuted. Coka remarks, "From the daily reports handed in I discovered that there was terrorism right under my nose. And those people flocked to the ICU as the ark which could convey them to safety."[14] Coka was issuing ICU membership cards in Vryheid and he knew what this meant, ". . . I wrote until my arm ached".

One of the factors which facilitated the spread of the ICU was the help and assistance it received from the ANC. There are many examples of this assistance but I shall confine myself to a few as a means of illustration. Selby Msimang, a founder member of the ANC, organized the ICU in Bloemfontein in 1919 and was arrested because of his ICU activities in March 1919. In August of that year he addressed an ICU meeting in Cape Town. From 1919 to 1921, Msimang was President of the ICU. Msimang reported on his activities in the ICU to the annual conference of the ANC in Queenstown in 1920. When Kadalie went to Durban in 1924, he was helped by J.T. Gumede, later to be President-General of the ANC (and who lived in Pietermaritzburg). In Johannesburg, assistance came from Selope Thema and many others: "Mvabaza, Mabaso and the Reverend Ngcayiya, also officials of Congress cordially welcomed the ICU and rendered [Kadalie] assistance."

A significant aspect of the relationship between the ANC and the ICU is the question of overlapping membership and common attitudes. There are many such examples, Masabalala is just one. In 1919, he was Secretary and Treasurer of the Cape ANC and later became prominent in the ICU in the 1920s; by 1930 he was again active in the ANC and obtained a position in the National Executive. Women activists also played their role in this early period. Maxeke was organizing the Women's League of the ANC and was also involved in the ICU. Kadalie says that he "did not wish to challenge the authority of the older South African Native National Congress",[15] but he attended the 1924 Bloemfontein Conference of the ANC as an ICU delegate and made suggestions and proposals, some of which were accepted and adopted by the ANC.

This does not mean, however, that the relationship between the two organizations had no problems. One difference that did emerge was the form of struggle to be pursued. Whereas the strike and mass campaigns (in short, class struggle) were accepted forms of protest and action in the ICU, the ANC was not yet accustomed to these forms of struggle and even tended to be unresponsive and sometimes unsympathetic to strikes.

At the international level, the ICU gained some support. It was invited to participate in the first "Negro Labour Congress" which took place in New York in May 1925. Kadalie did not attend because he could not get a passport:

> This invitation was a great honour as it was now apparent that an international association was being forged for me as well as for the ICU. Before this invitation I had contributed some articles to an American Negro Magazine, the *Messenger*. Through these articles my name and that of the ICU became internationally known.[16]

When Kadalie invited Tom Mann, the British trade unionist and communist, to attend and speak at the Third Conference of the ICU in Cape Town on 17-25 January 1923, he unwittingly invited the anger, vilification and misrepresentation, of the enemy and anti-communist forces. When Mann visited Lovedale at Alice, together with J.A. La Guma, ICU Assistant Secretary-General and a communist, *The African Voice* run by I.B. Nyembolo and S.M. Bennet Mcwana, wrote in big headlines, "Bolsheviks visit Lovedale". On the other hand, Mann was so impressed by this invitation during his four-month stay in South Africa that at the Fifth World Congress of the Comintern in 1924, which discussed the colonial question, he reported enthusiastically and at length about his participation at the ICU conference.

This brings us to the question: What was Kadalie's relationship with the Communist Party (CP) of South Africa? Even before the formation of the CP, its predecessor, the ISL, maintained good contacts with the ICU. Members of the ISL in Cape Town had assisted in drafting the preamble and constitution of the ICU. Stanley Silwana, Thomas Mbeki and other Communist Youth League members helped Kadalie establish his headquarters in Johannesburg in 1925 after he had moved from Cape Town. Members of the CP were so active that five of them were on the National Council of the ICU - two Africans, two Coloureds and one Indian. These were: Thomas Mbeki (Transvaal Provincial Secretary); E.J. Khaile (Financial Secretary); J. La Guma (Assistant General Secretary); J. Gomas (Cape Provincial Secretary); and R. de Norman (member of the Cape Town Committee). Kadalie was even enthusiastic about the Soviet Union. "No government in the world is sympathetic to the workers except the government of Russia."[17]

But clouds were beginning to gather over the ICU. Dissatisfaction developed amongst workers and ICU members because the leadership could not deliver the goods: the thousands who had joined the ICU saw no improvement in their conditions. Indeed, repression intensified for ICU members. White farmers organized campaigns, evicted hundreds of African families from their land and refused to have tenants who were members of the ICU. They spied on them; felled their huts to the ground, burnt them and threw the tenants onto the roads, confiscating their stock if they did not leave quickly enough. In Natal white farmers attacked and raided the ICU offices at Krantzkop, Weenen and Greytown and even marched to Pietermaritzburg:

> It was now a question of endurance . . . Africans were ready to do anything in order to throw off the chains of servitude and slavery. Everything rested with the higher officials. A general strike, passive or even active resistance, demonstrations, or any militant move would, at that time, have changed the history of the Union. The masses were ready to follow the lead even to death. The news of the outrages had har-

dened their determination to strive to the last. Everything depended upon the leaders; and they gave no lead. [18]

The lack of militant policy combined with mass action and the lack of a clear ideology led to a situation where peasant ideas of Messianism entered the labour movement. These ideas were consolidated by Kadalie who, because of his personal ambitions, became an increasingly despotic leader, refusing to respond to a democratic demand for the checking and control of finances.

People came to the ICU offices for assistance but "instead secretaries enjoyed joy-rides in cars, lived fast and ran up and down the countryside". The ICU head office in Ferreirastown in Johannesburg "showed all signs of anarchism and laxity"; money was squandered; there was maladministration and the habit of engaging lawyers for trifles.

The salaries of officials were extravagantly high. Yet just near the office, workers were underfed and ill-clad, ignorant and undernourished; buildings were dilapidated, more fit for pigs than for human beings, ill-ventilated and full of vermin. Unemployment led to deplorable conditions with people becoming drug pushers, bootleggers, prostitutes, thieves and gamblers. The people paid exorbitant rents and were unable to educate their children who led wild, violent and criminal lives amidst insecurity, squalor, crime (such as stabbings), disease and poverty. Wages for those who got jobs had to go on rent, wood, coal, candles and food: nothing was left for clothing or the education of the children. To add insult to injury the African workers who tried to form trade unions were victimized or detained and thus could not collectively bargain for their labour. No matter how bad conditions were, no African could go on strike, for that was a criminal offence. Africans were supposed to accept whatever wages and conditions the bosses imposed.

Coka had the opportunity to go through the ICU files and "he learnt the key to many riddles": "I discovered how an opportunity for raising the working class to fight for better conditions had been missed by a policy of opportunism. There was no lead given except an appeal for funds. That done, all would be well." [19]

All this led to a crisis at the meeting of the National Council of the ICU in Port Elizabeth on 16 December 1926. Two wings emerged: a militant one led by the communists and a reformist one led by Kadalie - Roux calls them the "hamba kahle" (go slowly) leaders. The issue at stake was the question of sending a delegate to the International Congress of the League against Imperialism which was to be held in Brussels in 1927. Kadalie was of the opinion that the "Brussels conference was a Bolshevik affair financed by Moscow."[20] James La Guma stated that the Brussels congress was a meeting of people with different political convictions and ideological complexions and that the South African Trade Union Congress (formed in 1926) and the ANC were attending. Kadalie was adamant and a resolution was proposed in which it was stated that no member of the ICU should be a member of the CP. Mbeki attempted to save the ICU from following anti-communist allies by suggesting that no functionary of the ICU should be victimized or expelled for being a member of the CP. The anti-communist resolution was, however, adopted by six votes against five.

There then followed an internal struggle within the ICU. The CP explained its trade-union policy, the content of which was the strengthening rather than the weakening of trade unions. The argument that CP members had a "double loyalty" or "served two masters" because they belonged to two organizations was refuted by the simple fact that the "expelled officials have never served two masters, but only one - the downtrodden workers of Africa".[21]

In April 1927 the annual conference of the ICU in Durban decided to send Kadalie to Europe where he used the opportunity to seek affiliation with the reformist International Federation of Trade Unions in Amsterdam. Meanwhile, George Champion became acting General Secretary. When Kadalie came back from Europe and gave a report about his tour to a special conference of the ICU in Kimberley, he suggested that he would like to bring a private secretary from England. A "buxom African woman" from Boksburg asked, "Kadalie, you went out black; have you returned white?"

To save himself from the people's anger Kadalie appealed to the instincts of the masses, and misused them: he identified the anti-racist and anti-colonial sentiments of the Africans with a hatred of whites. He tried to direct the national feelings of the masses not against the racist government but against the "white communists". He hoped to separate white communists from black ones, to isolate the white communists from the masses so as to weaken the influence of the black communists.

What were the reasons for this development in the ICU? What were the objective and subjective reasons that led such a powerful working-class organization to eventually disappear from the face of history? Was it only a question of political opportunism? What were the causes of this opportunism?

The emergence of trade-union reformism in South Africa had social causes and was determined by internal and external factors. The hostile attitude of the white workers contributed to the fact that African trade unions had such weaknesses.[22] The CP at this time (1926) did not have many African members and thus it sometimes hesitated to take the initiative. Unscrupulous black nationalists then misused this to "prove" that the CP was a "white party". The ANC was weak and its social composition (with only a small number of workers) at this time did not help much to strengthen the trade unions, let alone lead them in the struggles. Structurally the ICU was loosely organized.

By the time the ICU was formed in 1919, the African people as a whole and the African working class in particular had had experience of a national political organization for less than a decade - the ANC was formed only in 1912. Up until then there existed a more-or-less negligible stable and structurally independent African working class. The difficulty of organizing at the time under conditions of increasingly severe colonialist-racist exploitation and oppression should not be underestimated. These conditions were not conducive to the emergence of an independent working-class movement and its leadership.

The final break up of the ICU into three (and later more) separate sections was a result of the contradictory nature of the ICU's political-ideological development and the character of its leadership, but this cannot be separated from the society in which the ICU was embedded. The personal traits and political methods of the ICU leaders related to the milieu of the time. The rise of "platform thunderers" like Kadalie, to popular prominence in the 1920s was integrally related to the level reached by the African mass movement, the level of political conscious-ness of the workers (especially the migrants) and the worker-peasants on the white farms. The essentially petit-bourgeois radical nature of the ICU's leadership which, although it had its positive aspects, found ex-pression in political vacillations and indiscipline (particularly with respect to money), evolved out of a specific social and political context. The weaknesses of the leaders reflected and were integrally related to the weaknesses of the mass movement which, in their turn, arose not out of racial characteristics, but out of the objective conditions which, amongst other things, produced a particular social psychology. Let us take the class consciousness of the African worker at that time as an ex-ample. He did not think of himself only as a worker: he was Zulu, Xhosa, Sotho, Tswana, Pedi, Tsonga, Venda and so on, first and foremost, and then a worker. He worked to buy cattle for lobola for his future wife and wanted to educate his children so that they could im-prove his future prospects. The fact that there were no channels open either for soft jobs or for African workers to improve their qualifica-tions was known; what was not known was what to do about it.

I have dealt with the internal factors that precipitated the break up of the ICU. There were also, however, international or external factors at work: South African blacks have never been totally encapsulated from outside influences. Theoretically, we need to understand that after the October Revolution in Russia (and as a counter to its influence), and with the rise of national liberation movements and trade-union organizations in the colonial world, the European Labour and Social Democratic Parties affiliated to the Second International were forced to abandon their policy of indifference towards the liberation movements and trade unions in the colonial world, and decided to burrow from within so as to divert these movements from their militant positions.

In an article on the ICU, Teresa Zania had explained the external influences on Kadalie.[23] She mentions Ethelreda Lewis, an English writer who had contacts in the Independent Labour Party of Britain, especially Winifred Holtby. Holtby came to South Africa in 1926, shortly before the expulsion of the communists from the ICU. She contacted Kadalie and worked with the Joint Councils and Welfare Societies in Johannesburg and Durban as well as with the church circles around Howard Pimm, Rheinald-Jones and Edgar Brookes. The correspondence between Holtby and Lewis in May 1928 is revealing: "I must do all I can to remain an unsuspected person in the eyes of the communists here . . . It would be a setback to my work with the ICU if it were known to everybody."[24] When the Scottish trade-union organizer W. Ballinger came to South Africa in 1928 to "advise" the ICU, he extended the undermining influence of white liberals.

These elements were crucial in persuading the leaders of the ICU to withdraw from radical positions. Eventually this led to the break-up and disappearance of the ICU from the historical scene. Nevertheless the early revolutionary period of Kadalie is still remembered by millions of African workers from whom he emerged.[25] It is also an important part of our history because in the coming battle the South African working class will have a significant and leading role to play.

It should be remembered that the white liberals also influenced the ANC. Let us take the case of Selope Thema as an example. At the end of 1915, Thema acted as Secretary-General of the ANC under the presidency of John Dube - Plaatje, the ANC Secretary-General, was in England at the time. When Thema went on an ANC delegation to England in 1919 he met the British left and was even interviewed by Sylvia Parkhurst, the editor of the left-wing weekly *Worker*. Thema was also influenced by the visit of Dr Aggrey - a liberal Gold Coast (now Ghana) African, then resident in the US - to South Africa in 1921 and the subsequent activities of some white liberals. These were Howard Pimm, Dr C.E. Loram, J.D. Rheinhold-Jones and others, who later launched what became known as the Joint Councils - a liberal institution of Africans and whites, a form of "race relations exercise". D.S.

Letanka, the Vice-President of the ANC, attacked Thema and he was forced to resign his position of "provincial secretary to the Congress".[26]

This was Thema's first step out of the ANC. He then launched the *Bantu World* in 1932 as a diversion from Congress politics, and ended up joining the Moral Rearmament movement in the 1950s. At that time he also led a group called the ANC National Minded Block which attacked the ANC, and he was ultimately expelled from the organization.

I relate Thema's story because it demonstrates a trend within the liberation movement - a trend away from the politics of liberation to downright reformism.

The ANC and the Communist Party (CP) (1921-28)

The CP was formed in 1921. Its history is relatively well-known. Our main concern here is its relationship with the ANC. It is a well-known fact that the CP originated within the radical wing of the white workers and white intelligentsia (see chapter 2). This does not mean that socialism is a "foreign ideology" in South Africa because the history of socialist thought teaches us that socialism originated in central Europe and spread to all countries of the world, where a working class or forces ready to assimilate that ideology, existed. The fact that in South Africa these forces were white radicals is historical - in a sense, incidental. But stating this does not means that we can hide the fact that this led to some problems in relation to theory and practical political questions. These were, however, later solved thanks to the assistance rendered by the Communist International, especially at its Sixth Congress in 1928 which decided on the "Black Republic" as a slogan for immediate revolution in South Africa. The "Black Republic" was viewed by the Comintern as a stage towards the workers' and peasants' Republic which, in turn, was viewed as a transition towards socialism.

The formation of the ICU in 1919 ushered in a new chapter even in the thinking of the white radicals. But the belief in the white workers being the main revolutionary force persisted and this was reinforced by the 1922 white miners' strike which the South African press erroneously dubbed as the "Red Revolt". This strike was suppressed by force by the government. The leaders received long prison sentences and some were even executed. This led to white workers becoming more demoralized, more hostile to Africans and eventually they became an appendage of the bourgeoisie: *events seemed to outstrip the theory* of the CP at this time.

There was a militant wing within the CP which emphasized that the main task of the Party was the "awakening of the African proletariat".

73

It gradually became more vocal and the 1924 conference of the Party adopted this line. Africans were recruited into the Party; black communists established ICU branches and therefore strengthened that organization and they were elected to the National Executive of the ICU. There emerged the first generation of African communist leaders such as Albert Nzulu, Johannes Nkosi, Moses Kotane, J.B. Marks, Edwin Mofutsanyana, Gana Makabeni, and many others.

In the late 1920s, important developments took place within the ANC. These were closely connected with the name, actions and ideas of Josiah Tshangana Gumede. Who was Gumede? What did he do and think?

Gumede's early life is little known. Born in Natal in the midnineteenth century, he attended school in Grahamstown (in the Cape) and taught for some time at Somerset East before going to Natal where he became adviser to Natal and Orange Free State chiefs. In 1899 Gumede and Saul Msane met Hariette Colenso to discuss the formation of an African political organization and in 1900, together with Martin Lutuli and Msane, he became a co-founder of the Natal Native Congress and was for several years its General-Secretary.

In 1906, Gumede was a member of a delegation to Britain over the land laws of the Orange Free State. He acted as the agent of the Sotho people who had bought land in the Orange Free State. For leaving Natal without a pass (for which he had applied but which had not been granted) he was arrested and fined £10 or three months imprisonment on his return. With Z.M. Mazuku he co-signed the constitution of Iliso Lesizwe Esimnyama (The Eye of the Black Nation) - an organization of Wesleyan Methodist converts and chiefs formed in the Dundee and Newcastle area of Natal in 1907.

Gumede belongs to the generation of the founding fathers of the ANC. He was a member of the ANC delegation which went to petition the British Government in 1919. His name appears and re-appears in the petitions of the time.

The ANC attended the inaugural congress of the League against Imperialism which took place in Brussels from 10-15 February 1927. At this congress at the Palais Egmont there were 174 anti-colonial fighters from all over the world. For the first time in history, representatives of the progressive labour movements of the capitalist countries were united with delegates from the labour movements and national liberation movements of the peoples still under the yoke of colonialism and imperialism on all continents. The aims of the participants were to take up the struggle for the independence of those countries, and to struggle against imperialism on a wide front.

J.T. Gumede represented the ANC, and the communist and ANC

leader J.A. La Guma was also there, as well as D. Colraine of the South African Trade Union Congress. There were communists, anti-colonial freedom fighters from Africa, Asia, Latin America and the Caribbean, bourgeois humanists and social democrats at the congress. Despite the heterogeneous nature of its composition and the difference in ideological and political conviction, the necessity and the will to unite was an overriding factor.

Gumede spoke twice in Brussels. According to Otto Schnudel from Switzerland who was at the congress: "His speeches made a deep impression on the assembly."[27] In his presentations, Gumede analysed the plight of our people; their living conditions and their resistance and, on an optimistic note, he stated:

> I am happy to say that there are communists in South Africa. I myself am not one, but it is my experience that the Communist Party is the only Party that stands behind us and from which we can expect something. We know there are now two powers at work: imperialism and the workers' republic in Russia. We hear little about the latter, although we would like to know more about it. But we take an interest and will soon find out who we have to ally ourselves with.[28]

Gumede was not making a "diplomatic" statement, he was sincere in what he was saying and this sincerity did not stem from moral or value judgements but from what he himself experienced. Gumede repeated this theme in his presidential report to the annual conference of the ANC in June 1927: "Of all political parties the Communist Party is the only one that honestly and sincerely fights for the oppressed people."[29] It is interesting to remember that Gumede, this sincere nationalist and devout Catholic had strongly opposed "Bolshevism" in 1917.

In Brussels, Gumede, La Guma and Colraine drafted a joint resolution and signed it as "South African delegates" before it was adopted by the congress. This unity of South African revolutionaries, though it took place outside the country, was significant. The resolution demanded the right to self-determination through the complete overthrow of capitalist and imperialist rule in South Africa. Jack and Ray Simons believe that this resolution introduced an impetus and a new dimension in our view of the struggle; a concept which was later incorporated in the slogan of the "Black Republic".

Gumede's trip to Brussels was a turning point in his life. He met anti-colonial revolutionaries from Asia (including Jawaharlal Nehru), Latin America and the Caribbean, some of whom were "blacker than myself, speaking languages I could not understand.[30] (he was surely referring to French). There was one other African leader - Lamine Senghor of Senegal.

After the congress, Gumede and La Guma travelled to Germany

where they addressed large crowds at rallies organized by the Communist Party of Germany. Schnudel has some interesting things to say about Gumede in Berlin:

> Following the Congress there was in Berlin an informal meeting of the delegates who had come to the German capital, among them our friend Gumede. Berlin was to be the seat of the League Against Imperialism formed in Brussels.
>
> I was present at that meeting, since for the next three years I was to work on the International Secretariat of the League Against Imperialism and for National Independence. Josiah Tshangana Gumede and I were standing side by side. He towered over most of those present with his tall, powerful figure. Most of the whites he had met until then had treated him with contempt, and that was why this Berlin meeting was infinitely important. For the first time he stood as an equal among people of all races, all colours and various beliefs, united in brotherhood with the purpose of putting an end to the contemptible system of colonialism. Josiah Tshangana Gumede was so overwhelmed by this experience that his eyes were filled with tears. "I am so happy!" he stammered. Then he drew himself up and added: "I am going to fight!"[31]

Gumede and La Guma proceeded to the Soviet Union. They returned to Moscow at the end of the year to attend the celebrations and commemoration of the tenth anniversary of the October Revolution. They also participated at the Congress of the Friends of the USSR. Gumede then made a trip through the Soviet Union, which included a visit to Georgia. A photograph of Gumede in Russian winter clothes with Georgian peasants shows how cheerful a man he was. Fifty years later, his former interpreter, A.F. Platé, then a student and now Professor of Chemistry at the Moscow State University, told *Sechaba:*

> In Tbilisi Gumede was given a good reception and had various conversations with Georgian leaders and Georgian peasants. One of these meetings was held in the "house of the peasant" a place where peasants coming to town could have a place to shop.
>
> Gumede asked the peasants about their lives in detail . . . We visited a number of Georgian villages and returning to the hotel everytime, Gumede compared the way of life of the Georgian peasants with the mode of life and labour (conditions) in his motherland . . .
>
> Gumede considered as one of the greatest achievements of our country that the Socialist Revolution managed to unite people of different nationalities in their struggle for common ideals. He emphasized the significance of this experience for all nationals struggling for their independence and considered that success in this struggle would highly depend on the unity of action of all forces fighting against racism and colonialism.[32]

Gumede never forgot this experience. Back in South Africa he told large crowds: "I have seen the world to come, where it has already begun. I have been to the new Jerusalem."[33]

The new message Gumede had was a call for a united front bringing together communists and non-communists. He even crossed the borders of South Africa into Basutoland where he addressed meetings of Lekhotla la Bafo (Common Man's League) which was led by Maputseng Lefela. The masses responded to Gumede's message: he was elected President-General of the ANC in 1927 and E.J. Khaile (a known communist) was elected Secretary-General.

The growing influence of the Soviet Union seems to have had an impact on many radical black leaders of the time. Dr Du Bois himself confessed in 1926:

> I stand in astonishment and wonder at the revelation of Russia that has come to me. I may be partially deceived and half-informed. But if what I have seen with my own eyes and heard with my ears in Russia is Bolshevism, I am a Bolshevik. [34]

Moreover, the fourth Congress of the Pan-African Movement in 1927 stated, "We thank the Soviet Government for its liberal attitude toward the coloured races and for the help which it has extended to them from time to time." [35]

These statements by leading black radicals demonstrate that Gumede's reactions were not an exception to the rule; the ANC was moving with the times and reflecting the dynamism characteristic of a revolutionary organization. The very existence of the Soviet Union; the fact that racism had been eradicated there and that the Soviet leaders treated any manifestation of racial chauvinism with great severity; and the fact that the Soviet people showed great sympathy, and actually rendered assistance, to the oppressed colonial people: these were the factors which impressed Gumede and other black radicals. Gumede was never a communist, he was a sincere nationalist. A devout Catholic, he had strongly opposed "Bolshevism" 10 years before he went to Moscow. Yet he is definitely one of those whom Nelson Mandela, in his Rivonia speech in 1964, characterized as "experienced African politicians [who] so readily accept communists as their friends". [36]

Though the ANC as a whole held different views from Gumede's, two trends are distinctly discernible. The first one expressed itself at a meeting of the Cape Town branch of the ANC, held in the International Hall, Caledon Street, Cape Town, on 9 May 1928, where the following resolution was adopted by a large majority:

> This General Meeting of the Cape Town Branch of the African National Congress, though it affirms the statement of the President, Mr J.T. Gumede, to the Convention of Chiefs held in Bloemfontein in April last, that the African National Congress is in no way attached to or affiliated to the Communist Party of South Africa, hereby places its full and unqualified confidence in the CPSA, in view of the fact that of all political parties of South Africa the Communist Party alone unreservedly advocates

freedom and equality for the non-European people of South Africa with other races.

Further, that it is the only party that champions the cause of the workers of South Africa irrespective of colour and knows no colour discrimination within its ranks.

Further, as the aims and objects outlined in the constitution of the Communist Party are the correct interpretation of the aims and aspirations of the workers of South Africa, this meeting calls upon the Headquarters Executive of the African National Congress to consider and explore every avenue towards the closest cooperation with the Communist Party as the only party correctly interpreting the aspirations of the working class of this country especially the subject peoples.[37]

At a subsequent meeting, held on 13 May 1928, and attended by a large gathering, the above resolution was reaffirmed in a motion by J. Mabitla, seconded by N. Maseti and carried by a large majority.

There was also, however, a conservative wing which could not remain neutral to the remarks and ideas of President-General Gumede. One chief warned, "The Tsar was a great man in his country, of royal blood like us chiefs and where is he now? . . . If the ANC continues to fraternise with them [the communists] we chiefs cannot continue to belong to it."[38] And another chief (fearing a future social revolution) said, "It will be a sad day for me when I am ruled by the man who milks my cow and ploughs my fields."[39]

I have already stated that the resolution of the Brussels congress introduced a new dimension to our concept of the struggle in South Africa. This was elaborated, enriched and developed in the discussions La Guma held with Bucharin and other Comintern leaders. These leaders viewed our struggle from a somewhat different angle. Whereas up to then the CP regarded the struggle in our country as a working-class struggle for socialism, the Comintern saw the importance of a national struggle uniting all oppressed people and classes against white domination and imperialism, and for national liberation. The Comintern suggested the adoption of the slogan, "An independent native republic as a stage towards a workers' and peasants' republic with full, equal rights for all races."[40]

The CP had up to then advocated working-class unity as the only way to socialism and equality between black and white, so this new call for the support of the liberation struggle led by the ANC was indeed a new departure. The CP had reservations about the ANC; they were ready to unite with the ANC *on specific campaigns* but they argued that the ANC was basically reformist. The question of communists working to build and strengthen the ANC was never raised, partly because the ANC was said to be serving the interests of the "African bourgeoisie", although some of these people called "bourgeois" were very poor indeed!

78

Speaking about this period and these attitudes, Forman remarks:

The party believed it was necessary to rally the masses on national slogans but under its own banner. Experience had still to teach the vital lesson that it was not *in spite of*, but *in alliance* with Congress that the party would lead the struggle against national oppression.[41]

In other words, the slogan for a black republic was a theoretical and practical political framework which set in clear perspective the relationship between African nationalism and socialism, by stating that the concept of class struggle in South Africa must of necessity incorporate the principle of national self-determination for Africans and other nationally oppressed blacks.

There are important reasons for dealing with this question of the genesis of the relationship between African nationalism and socialism in South Africa. First, our enemy - whatever form or colour it takes - has always deliberately distorted the relationship between the ANC and the CP. The ANC is portrayed as a brainless organization, without independent thought or initiative, "controlled" by communists who are white. The reasoning behind this distortion is clear: they are trying to tell our people that whether you are inside or outside the ANC it is the same - "white control" is everywhere. They are trying to demoralize our people, disarm them and instill a sense of hopelessness preventing them from joining the ranks of the freedom fighters.

Second, it is important to stress the contribution of the ANC to the realization of the urgent need for a solution of the national question. Even if the ANC was not always articulate enough in bringing this point home, its very existence spoke louder than words. This was an independent contribution, but that does not mean that the ANC was immune or encapsulated from the liberating ideas of the ICU and CP. There is, however, a difference between influence and control.

Third, the question of relations between the ANC and CP was not only a theoretical issue; it was fundamental to the success of the anti-racist and anti-colonial movement. The two organizations emerged separately and independently of each other; their campaigns were based on different premises. At times they ran parallel but as the struggle developed they came closer to each other. As happens in such cases, the great teacher was our common experience and the school was the practical political struggle. At times, the fees were high - our sacrifices were great - but we were sure to graduate at this school as comrades, friends, equals and countrymen.

The period from the formation of the ANC up to 1928 is important because it demonstrates the creative thinking and positive initiatives

79

taken by Africans to redress their grievances. The formation of the ANC was a reaction to an unsolved national question and was an attempt to solve it. Black intellectuals played a key role at this time and, indeed, the very existence of this social group disproved racist theories about the so-called inherent inferiority of Africans. This period also, however, showed the limitations of the intellectuals. To illustrate this point let us take the example of John Langalibalele Dube.

Dube was born in Natal in 1871. He was the son of the Revd James Dube, one of the first ordained pastors of the American Zulu Mission. He was educated at Inanda and Amanzimtoti Theological School (later Adams College). In 1887, he accompanied the missionary W.C. Wilcox to America, where he studied at Oberlin College, supporting himself through a variety of jobs. He went back to Natal but did not stay long before returning to the US for further training and to collect funds for a Zulu industrial school along the lines of Tuskegee, the black American college founded by Booker T. Washington. Indeed, the influence of Booker T. Washington manifested itself in Dube's emphasis on the virtues of thrift and industry, education and capital accumulation.

In 1901, Dube built a school called Ohlange on 200 acres of land in the Inanda district in Natal, and 200 students were enrolled. He founded the Zulu-English newspaper *Ilanga lase Natal*. He raised funds for Ohlange (again in the US) and because of his political reputation was elected the first President-General of the ANC in 1912. Dube fought against the Native Land Act of 1913 which affected every stratum of African rural society and he was part of the delegation of the ANC in 1914 which went to London to protest against this Act. His presidency of the ANC lasted until 1917. From then onwards he concentrated not so much on national issues as on the activities of the Natal Branch of the ANC. In the 1920s he, like many intellectuals of his generation, became closely involved in "liberal" attempts to establish "racial harmony" between black and white through the Joint Council movement and many missionary conferences. He was one of the South African delegates to the international missionary conference at Le Zoute in Belgium in 1926. In 1935, he became a member of the executive of the All-African Convention. The University of South Africa awarded him an honourary doctorate in the mid-1930s. He died in 1946.[42]

The strategy and ideology of the early ANC leaders such as John Dube did not move with the times. This is not to say that they changed from their early radicalism - they did not become "reactionary" - but the world around them changed. Their theories about and demands for racial equality, justice and African unity challenged the very basis of white power, but they tended to "mediate between two unequal societies", to swing "between belligerence and servility" in their attitude to the whites. [43]

This generation of leaders straddled two historical periods. They witnessed the dramatic changes in African society as a result of industrialization; saw the final destruction of African independence; the conversion of African peasants into dispossessed rural and urban wage-earners; and the emergence of the African proletariat. Some of them articulated the grievances of the emergent African working class, but they could not provide it with proper leadership. The ICU, under Kadalie and Champion, offered leadership for some time but this did not last. In an effort to broaden its constituency and mandate, the ANC sought collaboration with other protest organizations, especially the ICU. Membership of both were overlapping and after the fragmentation of the ICU, some of its leaders such as Champion, Mbeki and Doyle Modiakgotla moved back into prominence within the ANC.

The ANC's ideology has always been African nationalism, but this has never been a narrow nationalism. Its approach has undergone changes with the passage of time, and this is due to the fact that the ANC itself has undergone changes and the South Africa of today is different from the South Africa of the 1920s. The nationalism of the ANC in this early period sought to unite the Africans in the struggle against colonial domination; it instilled a feeling of belonging to an oppressed people whose existence was threatened; it sought cohesion, consolidation, a defence of national values and an assertion of national identity; it defended the rights, customs and traditions of our people; fought against the loss of land, liberty and independence and for the preservation of African culture. The mobilizing slogan during this period was "Freedom in the land of our Fathers".

4
Fundamental Changes
(1930-49)

The early 1930s were times of widespread misery for Africans in both urban and rural areas of South Africa. Previously poor conditions were aggravated by drought, over-population on the African reserves, and declining crop yields. This led to real starvation and thousands of African peasants were forced to the towns and cities in search of employment.

The composition of African society was changing in many ways. Traditional chiefs, many of whom had been in the forefront of campaigns to improve the conditions of their communities, began to be replaced by new incumbents who were now paid servants of the government - tools of the white exploiters, the Native Recruiting Corporation, the Chamber of Mines, and Boer landowners. Increasing industrialization and urbanization led to a growing African working class and this resulted in the emergence of a new breed of African revolutionaries with a distinctively working-class outlook, and a new generation of intellectuals.

Throughout the world this was a period when revolutionary movements had serious problems. It was the time that saw the rise of fascism in Europe and militarism in Japan. Within South Africa, the more militant ANC leadership of Gumede and Khaile was ousted and replaced by the ageing Seme and the not-so-radical Revd Mahabane - leaders who could not cope with the changes taking place in African society. Seme's weak leadership as President-General caused the ANC to become ineffective. Furthermore, the ICU was by now fragmented and the CP was divided by sectarianism.

The ANC's policy at this time was to fight for the integration of Africans into the "common society", whereas the CP's programme was the destruction of the state apparatus and its replacement by a predominantly black-run state - the "Black Republic". Within the

ANC, only Gumede and a few others supported the creation of a black republic. Even organizations allied to or created by the CP, such as the League of African Rights (initiated by Bunting after a successful Transkei campaign in 1929), were closer to ANC policy than to the CP. The League of African Rights, for instance, demanded:

(a) no tampering with the Cape (African) vote and the extension of the vote to blacks throughout South Africa on the same basis as whites;
(b) abolition of the pass laws;
(c) universal free education for black children;
(d) free speech and the right to public meetings irrespective of race;
(e) no restriction on black acquisition of land and a radical increase of land in the African areas.

Many of the ANC leaders, as well as rank and file members, were religious, and some of the differences at this time between the ANC and CP related to the question of religion versus atheism - the latter being regarded as a communist doctrine. "According to Mofutsanyana, the educated "good boys" and, alas, thousands of black workers were being doped by "Skokiaan branded religion"."[1] Yet this view is not really accurate. It is true that Marx defined religion as "the opiate" of the people, but the religion of blacks in South Africa, especially those associated with the ANC, has been unusual. African converts, since Nehemiah Tile in the 1880s, had rejected white Christianity and therefore one cannot equate black religion in South Africa with religion in general. Today this difference continues and is expounded in a conscious theology of liberation - a religion of the oppressed against the oppressor, something akin to the theology of liberation in Nicaragua and other Latin American countries.[2]

Towards the end of the thirties, however, there was a rapprochement between the ANC and CP, especially after the 1937 celebrations of the ANC's silver jubilee. The growing threat of fascism throughout the world brought together anti-fascist organizations. Mussolini's attack on Ethiopia in 1935 aroused great feelings of indignation amongst our people. This "made Africa sharply aware of being part of one great continent . . . black pride was high and African newspapers, full of reports of the war and pictures of Ethiopian soldiers, had record sales".[3]

The formation of the Hertzog-Smuts coalition government in 1933; its endorsement by the white electorate in the "general election" later and the economic recovery from world-wide depression filled the South African racists with new confidence and added urgency to the Africans' political campaign. A two-thirds majority of both houses of Parliament, the number required by the Act of Union to amend the entrenched clause protecting the black franchise in the Cape, was ensured. In 1936, Prime Minister Hertzog and Jan Smuts removed the Cape African voters from the common voters' roll.

The Representation of Native Bill and Native Trust and Land Bill excluded the African voters from the common roll and entrenched the 1913 Land Act, increasing the land occupied by Africans from 7,5 to 13 per cent with no hope of any further purchase of land. They also laid the basis for the creation of the Natives' Representative Council (NRC), a body in which 12 African representatives indirectly elected by Africans throughout the country would sit with four Africans chosen by the government and with white Native Commissioners under the chairmanship of the Secretary for Native Affairs. The Africans in the Cape, and throughout South Africa, who had hoped that there would be an evolution of the democratic process, extending the African vote to other provinces, saw these Acts as a total onslaught on their remaining rights.

These were some of the immediate issues agitating the Africans in South Africa. There was also the question of support for the struggle of the people of the High Commission Territories - Basutoland, Swaziland, Bechuanaland and Namibia - against incorporation into South Africa.

The All-African Convention (AAC)

It was to try to co-ordinate African action on these issues that Professor Jabavu, a distinguished academic, together with Pixley ka Isaka Seme, President-General of the ANC, called on all Africans and other blacks from all shades of the political spectrum and all parts of South Africa, to converge on Bloemfontein in December 1935. The Boers were celebrating the ninety-seventh anniversary of the Battle of Blood River - where they had killed Africans in Natal. The Africans on the other hand viewed the venue from a different angle: it was in Bloemfontein in 1909 that Africans formulated their protests against the Act of Union and where, in 1912, the ANC was formed.

The All-African Convention (AAC) was formed at this meeting. It was to be an umbrella organization within which all existing African political groups could be linked, and was not meant to phase out or replace organizations such as the ANC. It attracted a wide spectrum of people: ANC leaders, ICU personalities, chiefs, church dignitaries, professionals, elected members of advisory boards, prominent women, representatives of a number of local organizations, including Coloureds from left-wing study circles in Cape Town and also CP members.

More than 400 delegates converged on Bloemfontein. Two hundred came from the Cape Province, 100 from the Transvaal, 70 from the Orange Free State, 30 from Natal, 10 from Basutoland and one delegate, representing the paramount chief, came from Swaziland.

It is important to note that the Hertzog Bills even alienated Africans normally regarded by the Government as moderates, for example, the United Transkeian Territories General Council, Ibunga (a Transkeian organization of elders), and also African professional men associated with Cape liberalism such as Professor Jabavu.

Despite the broadness of approach, diversity in thinking and ideology, the general tone was the rejection of the Hertzog Bills. At the AAC B. Mashologu of Basutoland maintained that the Cape vote (first granted in 1854) was not a real franchise, for the Africans there could not send people they wanted to Parliament, but were bound to send white candidates elected by other people. No race could be adequately represented by another, he contended. The Cape Africans had the shadow of a vote without the substance. [4]

Mashologu was right. But there were two problems here. There was the question of reformism, of a "half a loaf", being "better than none", and there was also the question of the relationship between reforms, the defence of what had been achieved, and further advance to new gains, that is, the question of defending existing standards. In practical terms this meant defending the Cape vote and extending it to other provinces. But this demand had to be accompanied by or be subordinate to the overall strategy which included even changing the form, essence and goal of the Cape vote.

The AAC, which was a conglomerate of diverse and contradictory forces, expressing both rebellion and subservience, was to prove inadequate to tackle these complex problems. But there were new ideas that emerged from its discussions:

> A rather novel idea of designating Europeans in South Africa was mooted with appreciable effect. One delegate strongly contended that it is erroneous to describe Africans in South Africa as "Non-Europeans" when to all intents they formed the indigenous population of the continent of Africa. He urged the Convention in all sincerity to adopt the nomenclature of "Non Africans" for all Europeans as distinct from Africans, arguing that here they lived in Africa, and not in Europe where the term "Non European" is conceivable and tolerable for strangers in the continent of Europe. This [was a] sign of race-consciousness. [5]

These sentiments, first expressed in the 1930s, were to become one of the central tenets of black consciousness in the 1970s.

Selby Msimang posed the question of dependency and rebellion - the question of divided loyalties, loyalty to the present government or to the people's demands:

let us now admit, both publicly and in our conscience, that Parliament and the white people of South Africa have disowned us, flirted and trifled with our loyalty. They have treated us as rebels, nay, they have declared we are not part of the South African community. Whatever it means, I am satisfied in my mind that if we do no longer form part of the community which constitutes Parliament and the Government of the Union of South Africa, we have to belong to some authority other than the present, or we shall have to admit that we are slaves and outcasts in our fatherland. If we refuse to be made slaves then we should seek emancipation by such means as the dictates of self-preservation may lead us to.[6]

It took the ANC decades of hard organizational and propaganda work, in short, practical political experience, before our people resolved the question of divided loyalties - loyalty to the government or to the ANC. Today the people are rendering South Africa ungovernable.

The AAC was intended to unite African opposition to the Native Trust and Land Bill of 1935. It also, however, sought to identify the role of imperialism in Africa and called for continental African unity and worldwide condemnation of imperialism:

a) The All-African Convention hereby expresses its utmost condemnation of the savage, unprovoked and unwarranted attack made by Italy upon Abyssinia and declares as its considered opinion that the ruthless action of Italy can only be regarded as large scale violence against fundamental human rights.

b) Further this convention sees in this action of Italy a continuation of the game of grab which the imperialist nations of Europe have played in this continent whereby millions of inhabitants have been deprived of their land, exploited and robbed of their labour.

c) This Convention hereby declares its conviction that imperialism which has thus resulted in the ruthless destruction of life, in violent acts of robbery, in increasing exploitation and in the destruction of African culture is an evil force to be exposed, condemned and resisted.

(d) The All-African Convention recognises the value and desirability of establishing contacts with Africans and African organizations in other parts of the world. To this end the All-African Convention believes that a call to internationalc onference of Africans and overseas peoples of African descent should receive the serious consideration of the Executive Committee.[7]

With reference to Basutoland, Bechuanaland and Swaziland, a resolution was unanimously adopted, that supported the struggle of the Africans in these territories against incorporation in the Union "as such incorporation would not be in the best interests of the people of the Protectorates". It further pledged to supply all information to the people of the Protectorates "with a view to assisting them to come to a proper conclusion if and when they are consulted by the British Government with regard to the question of their inclusion in the Union".[8]

These sentiments showed how the liberation movement in South

Africa was no longer dependent on deputations to the racist regime. It was openly identifying and associating itself with colonized people throughout Africa.

Nevertheless, the contradictions between different elements and organizations in the AAC were a source of weakness. It tried to be all things to all people. Moreover the ACC; "had no organizational basis save fragmented and emaciated factions" and "in the long run" it was the ANC rather than the AAC that held hope for the future. Jack and Ray Simons write, "Unable to develop a mass basis, the Convention lapsed into inactivity until the early forties when Coloured and African radicals in the western Cape revived it with the aim of putting themselves at the head of the liberation movement."[9]

This raised the question of whether another form of united front should be brought together, and led to the birth of the Non-European United Front in Cape Town on 8 April 1939. Communists, nationalists, Trotskyists and others came together to work out a new strategy under new conditions. Those elected to the national council included Mrs Gool (President); R.G. Baloyi (Senior Vice-President); M. Kotane (Secretary); W.H. Andrews (Treasurer); Dr Dadoo and H.A. Naidoo. The Non-European United Front represented "a seed of a grand non-racial alliance" that had been planted, "but seventeen years were to pass before it bore fruit" (see chapter 5).[10]

Resurrection of the ANC

One of the reasons the AAC could not establish itself as a permanent federal body was that it tried to do so at the time the ANC began to re-establish itself. From 1939 onwards the ANC underwent a gradual process of revival, rejuvenation and re-emergence as the central body co-ordinating and expressing the views and opinions of Africans in South Africa.

In 1939 the ANC Secretary-General, the Revd Calata, and the President-General, the Revd Mahabane, embarked on a tour of the whole of South Africa. It took three years, until 1939, to cover all four provinces. Local problems were solved in the process; provincial activity was initiated and younger blood drawn into the organization. Other bodies, such as R.H. Godlo's Advisory Boards Congress, were also drawn into collaboration with the ANC, and even began to articulate ANC policies. Godlo himself, as President of the Advisory Boards Congress, regularly attended ANC meetings. This nationwide tour provided an important impetus for a revival of the ANC. Nevertheless, this was to be a slow and painstaking recovery.

Writing from the Transkei in 1941, Govan Mbeki reported that "The Transkei is, to be frank, politically in midnight slumber."[11] Calata was also pessimistic when reporting on his experience in Natal in 1942:

In passing through Pietermaritzburg I addressed a meeting which was presided over by Mr J.T. Gumede, former President-General of the ANC. I am afraid that Natal requires a special attention. Congress is dying in that province . . . There are no branches which are alive. There are some people called officials but they do nothing for the Congress and the people are suffering.[12]

Godlo, writing from East London, also complained, "Sorry to have to report that Congress is not making much progress in this town."[13]

Similar complaints came from other areas. This was the period when ANC membership was estimated by Molema at 253! "Congress lost its glamour; the Africans lost faith and interest in it," Molema wrote in 1943 - the year in which the ANC Youth League was formed and only six years before the adoption of the famous Programme of Action.

Dr A.B. Xuma became President-General of the ANC in 1940 - the year in which Dr Abdurahman, President of APO, died. Xuma was by no means a radical; he was a reformer. In 1932, he wrote about himself, "I am a medical practitioner by profession. I studied in the United States of America, in Austria-Hungary and at Edinburgh. I am neither a politician or agitator or racialist. I am merely an interested student of human relations."[14] Perhaps he was right. But eight years later, this "merely interested student of human relations", who was neither "a politician nor agitator", had become President-General of the ANC.

One of the factors which "radicalized" Xuma's ideas was the paternalistic and patronizing attitude of white liberals such as Heaton Nichols, Senator Brookes and Marwick, who portrayed themselves as "experts", "specialists" and "authorities" on the "Native Question". Xuma as President-General of the ANC wrote to Professor R.F. Alfred Hoenle, the President of the South African Institute for Race Relations, in September 1942, saying:

No individual European elected to the Senate is going to save the African people from disaster. They may help but one need not go to Parliament to serve the cause of better relations. There are many Europeans - unsung heroes - who are doing their bit quietly. The salvation of the African people from disaster is the African himself through his organisation which finally (implies) his proper representation. Any philosophy of doing or working for the African instead of working through and with the Africans, means humanely enslaving the Africans, as it does not advance him in any way.

Six months later, he repeated his message, in a somewhat different context:

The best thing to be done is for Europeans who believe in Christianity, democracy and human decency, to back up the stand taken by African organisations led by Africans, financially and otherwise, instead of them setting up organisations staffed by Europeans in which Africans become mere passengers . . . The emancipation of the African people shall come from Congress, this can come about when Congress is well organised.[15]

Letters to Xuma from Mbelle, nephew of A.S. Bud Mbelle (Plaatje's brother-in-law and, his successor as chief interpreter for the Native Affairs Department) were also critical of white liberals and of the way African leaders conducted their affairs. It is interesting to note the similarity between Xuma and Mbelle's language and the ideas of what later came to be known as "black consciousness" in South Africa. It demonstrates the depth of the roots of "black consciousness" in our people, in the ANC, and that in the South African context it was a radical perspective.

One of the problems the ANC faced in spreading its ideas was the lack of an African press. *Abantu-Batho*, the official organ of the ANC, finally closed down in 1931, forced to do so by competition from the white-owned *Bantu World* and because of the weakness of the ANC at that time. Govan Mbeki expressed concern about this when he wrote to Xuma on 7 May 1941 about the "futility of our attempts without a press to prepare the minds of the people for what we plan to do, and to strengthen them once they have undertaken to do a thing". The problem of the lack of an African press was, therefore, not unrelated to the broader problem of the reorganization of the ANC as a liberation movement.

At the annual conference of the ANC in Bloemfontein on 15-16 December 1941, Xuma spoke about the need for unity and self-sacrifice. Evaluating the positive traditions of the ANC since its foundation, he did not shy away from the problems it faced, the weaknesses in the movement, and their serious political consequences, stating that political inactivity "led to a belief that organizations led by non-Africans were more dignified than African organizations and thus we abandoned our organization and surrendered our leadership to others".

Xuma reiterated the aims of Congress: to unite the Africans and to fight for their rights - "unity means strength and hope" to educate African people on their rights, duties and obligations; and to promote mutual help, a feeling of fellowship and a spirit of brotherhood. He spoke of bringing people together "in common action" as "one political people" by means of "combined effort" in a "united political organization" - as a means to "discourage and contend against racialism and tribal feuds or to secure the elimination of racialism and tribal feuds; jealousy and petty quarrels by economic combination, education, goodwill and by other means."[16] The ANC was to "formulate a standard policy on Native Affairs for the benefit and guidance of the Union Government and Parliament". Its other task was:

To educate Parliament and Provincial Councils, Municipalities, other bodies and the public generally regarding the requirements and aspirations of the native people; and to enlist the sympathy and support of such European Societies, Leagues or Unions as might be willing to espouse the cause of right and fair treatment.

The ANC was the mouthpiece of the African people: "all its efforts are and must be concentrated upon raising the status of the African people from their semi-serfdom to citizenship". This was all the more so because the "Africans have no vote and therefore no voice in South African affairs".[17]

The adequate representation and right of franchise for Africans, participation of Africans as voters and citizens in the building of a Union policy acceptable to all sections of the community, representation of Africans in all government chambers and government departments, were all issues seen as part and parcel of the struggle for democracy in South Africa. Other crucial issues were the land question, the pass laws and the lack of social welfare for Africans.

The provisions of the 1913 Native Land Act had been reinforced by the Native Land Trust Act Amendment of 1935. Africans had no land and the problems posed by stock limitation ruled out the possibility of the improvement of the quality of stock. Land prices were greatly inflated and this resulted in problems of African overcrowding on small portions of land, leading to starvation and undermining the physique and health of African people for generations.

The pass laws, which restricted Africans' freedom of movement also limited their bargaining power; exposed them to exploitation and excluded them from enjoying the "rights" of white workers. Africans were paid far below the cost of living, debarred from skilled trades, and forced to live below the breadline.

Africans were the worst paid and consequently the poorest section of the community; they had no margin from their earnings to set aside for a rainy day, or for their old age; disablement or unemployment found them with nothing to support themselves. They have always been more in need of benefits from the social welfare departments than any other section of South African society. Therefore the questions of old-age pensions for Africans; disability and disablement pensions; extensions of the provisions of the Children's Act to meet the social requirements of destitute African children (that is, adequate maintenance grants) were bread-and-butter issues for the ANC. The Africans had the highest infantile mortality rate, and the highest mortality and morbidity rates - caused by the low wages, poor living and working conditions, lack of adequate food and, therefore, low resistance to disease.

Xuma spoke of the ANC's need to tackle all these issues and concretized the demands of the ANC as follows:

(1) the removal of industrial and commercial restrictions against the African;
(2) a living wage and better working conditions;
(3) the right of all African workers to organize into trade unions;
(4) the recognition and registration of African trade unions under African leadership by the Union Labour Department with all rights privileges and immunities appertaining to such organizations under the Industrial Conciliation Act;
(5) the right of Africans to learn skilled trades and engage in them;
(6) trading rights for Africans anywhere; and
(7) the abolition of the pass laws, Natives' Service Contract Act, Masters and Servants Act and other special disabilities.

Another problem which worried the ANC at this time was the question of African soldiers who were fighting in the Second World War. These Africans had volunteered to fight against fascism, mainly in North Africa, but were restricted to manual labour. Their wages were deplorably low - one shilling and sixpence a day for unmarried African soldiers, "just sixpence more than the allowance which, I understand, was given to internees, enemies of the state, whose dependents were receiving £2 10s to £5 allowance in addition and that for working against the government".[18] Here Xuma was referring to those whites such as John B. Vorster who were interned in South Africa for their pro-Nazi activities - the later rulers of South Africa after the Afrikaner National Party came to power in 1948.

African soldiers could not rise higher than the position of sergeant; they could not receive the extra shilling a day allowed for doing work such as training transport drivers and electrical work. There was also the problem of the disabled and discharged soldiers. Indeed, said Xuma, Africans had given from their meagre earnings, from their dire poverty, more than their proportionate share towards the various war funds.

The attitude of the ANC towards the war demonstrated another, broader dimension - a spirit of solidarity with the Soviet Union which was being attacked and occupied by the Nazis. This was expressed at a meeting of the Johannesburg branch of the Transvaal ANC when, on 16 November 1941, the Chairman said:

Soviet Russia has been drawn into conflict under such obviously vague pretences, that I feel it would be idle on my part to mention them . . . We sympathise with the Soviet people who are living in a fatherland so occupied. We Africans are competent to express sympathy with people under ambitious elements because we know what it is to be under such elements. Our sense of pity is aroused when we read about atrocities in Europe because we Africans are going through the same mills in South Africa. [19]

This spirit of solidarity and identity with the oppressed in other countries: "because we know what it is to be under such elements", shows the farsightedness of the ANC leaders at that time - it was miles ahead of the thinking of the founding fathers of the ANC.

In 1927 Gumede had praised the achievements of the Soviet Union. Msimang went even further, "We may live to see, if we have the soul and the righteous determination to do and dare, the history of the overthrow of the Russian Empire by the governed, repeated in our dear Fatherland." [20]

Msimang was by no means a communist, neither was he a friend of the communists - we are not even sure whether he was for or against what he described above - but one thing we are sure of, he was expressing his sincere feelings: he was a patriot. These trends and tendencies within the ANC demonstrate clearly that the ANC has always been a "parliament of the African people", incorporating within its ranks people of different political persuasion and ideological complexions, including internationalists.

At the November 1941 meeting of the Johannesburg ANC branch, recommendations to the national ANC through the provincial body were discussed. The amendment of the constitution of the ANC was seen as of crucial importance, "As a matter of fact the whole constitution as it stands today is so antiquated that those of us who are charged with the administration of the Congress are finding it hard to be guided by it." [21] At the same time, however, it was also acknowledged that "nobody is more proud than us to have been the inheritors of this legacy. We are pleased to have had predecessors who have left us a foundation capable of many storeys". This dual process of continuity and renewal has characterized the history of the ANC; today it has become an established custom.

Suggestions were made at the meeting on the composition of the National Executive Committee, including the appointment of a Working Committee to carry out the basic administrative and campaigning work, which would consist of members of the National Executive Committee (or others by co-option) resident in the same district as the President-General, which was to be the headquarters of the ANC for the time being. This was due to the fact that the members of the National Executive were scattered and could not meet with ease.

There were also decisions taken on the organizational form and structure of provincial congresses and financial arrangements. This was connected with discussions on amending the constitution, which was said to be unsatisfactory, verbose and bulky. It was to be substituted by one which would provide for a fairly simple organizational structure and financial arrangements; that would not be overburdened with details, but that would confine itself to the basic requirements. If necessary, this was to be supplemented by a set of rules to be added to as circumstances required. In other words, the aims of the ANC were to be simply set forth in the constitution in a readily understandable form based on the statement of policy recently issued by the President-General, Dr Xuma.

The discussion on the constitution was of significance in the great task of politicizing the masses, educating them about the aims of the ANC, inspiring them with hope and above all in organizing the ANC, ensuring discipline and acceptance of the authority of the mother-body and regulating relations between the various provinces and the mother-body, for example through the issue of uniform membership cards and the reorganization of the ANC in the Cape where there existed three congresses - in the Transkei, the eastern Cape and the western Cape.

Earlier on I dealt with the women's struggles in 1913. These struggles continued under the new and difficult conditions imposed by the First World War. Then in 1918 the Bantu Women's League was formed as a "branch of the ANC", with Charlotte Maxeke as the moving force behind it.

Maxeke died in 1939 but her spirit did not die. One of the resolutions adopted at the annual conference of the ANC held at Bloemfontein on 14-16 December 1941 was the "Resolution on the Women Section" which read:

That this conference recommends to the parent body the necessity of reviving the women's section of the Congress in terms of the provisions of the constitution. Further, the women be accorded the same status as men in the classification of membership. That the following means be made to attract the women:

(a) to make the programme of the Congress as attractive as possible to women;
(b) a careful choice of leadership. [22]

In 1943, the ANC Women's League was formed under the leadership of Madi-Hall Xuma and it was inaugurated at the 1948 Annual General Conference of the ANC.

The African Claims 1943

Besides the question of dealing with organizational problems and modernizing the constitution, the ANC was faced with the problem of mapping out a future South Africa. Moreover the organization was also affected by the international debate about the nature of the post-war world. After Roosevelt and Churchill signed the eight-point Atlantic Charter on a post-war settlement in 1942, Xuma organized a committee whose brief was to discuss the Charter "from the African's point of view". The committee met at Bloemfontein on 13-14 December 1943. Z.K. Mathews was elected chairman, with L.T. Mtimkulu as secretary, and a sub-committee consisting of S.B. Ngcobo, M.L. Kabane and J.M. Nhlapo, with the chairman and secretary as ex-officio members. The sub-committee drafted the African position on the Atlantic Charter.

The Atlantic Charter Committee (as it was then called) was guided throughout by Xuma. It consisted of: R.G. Baloyi; Dr R.T. Bokwe; the Revd J. Calata; R.H. Godlo; M.L. Kabane; M. Kotane; E.M. Lepolisa; the Revd Z.S. Mahabane; G. Makabeni; T.M. Mapikela; Z.K. Matthews; C. Mbata; G.A. Mbeki; M.T. Moerane; E.T. Mofutsanyane; Dr S.M. Molema; Dr J.S. Moroka; the Revd Mpitso; the Revd Abner Mtimkulu; D. Mtimkulu; L. Mtimkulu; J.M. Nhlapo; S. Ngcobo; Dr I.P. ka Seme; Dr Setlogelo; R.V. Selope-Thema; B.B. Xiniwe and Dr A.B. Xuma.

This list is in alphabetical order. It includes leading members of the ANC (Xuma, Calata and Baloyi - the Treasurer-General); Kotane - the Secretary-General of the CP; leading provincial and local leaders of the ANC; intellectuals and academics; peasant leaders; religious personalities and friends of the ANC. Dr Xuma, the President-General of the ANC and Secretary-Organizer of the Atlantic Charter Committee, had this to say about it:

> The list of names of the members of the committee who produced this document tells a story for those who would understand. These fruits of their labours are a legacy, nay, a heritage, which will leave behind for future generations to enjoy. For it, and to them, we are all forever indebted ... We realize that for the African this is only a beginning of a long struggle entailing great sacrifices of time, means and even life itself. To the African people the declaration is a challenge to organise and unite themselves under the mass liberation movement, the African National Congress. The struggle is on right now and it must be persistent and insistent. In a mass liberation movement there is no room for divisions or for personal ambitions. The goal is one, namely, freedom for all. It should be the central and only aim for [sic] objective of all true African nationals. Divisions and gratification of personal ambitions under the circumstances will be a betrayal of this great course. [23]

The terms of reference of this committee were to study and discuss the problems arising out of the Atlantic Charter in so far as they related to Africa, to formulate a comprehensive statement embodying an African Charter, and to draw up a Bill of Rights which Africans were demanding as essential to guarantee them a worthy place in the post-war world.

Of particular interest was Clause 3 of the Atlantic Charter, which demanded, "the right of all peoples to choose the form of government under which they may wish to live and . . . sovereign rights and self-government restored to those who have been forcibly deprived of them."[24] The imperialist countries, however, maintained that this clause was only applicable to "occupied territories" in Europe and not to colonies. This interpretation raised the question whether the meaning of "nations", "states", "peoples" and "men" included colonial people or not. No wonder Xuma remarked, "The Africans in Southern Africa should draw up their own Atlantic Charter."[25]

The African Claims, that is the Atlantic Charter "from the standpoint of the Africans within the Union of South Africa", was adopted by the Annual Conference of the ANC at Bloemfontein on 16 December 1945. It started off by demanding the safeguard of the status, independence and the right to sovereignty of Abyssinia (now Ethiopia) which was being attacked by fascist Italy, and went on to demand that "the former Italian colonies in Africa should be granted independence and their security provided for under the future system of World Security". As far as the High Commission Territories (Bechuanaland, Basutoland, Swaziland and Namibia) were concerned, the African Claims rejected the idea that these territories, be incorporated into South Africa: "Africans therefore, are definitely opposed to the transfer of the Protectorates to the South African state."

It was on the question of self-determination that the African Claims became most eloquent: "this principle of self-determination necessarily raises not only issues relating to the independent existence of small nations besides their more powerful neighbours but those also concerning the political rights and status of minorities and of Africans now held under European tutelage". It went on to characterize the situation in Africa where "European aggression and conquest has resulted in the establishment of alien governments which . . . are not accountable to the indigenous inhabitants." The document stated categorically: "Africans are still very conscious of the loss of their independence, freedom and the right of choosing the form of government under which they will live. It is the inalienable right of all peoples to choose the form of government under which they will live."

It is interesting to see how the ANC treated the struggle in Africa in those days. The document states that "in certain parts of Africa" it should be possible to "accord Africans sovereign rights and to establish administration of their choosing", but "in other parts of Africa", where a ruling white minority has politically entrenched itself "the demands of the Africans for full citizenship rights and direct participation in all the councils of the state should be recognized". This was said to be the "most urgent" in South Africa.[26]

This differentiation of tasks in the anti-colonial struggle in Africa was a result of the realization of the fact that the African revolution was not homogeneous, that in countries where there were no white settlers the struggle and the tasks facing the anti-colonial fighters were relatively straightforward. This shows a sense of realism in the ANC and at the same time testifies to the fact that the ANC was never at any time anti-white - it has always been against white *domination*. Though the ANC today continues the policies followed by our predecessors, there has been a change of emphasis in its policies over the decades. Then the ANC was fighting for "full citizenship rights and direct participation in all councils of the state", today these demands have expanded and include not only the national liberation of the Africans, but of all blacks (Coloureds and Indians as well) and the social emancipation of the whites as well as the abolition of apartheid.

Massive Indian resistance (1946-49)

I have already discussed the early beginnings of Indian protest in South Africa. These did not, however, meet with a corresponding organizational preparedness. There was no viable organization which could harness Indian anger and hatred of the South African system: necessary preparations had to be made. This was not unconnected with the period of weakness of the ANC. Indeed, the reorganization of the ANC had an impact on the Indian community and vice versa.

The first conference of the South African Indian Congress was convened in Cape Town in January 1919 by the Cape Indian Congress, but the constitution was not adopted until the third conference held in June 1923. There were still problems, differences of opinion and even splits, but by February 1928, at the eighth conference of the South African Indian Congress, these had mostly been overcome.

It was in the thirties that younger men infused with enthusiasm and vigour saw the need to change the form and nature of the Indian Congresses. These were men like Dr Dadoo, Mulvi Cachalia, Nana Sita, Jasmat Nana-Bhai, Naransammy Naidoo and G.H.I. Pahad. In the Transvaal Indian Congress there was a clash between the moderates

and the radicals. For the radicals, the issues were:
- a more militant and democratic Transvaal Indian Congress;
- development of links with African and Coloured organizations;
- that Indian women be more involved in the struggle and the Transvaal Indian Congress should guarantee their full participation.

The moving spirit was Dr Dadoo, a young militant communist who became involved in politics in 1936 after qualifying as a doctor in Britain.

In Natal a similar process took place. The main leaders in this drive were militants like H.A. Naidoo, Dr G.M. Naicker, George Singh, M.D. Naidoo and G. Ponen. These radicals were either members of or had contacts with the CP and trade unions.

The battle was won when the militants managed to oust the moderate leaders, but it was not all a smooth and non-violent path.

Besides these internal problems within the Indian Congresses, there was a bigger problem: the racist onslaught against the Indians. In 1940 the racist regime, worried about the extent of what they called Indian "penetration" of white areas in Natal and the Transvaal, set up the Broome Commission to enquire into this question. This commission led to the Asiatic Land and Trading (Transvaal) Act in 1941. On 15 March 1946 Prime Minister Jan Smuts introduced into parliament the Asiatic Land Tenure Act and Indian Representation Bill, which curtailed the movement of the Indians and circumscribed where Indians could reside and trade; prohibited any land transfers between Indians and non-Indians in the Transvaal and Natal, and went even further to propose "in return" token representation of Indians by three whites in parliament. This law, which was an insult to the national honour and dignity of the Indian people, anticipated the Group Areas Act of the racist regime.

In February 1946, the South African Indian Congress held a conference in Cape Town which resolved to oppose the new law with concerted and prolonged resistance and Passive Resistance Councils were appointed in Natal and Transvaal. The "Ghetto Bill" (as the bill became known) became law on 3 June 1946 and the Indian community replied by proclaiming 13 June "Resistance Day" in which a complete "Hartal" (strike and closing of businesses) was observed throughout the country. Mass meetings of 15 000 in Durban, the main centre of the Indian population, hailed the first batch of volunteers, headed by Dr Naicker and M.D. Naidoo, who pitched tents on land reserved for whites. White hooligans in full view of the police attacked the "Resistance camp". "The unprovoked vicious attacks continued until finally an Indian - ironically a policeman off duty - was killed. In a manifestation of solidarity 10 000 people attended the biggest funeral ever given to a policeman."[27]

On 27 June, the first group to be jailed included Dr Dadoo and Dr Naicker. Within two months, over 2 000 resisters (including 300 women) were sentenced. Dadoo and Naicker were sentenced to six months' hard labour. The campaign continued until 1948 and one of its by-products was the publication of a weekly paper, *Passive Resister*, from July 1946 until the end of 1948, edited by I.C. Meer. Many young Indian youths interrupted their studies to do full-time work in the resistance. One typical example was Ahmed Kathrada, who joined the passive resistance campaign at the age of 15 (he was already involved in politics at the age of 12) and who since then has known no other life except that of being a practical revolutionary. He was one of the defendants in the 1964 Rivonia Trial (see chapter 6) and is now serving a life sentence in Pollsmoor Prison, having been transferred from Robben Island. Essop Pahad, states "By June 1947, 1,710 resisters had courted imprisonment . . . As well as Indians, there were 47 Coloured, 15 Africans and eight white resisters imprisoned."[28]

The slogans of the resistance were "Down with the Ghetto Bill" and "To Hell with the Ghetto Bill". Pahad quotes a message from Joshua Fritz Makue, an African speaking at a mass meeting after his release from prison (before the Indian resistance) who said:

> The present struggle is not a struggle of the Indian people alone. It is part of the struggle of the oppressed people of the world. By struggle alone we can liberate our people . . . I am prepared to go back to prison for we must make the necessary sacrifices. I appeal to all the Non-European people to join in a mighty battle for freedom.[29]

"A resister" wrote to Dadoo:

> I felt proud to be a member of the Indian community for in you we have a leader who symbolises our hopes and aspirations to be free. It was difficult to say goodbye to you but we all felt that with you as our leader our community was destined to make a glorious contribution to bringing about democracy in South Africa . . . You may be in jail, but the spirit of freedom is already sweeping the cities and open roads of South Africa . . . and in the new dawn of freedom, men, women, and children will forever remember your name, the name of Dr Dadoo, the torch bearer of freedom.

And a message from the ANC Youth League (see later in this chapter) read:

> We salute the Indian people whose resolve to carry on the struggle against the Colour bar and race domination is a struggle for fundamental human rights. Onward. Forward to Freedom.[30]

What was the philosophy of this resistance? It is usually said that the philosophy of "passive resistance" was Gandhism, a non-violent philosophy of Gandhi. Yet these campaigns, although known as "passive" resistance campaigns, were in fact active campaigns of protest and defiance.[31] It is true that some people shared and embraced Gandhi's non-violent philosophy, but the movement was broader than this and included communists and other revolutionaries. Concerning methods and techniques of struggle, our people and movement have never been dogmatic and inflexible; what is important is that the method of struggle should go beyond verbal protests, petitions and deputations, and the people should understand and accept this so that they can back the movement with mass demonstrations and strikes.

The resistance campaign aroused the Indian people to a higher level of political consciousness and militancy. It also gained general admiration and support from African and Coloured people and democratically minded whites. It certainly stimulated and inspired the struggles of our people in the 1950s. The Indian community thrust up its own leaders and organizers - Dadoo and Naicker being the most outstanding. Indian women and girls took part in the demonstrations, withstanding attacks from white hooligans, and Michael Scott, an English priest, also took part in the Indian mass demonstration. The Indian organizations increased their working-class membership and the Natal Indian Congress grew from a few hundred to about 35 000. This in turn radicalized the South African Indian Congress, with the result that the existing conservative leadership was ousted and a new, radical leadership took over; Dr Naicker became President in Natal, and Dr Dadoo the President of the Transvaal Indian Congress.

It is then no wonder that in 1947 the three doctors - Xuma, Dadoo and Naicker - signed the famous pact of co-operation: Africans and Indians decided voluntarily to join forces in the common struggle against the common enemy. The precondition was overcoming reformism. The rout of the right wing of the Indian Congress led to closer relations between Indians and Africans. In June 1946 the Indian Government recalled its High Commissioner from South Africa and this signalled the beginning of a worldwide condemnation and boycott of South Africa at the United Nations (UN) and internationally.

While these progressive developments were taking place, other, not so progressive, developments also occurred. In January 1949, riots broke out between Africans and Indians in Durban. These were sparked off by a seemingly insignificant incident: an assault of an African youth by an Indian. When the riots started, the authorities stood aside and did not avert them. Then the army and police opened fire indiscriminately. "The casualty figures were as follows: Dead - 142; 87 Africans, 50 Indians, 1 European and 4 who were not identified. Injured - 1,087: 541 Africans, 503 Indians, 11 Coloureds and 32

Europeans. Fifty-eight of the injured died later."[32]

The ANC (Natal) and the Natal Indian Congress appealed to the African and Indian people of Durban to do everything in their power to prevent any further disturbances and later, on 20 January, the Working Committee of the ANC expressed its appreciation of President-General Dr A.B. Xuma "for his timely visit to Durban during the riots, and for his cooperation and consultations with African leaders in Natal in their efforts to bring the race riots between Indians and Africans to an end".[33] African communists from the Transvaal also went to Natal to join with local communists, and ANC and Indian leaders in trying to end the riots.

These attempts by the ANC to grapple with this problem led to an "historic joint meeting" of the representatives of the national organizations of the African and Indian people, representing the Executives of the ANC and the South African Indian Congress and other leaders, held in Durban on 6 February 1949. These were:

- *For the African National Congress:* Dr A.B. Xuma, President-General; A.W.G. Champion, President (Natal); C.S. Ramahanoe, President (Transvaal); R.G. Baloyi, Treasurer-General; H. Selby Msimang; J.B. Marks; J. Malangabi; G. Makabeni; Moses M. Kotane; L.K. Ntlabati; O.R. Tambo.

- *For the South African Indian Congress:* Dr G.M. Naicker, President; A.I. Meer, Joint Hon. Secretary; J.N. Singh, Joint Hon. Secretary; Dr A.H. Sadler, Joint Hon. Treasurer; Y.A. Cachalia; T.N. Naidoo; V. Lawrence; I.C. Meer; M.D. Naidoo; Debi Singh; Nana Sita; Y. Cachalia; G.H.I. Pahad.

- *Other Indian and African leaders:* Professor D.D.T. Jabavu; the Revd Z.R. Mahabane (ANC) of the Orange Free State; N. Mkele, Observer, All-African Convention; D.W. Moshe; S.B. Ngcobo; S.R. Naidoo (Cape); T.B. Gwala; E.O. Msimang (ANC); A.N. Ntuli; J.G. Mgadi.

While expressing its deep and heartfelt sympathy with the relatives of all the victims of this "unhappy tragedy" and all those who suffered, the statement issued by this joint meeting went further to say:

Whatever are the immediate causes which may have precipitated the outburst, and which are receiving the attention of this meeting, this meeting is convinced that the fundamental and basic causes of the disturbances are traceable to the political, economic and social structure of this country, based on differential and discriminatory treatment of the various racial groups and the preaching in high places of racial hatred and intolerance. Any disturbances such as the recent riots are therefore the fruits and results of such a policy as well as the responsibility of those who create and maintain such an artificial social framework.[34]

A strategy for the respective peoples was formulated:
(a)   to view the problems in this perspective;
(b)   to devise ways and means for closer co-operation and mutual
      understanding through the existing national organizations;
(c)   to stand together in the fight for national liberation and mutual
      political, economic and social advancement and security.

The meeting gave directives to the constituent bodies, particularly
the ANC (Natal) and the Natal Indian Congress, to constitute a joint
council and to establish thereunder local committees to advance and
promote mutual understanding and goodwill among the respective
peoples. These were the beginnings of unity which found organizational expression in the 1950s and later.

Workers set the pace : the great mineworkers' strike of 1946

The period between 1933 and 1946 was a period in which South Africa
saw a rapid economic development and significant changes in the
structure of production. The economy was stimulated by the rise in the
price of gold after abandonment of the Gold Standard in 1932 and
then by wartime production - it expanded in the periods 1933-39 and
1940-46. The total dependence on agriculture and mineral exports was
transformed into a high level of industrialization. "The contribution of
manufacturing to National Income first surpassed agriculture in 1930
and outstripped mining in 1943."[35]This "boom" expressed itself in an
increase in the number of manufacturing establishments which rose
from 6 543 in 1933 to 8 505 in 1939, and by 1946 one could count 9 999.

This industrial development also affected the social composition of
the African population: by 1946, almost one in four Africans was an
urban dweller. The permanency of urbanization was guaranteed by the
increasing ratio of African women to men in the urban areas, from
under 1:5 in 1921 to 1:3 in 1946. Between 1933 and 1939, an additional
240 000 Africans entered industrial employment, but mine labour still
remained migrant labour.

Following the Land Act of 1913, the rural areas became increasingly
impoverished. This expressed itself in the fall in productivity and land-
lessness became more acute. The 1948 Fagan Commission revealed the
existence of three broad "classes" in the African reserves: owners or
occupiers of land; the landless who owned cattle; and the landless
whose cattle were grazed on common land. It was found out that in the

Ciskei, for example, 30 per cent of the families were landless, over 60 per cent owned five or fewer cattle, and 29 per cent owned nothing. The vast majority of the recruits to the mines came from the landless. This explains why the African mine labour force increased by 135 000 or 40 per cent in this period.

Despite the rapid economic development, this period (1933-46) did not see the rise of an African bourgeoisie. It is true that a small trading petty bourgeoisie emerged dealing mostly in foodstuffs, and there was a small stratum of professional men and administrative and clerical workers. This stratum comprised 0,2 per cent of all adult Africans in 1921; 0,9 per cent in 1926 and 1,2 per cent or a total of 62 246 individuals in 1946:

> The exploitation of the African proletariat produced no material benefit for the African petty bourgeoisie, *but was in fact the direct cause of their political oppression.* The labour policies of the state which differentiated between skilled and unskilled on racial grounds closed off avenues of mobility to this class and in effect lumped them together with the proletariat as politically rightless and economically exploitable.[36]

Indeed, it should be remembered that this was also the period of acute political contradictions sharpened by the Hertzog Bills which disenfranchised Cape Africans.

During the war, the living conditions of the black masses further deteriorated, through low wages, the pass laws, the need for more and better education, miserable housing conditions, insanitary overcrowded slums without street and house lighting, bad roads, often nonexistent sanitation, long distances to and from work, no proper transport system and so on.

In Alexandra township, Johannesburg, bus fares were raised from four pence to five pence in 1943. The average African wage was fixed at £5 2s 11d a month and the fares alone would have been tantamount to one-fifth of that! So the Africans decided to walk: 1 500 men and women boycotted the buses and walked nine or more miles to work. After nine days, the bus company gave in and reduced the fares to four pence again. This was in August, in mid-winter, and the bleak cold of the highveld. Two years later, in 1945, a similar thing happened. This time the boycott lasted for seven weeks and the Utility Company was forced to take over the bus service and revert to the original fare. There were riots in Marabastad, Pretoria, in which 16 Africans and one European were killed, and many wounded. In 1944, tens of thousands of Africans, who had been homeless for years, followed James Mpanza, nicknamed "Sofasonke" (We shall all die) to squat, setting up shanties near Orlando.

The growing number of African workers, especially on the mines, experiencing extreme poverty and beginning to act to try and change their living and working conditions, soon formed a co-ordinating committee of African trade unions. The Council of Non-European Trade Unions (CNETU) was formed at a conference held at the Trades Hall in Johannesburg on 29-30 November 1941. It was formed by African and Coloured workers. In 1942, a number of strikes in CNETU's campaign for a 40 shillings weekly minimum wage led directly to state action against African unions. War Measure 145 of December 1942 outlawed strikes by Africans; severe penalties and persecutions were threatened but this did not deter the workers. The Department of Labour complained that "Natives seem to be ignoring War Measure 145."[37] Without official recognition, subjected to a wide range of legal and other restraints, the CNETU nevertheless had, by September 1945, a national membership of 158 000 in 119 unions, embracing more than 40 per cent of the 390 000 Africans employed in commerce and manufacturing. The growth of African trade unions between 1930 and 1945 saw a corresponding growth in militancy, especially during the Second World War: in the period 1940-45, more than 52 494 Africans went on strike.

There was also another dimension in the organization of African workers - the mobilization of African miners. In a circular of 9 June 1941, Gauer Radebe, the Transvaal ANC Secretary of Mines, proposed a conference to be held at the Ritz Hall, Johannesburg, on 3 August 1941. The agenda was straightforward:
(1)   Report on condition of African miners.
(2)   Ways and means of organizing them.
(3)   Discussions and resolutions.
(4)   Election of a committee.[38]
He went on to explain the bad working conditions of the 400 000 African mineworkers employed on the mines; they were completely unorganized; had to work under extremely bad conditions at very low wages; they were injured and killed in mine accidents every year, thousands more got mine pthisis (which affects the lungs) and had to be sent back "home".

The circular went on to urge that miners' working conditions be improved stating that the organization of this sector of black workers could give great encouragement to African trade unionism; they would become a source of new life and strength to the African trade-union movement and this would help overcome "tribal" friction and create an organized body capable of taking its proper place in the advance of the African people out of national oppression. This would carry with it the possibility of advance of other sectors of the population suffering under discriminatory legislation. The circular stated, "This matter has engaged the Transvaal African Congress for some time and a serious study has been made of the conditions of the African miners and of the best methods to be adopted in organizing them."[39]

The two largest groups of African workers - the mineworkers and farm labourers - remained unorganized during the growth of trade unionism until Gauer Radebe (Secretary of Mines and Employment in the Transvaal ANC) and Edwin Mofutsanyana (responsible for Labour in the ANC National Executive Committee) organized the above-mentioned conference in August 1941 to discuss the formation of an African mineworkers' union. Eighty delegates from 41 organizations attended. They resolved to organize workers both on the mines and before recruitment in the reserves. The ANC played a crucial role in establishing the union, with the active participation of a number of communists. A committee of 15 was elected to raise funds and to build the union. J.B. Marks became president and J.J. Majoro, a leading member of the Witwatersrand Native Mine Clerks' Association, became secretary. The election of Majoro, a mine clerk, was very significant because the African mine clerks had their own grievances: Proclamation 110 of 1942 excluded "mine labourer'" from the statutory cost of living allowance payable to all industrial employees - the Chamber of Mines ruled that the 1 935 African clerks fell within the category of "mine labourers" and refused them the allowance. This was one of the reasons why the Native Mine Clerks' Association affiliated to the African Mine Workers' Union (AMWU). The mine clerks were also important, however, for another reason: they acted as a liaison between the miners and the AMWU. This was all the more important because the mine compounds were closed to AMWU officials. Nevertheless the union grew in numbers and ideology: by 1944 it had 25 000 members. There was a series of work stoppages in 1943 and AMWU and the African Gas and Power Workers' Union made representations to the employers.

The government then decided to appoint a commission - the Lansdowne Commission of Inquiry - to investigate the wages and conditions of African miners. At this time there were 308 374 Africans on the Witwatersrand gold mines. Working a six-day week, the average wage was two shillings one penny per shift for surface workers. There were no overtime rates and sick or holiday pay was not granted. There were also deductions for boots, mattresses and other items, totalling 15 per cent of gross earnings.

AMWU gave evidence on these conditions to the commission. It called for an end to cheap migrant labour and put forward five basic demands:

(1)   regular wage increases;
(2)   payment of a cost-of-living allowance;
(3)   a minimum statutory wage, and a wage board enquiry;
(4)   a total abolition of the compound system, the "tribal" division of the workforce and all restrictions on freedom of movement; and
(5)   recognition of AMWU.

The commission did little to help solve these problems. Both the Chamber of Mines and the government attempted to stifle the work of AMWU. "The Chamber persistently pressurised the government to detain Marks and Majoro,"[40] as an attempt to victimize and intimidate active members of AMWU. All the mines followed the Chamber's policy to get rid of anybody trying to organize workers. "At one mine alone, 102 AMWU members were arrested for intimidation."[41]

On the advice of the Chamber of Mines, the government proclaimed War Measure 1425 in August 1944. According to this proclamation, gatherings of more than 20 people on proclaimed mining ground were prohibited. Meetings had now to be held clandestinely at night under mine dumps.

In August 1944, the Report of the Lansdowne Commission was considered by the annual AMWU conference, attended by delegates from every mine, and a mass emergency conference of March 1945 demanded the repeal of the War Measure and the retrospective enforcement of the Lansdowne recommendations. In June 1945, the AMWU delegation met the Acting Prime Minister and other members of the cabinet but it failed to convince them of the workers' case.

South Africa at this time was suffering food shortages. In 1945 rations were cut on all mines and canned beef was substituted for fresh meat. This deteriorating quality and quantity of food aggravated the grievances of the miners, who formed workers' committees to demand better food. Food riots broke out on at least 10 mines and a miner was killed and 40 injured when police broke up a protest outside the kitchen at the Modderfontein East mine. The clouds were gathering before the storm.

In April 1946, 2 000 delegates attended the AMWU conference. They demanded:
● a minimum daily wage of 10 shillings;
● family housing;
● two weeks' paid annual leave;
● A £1 000 gratuity after 15 years' service;
● payment of repatriation fares;
● repeat of War Measure 1425;
● an end to migratory labour.

The Chamber remained intransigent and the fact that numerous letters from AMWU went unanswered reflected the Chamber's policy, which acknowledged neither the existence of the union nor the miners' grievances.

In June the conference of the CNETU unanimously pledged full support to the AMWU in the event of a strike. At a special open-air conference on Sunday 4 August, a resolution to strike was unanimously adopted by the 1 000 delegates. On Monday 12 August 1946, in response to a call by AMWU, over 60 000 African miners on the Witwatersrand went on strike. Mary Benson describes the day:

> it was a cold clear night on the highveld. All along the Reef from hundreds of shaftheads African miners surfaced at the end of their shift and walked out in the wintry night, back to the compound. Some, as they tramped wearily along, passed others, waiting to go underground. But on seven mines they passed no one. The cages went down empty. The huge fly-wheels stopped. The great mine strike had begun.[42]

Estimates of the number of participants vary between 50 000 and 100 000; monthly production fell that month in 31 out of the 45 mines; the total monthly production went down by 169 000 tons to the lowest since 1937.

Official reaction was swift and violent because the strike was considered to be a result of agitation and not of legitimate grievances; "appropriate action" had to be taken and "ringleaders" were to be arrested. This is the language of our oppressors and it meant nothing more than that the leadership of AMWU had to be paralysed and at the same time this was seen as an incitement to the police to attack the miners with rifles and clubs. Sixteen hundred police were put on special duty; reinforcements were rushed to the Witwatersrand; compounds were sealed off under armed guard. "The strikers were thus put out of touch with the Union organizers and with no news from other mines or compounds."[43]

The police fired on strikers at the Sub-Nigel mine. Six were reported killed by rifle fire and a further six trampled to death in the ensuing panic; at the West Springs mine, 324 casualties were reported, including one policeman bayonetted by a miner. On the following day, the miners staged a sit-down strike underground - they were baton-charged and driven up "step by step, level by level" to the surface and back into the compounds. Miners from the City Deep, West Springs, Simmer and Jack and Robinson Deep mines marched towards Johannesburg to see the Chief Native Commissioner. They were "dispersed" by the police.

An emergency meeting of the CNETU was held on 13 August and it issued a call for a general strike in 48 hours. The ANC President-

General, Xuma, and the Transvaal ANC and Indian Passive Resistance Councils pledged full support. Police burst into the meeting and arrested J.B. Marks, AMWU President, and raided the AMWU offices.

The 1946 mineworkers' strike was indeed a turning point in many respects in the history of the South African liberation struggle. The migrant workers - the miners - launched the largest strike in South African history. The violence of the state's response indicated the degree to which it felt threatened. The strike did not only arouse widespread support among the ranks of the working class and national liberation movement, however, it also strengthened the solidarity between the African and Indian community who were fighting against anti-Indian legislation, for instance the Durban Indian resisters sent £100 for the strike fund. Scores of resisters helped to duplicate leaflets and distribute them to the compounds from Randfontein to Springs. A crucial role was played by CP and ANC members in the Transvaal, who went out night after night to distribute union leaflets and bulletins at the mine shafts after the entire AMWU leadership had been arrested or immobilized. Because of this work, the strike kept spreading to new mines.

The miners' strike opened the eyes of our people to the power and indeed the role of the working class, especially the miners, in our national liberation movement. In August 1946, the ANC Youth League issued a flyer: "The African Mine Workers' Strike - A National Struggle" in which they pledged their support to the miners' strike:

> The African National Congress Youth League calls upon all Africans - in all spheres of life and occupation and employment - to lend active support to the mine workers' struggle. The African Mine Workers' struggle is our struggle. They are fighting political colour bar and economic discrimination against Africans.[44]

One immediate result of the strike was the trial of 53 trade-union, ANC and CP officials for aiding and abetting an "illegal strike", followed by the trial of the entire CP Central Committee on sedition charges, "even Dr Dadoo, who was brought from prison in Natal where he was still serving his sentence for passive resistance".[45] The miners' strike helped to bring to the fore the convergence of interests among the different sections of the liberation movement. Joint practical action strengthened the ties between the ANC and CP, producing a broad set of leadership contacts of vital importance in the years to come. This also helped to radicalize the ANC. In the words of Michael Harmel:

The miners' strike of 1946 was one of those great social events which at once illuminate and accelerate history: brillantly showing up and hastening the main conflicts which determine social development, pitilessly exposing the hypocrisy, cowardice or futility of those who seek to evade those conflicts and stand on the sidelines. The strike destroyed, once and for all, the myth of the state as a "neutral" body, standing above the conflict between employer and employed, rich and poor. It spelt the end of the compromising, concession-begging tendencies which had hitherto dominated African politics . . .

The courage and class consciousness of the miners inspired and awakened tens of thousands of oppressed African workers: the miners of 46 were the forerunners of the protest strikers of May Day and the 26th of June, the defiance volunteers, the brave men and women who have stood by the Congress movement through the grim days of Nationalist repression.[46]

The formation of the ANC Youth League (1943-49)

In the mid 1940s young men and women in their mid-twenties or early thirties, mainly teachers or students of medicine or law, became dissatisfied with the manner in which things were done by the ANC and the pace at which they were done. They came from the Anglican (Episcopal) Secondary School of St Peters in Johannesburg, from Lovedale or Healdtown, Adam's College and Fort Hare. Walter Sisulu, as a worker, was a noticeable exception.

These were prominent members of provincial and/or local student associations who articulated the aspirations of their generation and the masses of our people as a whole. They held political discussions frequently. These young Africans were concerned with the deteriorating conditions of our people, the rise of fascism in Germany and with Mussolini's attack on Ethiopia. The growth and new militancy of African trade unions, the activities of the CP and their own participation in militant mass action were other influences that radicalized them.

In response to this upsurge of militant youth the annual conference of the ANC on 21 December 1942 authorized "the Executive to institute a Youth League of the African National Congress to include students at Fort Hare",[47] and the 1943 annual conference adopted a similar resolution. After consultations between these young men and women and the ANC leadership, especially Dr Xuma, the ANC Youth League was formally established at an inaugural meeting held at the Bantu Men's Social Centre in Johannesburg in April 1944. Anton Muziwake Lembede became its first president and Nelson Rolihlahla Mandela its secretary. Their aim was simple and honest: a desire to remould the ANC. They set about recruiting a broader membership and organizing a permanent youth league within the ANC.

Before we take a closer look at their ideas and ideology, let us answer the question: Who were these youth leaguers? The most notable were Lembede, Mandela, Tambo, Mda, Walter Sisulu, Dr James Njongwe, Dr William Nkomo, Jordan Ngubane, Robert Sobukwe, Ntsu Mokhehle and others. Lembede was definitely the most dynamic and articulate.

Born in the rural district of Georgedale near Durban in Natal in 1914, Lembede was of peasant origin. His parents were extremely poor. He went to Adam's College on a bursary in 1933 to train as a teacher. During his spare time he studied for his matriculation, which he passed in 1937 with a distinction in Latin. He taught in Natal and the Orange Free State at the age of 29 and at the same time learnt Sesotho and Afrikaans. In 1943, he obtained a BA degree through correspondence with the University of South Africa and, again through self-education, he obtained an LL.B degree. Pixley ka Isaka Seme agreed to article Lembede as a law clerk and he became a full partner - the firm became "Seme and Lembede" in 1946. He later achieved an MA degree in philosophy.

Lembede was militantly nationalistic, with very strong views on the Africanness of our struggle. He called his philosophy "Africanism". He was a practising Catholic and this perhaps explains his mysticism in his ideological concepts. He was a controversial figure and his ideas were full of contradictions. T. Singh has assessed the ideas and concepts of Lembede.[48] He says Lembede was preoccupied with working out a "nation-building faith", the philosophy of "Africanism". Lembede claimed that "the dynamic human energy that will be released by African Nationalism will be more powerful and devastating in its effects than . . . atomic energy".[49] He had an idealistic belief in self-reliance that denied the need for solidarity and unity. But he was not alone - he was part of a bigger collective.

Let us take a closer look at the ideas of this collective, starting with the manifesto issued by the Provincial Committee of the ANC Youth League in March 1944, a month before the actual formation of the Youth League.[50]

The preamble of this document stated that "Africanism must be promoted" and this meant that Africans should struggle for development, progress and national liberation so as to occupy their rightful and honourable place among nations of the world; that the African youth should be united, consolidated, trained and disciplined because from their ranks future leaders would be recruited. The document went on to explain the policy of the ANC Youth League, which was based on

109

the conviction that "the contact of the white race with the black has resulted in the emergence of a set of conflicting living conditions and outlooks on life which seriously hamper South Africa's progress to nationhood". The whites, said the youth leaguers, possessed superior military strength and superior organizing skills, and therefore had arrogated to themselves the ownership of the land and invested themselves with authority and right "to regard South Africa as a white man's land".

On civilization it was stated that:

The African regards civilization as the common heritage of all Mankind and claims as full a right to make his contribution to its advancement and to live free as any white South African: further, he claims the right to all sources and agencies to enjoy rights and fulfil duties which will place him on a footing of equality with every other racial group.

The devastating effects of the Land Act were dealt with at length and the Colour Bar Acts were also scrutinized, as were the Mines and Works Act of 1926, "which shuts Africans from skilled trades"; the 1923 Urban Areas Act "which warned Africans clearly that they were bidding farewell to freedom"; and the 1927 Native Administration Act, which "established the white race as the Supreme Chief of the African people. The conquest of the African was complete". The 1937 Native Laws Amendment Act, it was said, closed up any other loophole through which the African could have forced his way to full citizenship.

The dilemma of the Africans during the Second World War was described thus: "South African blood - of Whites and Africans alike - has been shed to free the white peoples of Europe while Africans within the Union remain in bondage."

On an optimistic note, however, the document went on:

These conditions have made the African lose all faith in all talks of Trusteeship. *He now elects to determine his future by his own efforts.* He has realized that to trust to the mere good grace of the white man will not free him as no action can free an oppressed group other than that group itself.

Self-determination is the philosophy of life which will save him from the disaster he clearly sees on his way ... The African is aware of the magnitude of the task before him but has learnt that promises, no matter from high source, are merely palliatives intended to drum him into yielding to *more* oppression. He has made up his mind to sweat for his freedom - determine his destiny himself and, *through his African National Congress is building a strong national unity front which will be his surest guarantee of victory over oppression* .

The ANC was described by its Youth League as "the symbol and embodiment of the African's will to present a united national front against all forms of oppression". But it was admitted that the ANC had not made progress and this had drawn criticism "in the last 20 years." The arguments of the critics were dealt with and the following conclusion was drawn:

> It does no good to stop at being noisy in condemning African leaders who went before us. Defects in the organisation of the people against oppression cannot be cured by mouthing criticism and not putting our heads together to build what has been damaged and to find a way out of the present suffering . . . In response to the demands of the times African Youth is *laying its services at the disposal of the national liberation movement, the African National Congress, in the firm belief, knowledge and conviction that the cause of Africa must and will triumph.*

This positive attitude towards the solution of the problems that faced the ANC at the time was accompanied by an articulation of a positive strategy which took the form of a programme, and clarified ideological questions in the process. This was expressed in the sub-section "Our Creed" which stated:

(a) We believe in the divine destiny of nations.
(b) The goal of all our struggles is Africanism and our motto is *Africa's cause must triumph* .
(c) We believe that the national liberation of Africans will be achieved by African themselves. We reject foreign leadership of Africa.
(d) We may borrow useful ideologies from foreign ideologies, but we reject the wholesale importation of foreign ideologies into Africa.
(e) We believe that leadership must be the personification and symbol of popular aspirations and ideals.
(f) We believe that practical leadership must be given to capable men, whatever their status in society.
(g) We believe in the scientific approach to all African problems.
(h) We combat moral disintegration among Africans by maintaining and upholding high ethical standards ourselves.
(i) We believe in the unity of all Africans from the Mediterranean Sea in the North to the Indian and Atlantic Oceans in the South — and that Africans must speak with one voice.

I have quoted at length from this important document because its adoption had far-reaching repercussions on the ANC as a whole. It also helps us to identify the trends and tendencies in the ideological struggle and the problems that faced the ANC at the time. The central theme of the document was the struggle for national self-determination which would be brought about by "building a strong national unity". The document was orientated towards mass action; action to strengthen the ANC and to fight for freedom.

At the ideological level one notices an attempt at defining an ideology that corresponds to reality in South Africa - a striving towards the

111

"Africanism" and its essence was to be found in the formulation: "We believe that the national liberation of Africans will be achieved by Africans themselves." This sounds like the philosophy of present-day "Black Consciousness" in South Africa which states: "Black Man! You are on your own!" This was interpreted to mean that Africans were struggling, through their own efforts, to occupy "their rightful and honourable place among nations of the world". The ANC Youth League's stress on "Africanism" was a radical departure from the predominantly "liberal" and traditionalist thinking of the ANC at that time.

There was a serious attempt by the ANC Youth League to work out an ideology for liberation and a need was expressed "to borrow useful ideologies from foreign ideologies, but we reject the wholesale importation of foreign ideologies in Africa". This statement was significant because it pointed out that ideology should be subject to popular demands and express popular aspirations. At the same time, the youth leaguers recognized their inadequacy - their ideas were not consistent and fully developed; they were still at a formative stage in the process of development.

Another important aspect of the Youth League Manifesto was that it viewed our struggle in the context of the wider struggle in Africa and expressed the idea of African unity: "from the Mediterranean Sea in the North to the Indian and Atlantic Oceans in the South - and that Africans must speak with one voice". This was 20 years before the formation of the OAU and definitely not a new idea.

In talking about the ideology of the Youth League, it is important to stress that the slogan of Marcus Garvey, "Africa for the African", was not mentioned in the Manifesto. Not that the slogan was wrong in itself but in the South African context it had the implication that whites and other non-Africans were irrelevant to the struggle. This is important to mention because in 1959, the Pan African Congress (PAC) claimed to be successors of the ANC Youth League under the slogan "Africa for the Africans". They failed to modify the aspirations of the Africans to suit the concrete reality of our country by accepting the historical fact that there is room in our movement for those whites who are prepared to fight side by side with the Africans and who are willing to accept the policy of the ANC under African leadership. What the PAC did was to latch on to aspects of the philosophy of young Lembede: self-reliance without solidarity; African exclusivism and anti-Marxism. But they ignored the fact that Lembede himself grew away from these ideas.

On 9 March 1947 a meeting of the Joint Committee of the ANC, the Natal Indian Congress and the Transvaal Indian Congress, was held in Johannesburg. Present were Dr Xuma, in the chair, Dr Dadoo

(Transvaal Indian Congress); Messrs Debi Singh (Natal Indian Congress); J.B. Marks (ANC); M.P. Naicker (Natal Indian Congress); D. Tloome (ANC); C.S. Ramohanoe (ANC); Y.A. Cachalia (Transvaal Indian Congress); J.N. Singh and A.B. Meer (both of the Natal Indian Congress); and, significantly, A.M. Lembede. The Joint Committee's purpose was to work out a practical basis of co-operation between the national organizations of the Africans and the Indians. A sub-committee, consisting of Drs Xuma and Dadoo; Messrs J.N. Singh, A.I. Meer and A.M. Lembede, was appointed to draft a joint declaration. This was then accepted by the Joint Committee. It stated "that the next meeting of the joint committee be held on 23 March 1947 at 11.00 a.m. in which representatives of APO should be invited to attend".[51] This was an appeal to the Coloured community to join ranks with the Africans and Indians.

This historic fact, that Lembede was part of the Joint Committee of Africans and Indians, that he was a member of a sub-committee which appealed to the Coloureds to join them as well, is of great political significance because it proves that it is the ANC which has upheld the tradition set by Lembede. Even ideologically, Lembede was changing his views about the CP, as Brian Bunting has remarked: "Before he died at the tragically early age of 33, Lembede had also changed his attitude towards the Communist Party. "They are workers, not just talkers," he admitted grudgingly to Kotane."[52]

Unfortunately, Lembede died in July 1947. But his ideas were changing before he died, reflecting the change in the social composition of African society when workers were beginning to play a more important role. This is what the PAC did not understand when they said they were the upholders of African nationalism "as expounded by Lembede". What they did was to cling to some of the early, immature concepts of Lembede; before he changed; before he realized the need for unity and solidarity; before he discarded his anti-communist attitudes. This "mistake" of the PAC is repeated by Gail Gerhard in her book on black power in South Africa.[53]

So that I should not be misunderstood, I am far from maintaining that Lembede had changed entirely; he was in the process of changing. He was becoming more and more socialist-inclined but his socialism was "African socialism". In an article on the "Policy of the Congress Youth League" in *Inkundla Yabantu* in May 1946, he wrote:

> Africans are naturally socialistic as illustrated in their social practices and customs. The achievement of national liberation will therefore herald or usher in a new era, the era of African socialism. Our immediate task, however, is not socialism, but national liberation. Our motto: Freedom in Our Life Time.[54]

113

In 1948 the ANC Youth League issued its Basic Policy Document,[55] which did not differ much from the 1944 Manifesto and therefore I shall not go to any length analysing it. This document articulated the basic aspects of the national question, stating: "We are oppressed not as a class, but as a people, as a Nation." However, this one-sided approach missed the point that the overwhelming majority of the blacks have been oppressed as a class and as a people, or a nation if you like. Let us take a closer look at the national question and the ideology of African nationalism as expressed in this document.

The ANC Youth League Policy Document explained the fundamental aim of African nationalism as:
(1)   the creation of a united nation out of the heterogeneous tribes;
(2)   the freeing of Africans from foreign domination and foreign leadership;
(3)   the creation of conditions which can enable Africa to make her own contribution to human progress and happiness.

It stated categorically that Africans had a primary, inherent and inalienable right to Africa, which was their continent and motherland, and that Africans as a whole had a divine destiny - to make Africa free among the peoples and nations of the earth. In order to achieve this, it was stated, the Africans should build a powerful national liberation movement which, in order to have inner strength and solidarity, should adopt the national liberation creed - African nationalism - "and it should be led by Africans themselves". There was, however, mention of a "possibility of a compromise" with whites on condition that:
(a)   the whites completely abandoned their domination of Africa;
(b)   they agreed to an equitable and proportionate redivision of land;
(c)   they assisted in establishing a free people's democracy in South Africa and Africa in general.

The history, bravery and "unparalleled heroism" of the struggle was recorded, and it was acknowledged that the struggle would be "long, bitter and unrelenting":

It is known, however, that a dominant group does not voluntarily give up its privileged position. That is why the Congress Youth puts forward African Nationalism as the militant outlook of an oppressed people seeking a solid basis for waging a long, bitter, and unrelenting struggle for its national freedom.

The Youth League refuted the accusation that African nationalism was one-sided and racialistic, and they also rejected what they called "pseudo-nationalism": "People who pretend to be Nationalists when in fact they are only imperialist or capitalist agents, using Nationalistic slogans in order to cloak their reactionary position." "Fascist agents", "Vendors of foreign method" and "tribalism" were equally denounced.

What was the attitude of the Youth League to other nationalities? The majority of the whites (then usually referred to as "Europeans") were said to be sharing the spoils of white domination; they had a vested interest in the "exploitive caste society" in South Africa:

A few of them love justice and condemn racial oppression, but their voice is negligible, and in the last analysis counts for nothing. In the struggle for freedom, the Africans will be wasting their time and deflecting their forces if they look up to the Europeans, either for inspiration or for help in their political struggle.

It is interesting to notice the similarity between this statement and many statements of the same kind uttered and published by the Black Consciousness Movement in the recent past. But the problem is that this statement was ambiguous and even controversial because there is no need for Africans to reject help from whites in the political struggle if it is forthcoming. This "help" might include direct participation, contribution and even commitment to the cause of the black masses!

The Indians were said to be oppressed as a group like Africans "but" they differ from Africans in their historical and cultural background "among other things". They had their mother country, India, "but thousands of them made South Africa and Africa their home". "They, however, did not come as conquerors and exploiters, but as the exploited. As long as they do not undermine or impede our liberation struggle we should not regard them as intruders or enemies." This reflects a specific stage in the development of African nationalism: an acceptance - though with reservation - of the Indians as allies. Four years later, when the Defiance Campaign was launched in 1952, this question did not arise at all.

The Coloureds were said to be like Indians in that they "differ from the Africans": "they are a distinct group, suffering group oppression". But their oppression differed in degree from that of the Africans, it was said. The Coloureds had no motherland to look up to and "but for historic accidents" they might be nearer to the Africans than the Indians, "seeing they descend in part at least from the aboriginal Hottentots who with the Africans and Bushmen are original children of black Africa."

Coloureds, like Indians, will never win their national freedom unless they organise a Coloured People's National Organization to lead in the struggle of the National Freedom of the Coloureds. The National Organizations of the Africa's Indians and Coloureds may cooperate on common issues.

The realisation and acceptance of national characteristics and distinctions was very important; what was more significant was the recognition of the need to "co-operate on common issues". Today this "co-operation" has reached a higher level which we call unity of the patriotic forces".

The philosophy of the Youth League comes out clearly in the summary of their ideas:

> South Africa is a country of four chief nationalities, three of which (The Europeans, Indians and Coloureds) are minorities and three of which (the Africans, Coloureds and Indians) suffer national oppression . . . It is to be clearly understood that we are not against the European as such - we are not against the European as a human being - but we are totally and irrevocably opposed to white domination and to oppression.

It is also interesting to record that the Youth League noted what they called the "Two streams of African Nationalism":

> Now it must be noted that there are two streams of African Nationalism. One centres round Marcus Garvey's slogan -"Africa for the Africans". It is based on the "Quit Africa" slogan and on the cry "Hurl the white man into the sea". This brand of African Nationalism is extreme and ultra-revolutionary.

> There is another stream of African Nationalism (Africanism) which is moderate, and which the Congress Youth League professes. We of the Youth League take account of the concrete situation in South Africa, and realise that the different racial groups have come to stay. But we insist that a condition for inter-racial peace and progress is the abandonment of white domination, and such a change in the basic structure of South African society that those relations which breed exploitation and human misery will disappear. Therefore our goal is the winning of National Freedom for the African people and the inauguration of a people's free society where racial oppression and persecution will be outlawed.

This statement was important for two reasons. First, the national liberation of the Africans was interconnected with another vitally important issue - social emancipation: "such a change in the basic structure of South African society that those relations which breed exploitation and human misery will disappear". Second, it took into consideration the reality which was different from many African countries. It must be said, in fairness to the youth leaguers, that they were not attacking Garvey's theories, which had a liberating effect on Africa. After all, Garvey is considered a heroic figure in Jamaica - his home country - and Jamaican revolutionaries assess his contribution to the liberation of black people all over the world positively. This attitude of the ANC Youth League was meant to emphasize South African reality - a multinational society - and to underline the non-racist and anti-racist policy of our movement.

The document concluded with a powerful message:

> The historic task of African Nationalism (it has become apparent) is the building of a self-confident and strong African Nation in South Africa. Therefore African

> Nationalism transcends the narrow limits imposed by any particular sectional organisation. It is all embracing in the sense that its field is the whole body of African people in this country . . . The strength, solidarity and permanence of such a front will, of course, depend not on accident or chance, but on the correctness of our front . . . the most vital aspect of our forward struggle is the political aspect.

Two things need to be said about the character of African nationalism as propounded by the Youth League. First, this was a "nationalism of an oppressed people, seeking freedom from foreign oppression". The youth leaguers were very much aware of this, as the letter A.P. Mda wrote to G.M. Pitje (24 August 1948) reflects:

> Please note that our Nationalism has nothing to do with Fascism and National Socialism (Hitleric version) nor with the imperialistic and Neo-Fascist Nationalism of the Afrikaners (the Malanite type). Ours is the pure Nationalism of an oppressed people, seeking freedom from foreign oppression.[56]

Second, though the ANC Youth League was African, it was not exclusive because its constitution stated that "young members of other sections of the community who live like and with Africans and whose general outlook on life is similar to that of Africans may become full members".[57]

The youth leaguers learnt a lot from the ANC leadership and they in turn contributed positively to the formulation of a new militant policy of the ANC. Some of their ideas were incorporated in the famous 1949 ANC Programme of Action. These were the emphasis on:

(1) The principle of self-determination.
(2) Rejection of white domination.
(3) Vigorous pro-African policy "under the banner of African nationalism."
(4) Injection of a spirit of self-confidence and pride in being African as opposed to racist theories and paternalistic attitudes of liberals who sought to instil a sense of self-pity, "shame" in and even "excuses" for being black.
(5) Demand for mass action: strikes, demonstrations, protests, and so on.

The Youth League contributed one more thing to the ANC, however. At the thirty-seventh annual conference of the ANC held in Bloemfontein on 15-19 December 1949, the Revd J.A. Calata explained the significance of raising the right thumb when singing the national anthem. The first four fingers symbolized unity, determination, solidarity and militancy, while the thumb was raised as a supplication for Africa to come back to us. The symbol was first introduced by the ANC Youth League in the Cape and it was found appropriate to adopt it universally in the ANC.

The concepts and ideas of the ANC about the principles of self-determination developed and were incorporated in the 1949 Programme of Action adopted by the annual conference. This conference received messages from Dr Naicker of the South African Indian Congress and from as far afield as Nyasaland, from the Nyasaland African National Congress. Mzamane gave a report of the co-ordinating committee of the Programme of Action, which was thoroughly scrutinized, paragraph by paragraph, and then accepted and adopted unanimously in its amended form. It was pointed out that only those people who signified their willingness to carry out this programme should be elected onto the incoming Executive. They were: President-General, Dr J.S. Moroka; Secretary-General, W.M. Sisulu; Treasurer-General, Dr S. Molema. The other Executive Committee members were Dr A.B. Xuma; Dr R.T. Bokwe; the Revd J.A. Calata; L.K. Ntlabati; O.R. Tambo; J.L.Z. Njongwe; G. Radebe; J.A. Mokoena; G.M. Pitje; D. Tloome; M.M. Kotane; R.G. Baloyi; and V.V.T. Mbobo.

The policy and line of the Youth League had triumphed. Now the ANC was put on a path of struggle with a more concrete and radical programme than ever before. Forman has characterized the Youth League as follows:

These Youth Leaguers were students and teachers and professional men - as petit bourgeois as their predecessors. They were men thrown up by the national struggle, and not the class struggle, and more significant still, although they were not Communists when they initiated and carried through their militant policies, many of them were afterwards drawn towards Marxism and the Communist Party.[58]

5
Defiance and New Strategies (1949 - 60)

The Defiance Campaign

The radicalization of the ANC cannot correctly be attributed to a specific event or incident. Overall it was a process that developed over a period of time and in which significant landmarks are readily recognizable. One of these landmarks was the "Defend Free Speech" convention organized by the Transvaal ANC, the Transvaal Indian Congress, APO and the Johannesburg District Committee of the CP, in March 1950.

Dr James S. Moroka, the ANC President-General, chaired the meeting. Militant demands were adopted: freedom of speech, movement and organization; land; and the ending of the colour bar. The meeting called for a general strike on 1 May. The workers responded enthusiastically and virtually all industry on the Witwatersrand came to a stop that day.

The government's reply was to ban meetings and gatherings on 1 May and in the evening the trigger-happy police opened fire on young Africans in Alexandra, killing and wounding over 30 people. Later in May the Unlawful Organisations Bill (Suppression of Communism Act) was introduced and the ANC called for an emergency conference in Johannesburg to campaign against it. The organizations represented at this conference were: the ANC, APO, the South African Indian Congress, the CP, the CNETU and the Witwatersrand Local Committee of the South African Trades and Labour Council. Dr Dadoo called for unity and the need to "forget the past differences". Mandela and Walter Sisulu spoke in the same vein. It was at this meeting that Tambo made the prophetic words: "Today it is the Communist Party. Tomorrow it will be our trade unions, our Indian Congress, our APO, our

119

African National Congress." [1]

On 26 June 1950, the ANC called for a one-day strike throughout the country in protest against the Suppression of Communism Act and against the shooting of 18 Africans by the police on May Day. This was called the National Day of Protest and Mourning and was the beginning of the commemoration of 26 June, - a date which later became significant in our freedom struggle and came to be called South African Freedom Day. The ANC's enlightened defence of the right of the communists to organize their own legal party was (and unfortunately remains) unparalleled among the national liberation movements in Africa. We are now talking of 1950. In those days the ANC took a radical position in the context of the politics of the time. It should be remembered that "communism" had always been misrepresented to the African community as a "deadly evil". For the ANC to rise above this narrow view, defy the Suppression of Communism Act and thereby associate itself with the right of the CP to exist in South Africa, was both radical and revolutionary. The ANC had realized that communists are to be judged by their political acts and record and not by the denunciations of the racist regime. After all, communists and the CP were on the side of the suffering oppressed Blacks in their struggle for liberation, they had become proven champions of the black man's struggle for freedom and independence.

It is important to note that the growing strength of the ANC is based on the huge reserves of mass support for the liberation struggle to be found among the South African people and that as the pace of the struggle increases and widens, so more and more sections of the people are inevitably brought into the struggle. As they come to reinforce our ranks our strength will continue to be reinforced.

In 1951, the Coloured people were hard hit by the introduction of the "Separate Representation of Voters' Bill" which sought to disenfranchise Coloured men in the Cape. In the same year, they formed the "Franchise Action Council" and over 15 000 Coloured people marched through the streets of Cape Town and converged on the Grand Parade.

This campaign enjoyed the warm support of the ANC and the South African Indian Congress. Indeed, preparations were then being made for the direct participation of the masses of the oppressed black population in joint direct action against the racist regime. On 29 July 1952, African, Indian and Coloured representatives for their three respective organizations met in Johannesburg and agreed to recommend to their conferences a campaign of peaceful resistance. A Joint Planning Council was established with Moroka, Marks and Sisulu representing the ANC; Dadoo and Cachalia, the South African Indian

Congress."

Although this campaign was primarily an ANC campaign, it was all-embracing and involved all the democratic forces within South Africa. The Defiance Campaign, as it came to be known, was directed against all racially discriminatory laws. But its immediate targets were: the pass laws; stock limitation; the Separate Representation of Voters' Act; Group Areas Act; Bantu authorities; and the Suppression of Communism Act. The object of the campaign was to deliberately violate the laws as an act of protest, that protest being organized, not spontaneous, and undertaken by disciplined volunteers. In this way over 8 000 volunteers - African, Indian, Coloured and white - defied the laws of the racist regime and went to prison.

The Defiance Campaign represented a new phase in the South African liberation struggle. It established two principles. First there can be no liberation of the oppressed without sacrifice and readiness to face imprisonment. The political consciousness of the blacks, through the Defiance Campaign, was raised to understanding that imprisonment was part of the legitimate process towards liberation: In the context of political struggle imprisonment was one of the inevitable paths towards liberation. It had to be recognized that freedom could not be achieved if the leadership as well as the membership was not prepared to fight, go to jail and even die for the principles in which they believed.

The second important principle the campaign established was the fact that the liberation of the oppressed people in South Africa could only come about as a result of extra-parliamentary struggle. Our duty as an oppressed people was to fight by all means possible including extra-parliamentary methods. That means that our struggle went beyond petitions and legal deputations and delegations. The struggle was a challenge against the state and could only effectively be conducted outside the legal mechanism of the state.

The regime's response to the Defiance Campaign was, as usual, violent. Hundreds of blacks were shot and killed by the police and thousands more were wounded. Special legislation was also introduced, the Criminal Law Amendment Act introducing lashing for anyone breaking the law "by way of protest". Nevertheless, the campaign proved to be an effective form of training disciplined volunteers and mobilizing the masses in non-violent action. It transformed the character of the ANC, strengthened the leadership and attracted many new recruits - the membership of the ANC rose from 4 000 to 100 000 "with many times that number of politically conscious supporters".[2] It stimulated the growth of militancy within other black organizations such as the Coloured People's Organisation (successor to the APO) and the

121

South African Indian Congress. It fulfilled and further strengthened the Xuma-Dadoo-Naicker pact of 1947 (see chapter 4), which laid the foundation for African and Indian solidarity and called on the Coloured community to join this alliance. The Defiance Campaign also initiated the emergence of the Congress of Democrats, a white organization committed to ANC policy.

During and after the Defiance Campaign, many ANC leaders were arrested and a leadership crisis emerged. Chief Albert Lutuli has this to say about this "crisis":

> While the Defiance Campaign was entering its last weeks, the African National Congress was confronted with an internal crisis. The President-General, Dr Moroka, had earlier been one of a batch of twenty volunteers. All were arrested and brought to trial (Regina vs. Walter Sisulu and Nineteen others). Moroka elected to be defended apart from the others by his own lawyer. This in itself cost him much prestige. But the real damage was done when at the end of the trial, his lawyer entered a separate plea in mitigation ... the lawyer argued that Dr Moroka enjoyed good relations with neighbouring white farmers, and that he had helped financially with the education of the white boys ... The leader of Congress dissociated himself from his fellow-accused; he appeared unready to go the whole way in defiance, and he asked Whites to shield him from the consequences of white laws, and from the consequence of his own stand.[3]

This "process of dissociation" of Moroka from the ANC was accompanied by another "process of dissociation" of the masses from Moroka. He was ousted as a leader and Lutuli was then chosen as President-General of the ANC, in December 1952. Before this election Lutuli was ANC President in Natal and Chief in the Groutville mission area. The Secretary of Native Affairs then summoned Chief Lutuli and told him to choose between remaining chief or a leader of the ANC. He refused to resign from either position and was immediately deposed as chief by the regime. But "his refusal to surrender had enormously enhanced his reputation throughout black South Africa". Moreover he continued to use the title "chief" as an act of protest against the regime.[4]

Lutuli's presidency of the ANC was characterized by a spread of activity and the radicalization of the organization. He was a farsighted man and campaigned vigorously for the adoption of a more militant approach. This meant a creative implementation of the 1949 Programme of Action. It was during Lutuli's presidency that the ANC involved the masses of people in direct struggle. This orientation towards mass participation transformed the ANC into a mass-based movement - the oppressed people became involved directly in the struggle for freedom. This embodied the process of radicalization and the principle that the oppressed people had the right to fight for their

122

freedom.

ANC National Executive Committee 1952 - 1960

1952-55	*1955-58*	*1958-60*
	President-General	
Chief A. J. Lutuli	Chief A. J Lutuli	Chief A. J. Lutuli
	Secretary-General	
W. M. Sisulu	O. R. Tambo	D. Nokwe
	Treasurer-General	
Dr S. M. Molema	Dr A. E. Letele	Dr A. E. Letele
	National Executive Committee	
W. Z. Conco	W. Z. Conco	W. Z. Conco
D. Tloome	A. Hutchinson	L. Massina
A. Hutchinson	J. Mafora	Z. K. Matthews
J. Mafora	L. Massina	C. Mayekiso
L. Massina	P. Mathole	P. Molaoa
C. Mayekiso	Z. K. Matthews	O. Mpeta
L. Ngoyi	C. Mayekiso	T. Mqota
J. Nkadimeng	L. Ngoyi	L. Ngoyi
D. Nokwe	J. Nkadimeng	G. S. D. Nyembe
M. Rokaoana	D. Nokwe	A. Nzo
R. Resha	M. Rakaoana	R. Resha
O. R. Tambo	G. Sibande	G. Sibande
M. B. Yengwa	T. Tshume	O. R. Tambo
	M. B. Yengwa	

The Freedom Charter

Even in the field of ideas there was noticeably a shift, a further radicalization. At the annual conference of the Cape ANC in Queenstown in August 1953, Professor S. K. Matthews articulated the idea of a Congress to draw up a people's charter of rights, the *Freedom Charter*.[5] This was done by convening a mass representative gathering of men and women of all national groups in the country to decide about the future South Africa they wanted. At a meeting of the ANC, South

African Indian Congress, Coloured People's Organization and Congress of Democrats, presided over by Chief Lutuli himself (held in March 1954, in the Lower Tugela, to which area Chief Lutuli was confined by the regime), it was decided that meetings be held all over the country, in urban and rural areas, to hear the people's demands and their grievances, which would then be forwarded to the organizers for incorporation in the Charter.

The preparation for this gathering took over a year and "literally millions of people participated in the campaign and sent their demands of the kind of South Africa they wished to live in".[6] On 25-26 June 1955, the Congress of the People took place in Kliptown, near Johannesburg. About 3 000 people attended, despite roadblocks and police cordons. These were workers and trade unionists, peasants and traders, intellectuals and clerks, men and women, youth and students, of all colours and ethnic groups, Christians, Moslems, Hindus, communists and non-communists. It was the most representative gathering in the history of South Africa. Chief Lutuli, Dr Dadoo and Father Trevor Huddleston were honoured with the traditional award "Isitwalandwe Scaperankoe" which has since become the highest honour in the ANC.

Father Trevor Huddleston, now Archbishop of the Indian Ocean and President of the British Anti-Apartheid Movement, arrived in South Africa in 1943 and was one of the few whites who identified themselves with the cause of the Africans. His popularity grew as his name became a household name in African townships. He, together with Bishop Ambrose Reeves and Michael Scott set a precedent for Christians like Archbishop Desmond Tutu, (whose son is named Trevor in honour of Trevor Huddleston) and Allan Boesak. I mention this to show the historical continuity.

The Congress of the People was the beginning of the Congress Alliance of the ANC, the South African Indian Congress, the Coloured People's Congress, the Congress of Democrats and the South African Congress of Trade Unions. It adopted the Freedom Charter, and the various organizations in the alliance also subsequently adopted it at their annual conferences. Thus the Freedom Charter became the common programme enshrining the hopes and aspirations of all the progressive people of South Africa.

What is the Freedom Charter? What is the essence of the demands in it? How are these demands to be realized? The Freedom Charter is a statement of aims. The method of achieving these aims, the forces of change, the strategy and tactics to be followed is spelt out clearly not in the Freedom Charter itself but in the 1969 Strategy and Tactics document of the ANC which I shall review later.

124

The preamble to the Freedom Charter states:

We the people of South Africa, declare for all our country and the world to know: that South Africa belongs to all who live in it, black and white, and that no government can justly claim authority unless it is based on the will of all people; that our people have been robbed of their birthright to land, liberty and peace by a form of government founded on injustice and inequality; that our country will never be prosperous or free until all our people live in brotherhood enjoying equal rights and opportunities; that only a democratic state, based on the will of all the people, can secure to all their birthright without distinction of colour, race, sex or belief; and therefore, we the people of South Africa, black and white together - equals, countrymen and brothers - adopt the Freedom Charter." [7]

The significance of this preamble - "South Africa belongs to all who live in it, black and white" - becomes very clear and even topical today when Africans are losing their South African citizenship and being forced into Bantustan citizenship. At the Morogoro Conference in 1969, the ANC made an analysis and evaluation of the Freedom Charter and stated that the conflicts in South Africa have largely centred on the relationship between the Africans and the whites and that the Coloured and Indian people are, like Africans, oppressed by the dominant white minority. The statement further emphasized the ANC principle:

In the face of the gravest injustices the ANC never once abandoned the principle that all those who had their home in the country of Africans were welcome, provided only that they accepted full and consistent equality and freedom for all. In this the ANC was not merely bowing to history and reality but believed that it was correct in principle to make their position clear. Over and over again in the face of manifest inhumanity, the ANC absolutely refused to be provoked into abandoning its democratic principles. [8]

Taking these historic realities into consideration, the democratic principles of the ANC became the cornerstone of our movement - for the national liberation of the African, Coloured and Indian. These became the most fundamental and essential tenets for the building of a revolutionary united front of all democratic anti-racist and anti-fascist forces in South Africa. The ANC made it clear that nobody is excluded by reason of race or colour. It therefore rejected totally all racist ideas; expressed the consistency of the ANC in its non-racial and anti-racist approach and offered an alternative to the reactionary philosophy of apartheid. There was no compromise with racism.

By stating that "no government can justly claim authority unless it is based on the will of the people" and that "our people have been robbed by a form of government founded on injustice and inequality", the Freedom Charter makes a distinction between oppressor and oppressed and "directs attention of the people to the source of their oppression, and by focussing accurately on the question of state power presents a profoundly revolutionary challenge to the existing order." [9]

Writing about the Freedom Charter, *Sechaba* has said that it

> Lays as a basis and is a precondition for further development and radicalisation of our revolution; its implementation will presuppose and demand the *destruction* of the white racist regime and the *abolition* of national, cultural, religious and language privileges of Whites over Blacks. This will encompass the *equality of all ethnic groups* - large or small, black or white - the satisfaction of their national rights and feelings, traditions and customs, aspirations and emotions, characteristics and features and the *development of their languages and culture,* and inter-ethnic contacts. [10]

It goes on to say:

> This entails the injection of hatred for the enemy and all that he stands for; imbuing the masses with a revolutionary consciousness and this should be accompanied by stimulation of national pride and identity, assertiveness and patriotism which are associated with the revolutionary traditions of anti-colonialism and anti-imperialism of all our people and ethnic groups and their positive contribution to the struggle for social progress. [11]

The demand for the transfer to the ownership of the people of the "national wealth, the heritage of all South Africans" and "mineral wealth beneath the soil, the banks and monopoly industry" demonstrates the anti-monopoly character of the Freedom Charter. The significance of this emphasis on the people as opposed to the individualistic, capitalist system cannot be over-emphasized. What this means is that the seizure of political power is meaningless without economic and social emancipation; it is impossible to think of the envisaged democratization of internal and foreign policy in a new South Africa without the destruction of state monopoly capitalism.

Though the paramount question in our country is the advocacy of equality of different ethnic groups and the impermissibility of all privileges in this respect, the Freedom Charter was not unmindful of our internationalist commitment. It states:

- South Africa shall be a fully independent state which respects the rights and sovereignty of all nations;
- South Africa shall strive to maintain world peace and the settlement of all international disputes by negotiation - not by war;
- Peace and friendship amongst all our people shall be secured by upholding the equal rights, opportunities and status of all;
- The people of the protectorates - Basutoland, Bechuanaland and Swaziland - shall be free to decide for themselves their own future;
- The rights of all peoples of Africa to independence and self government shall be recognised and shall be the basis of close cooperation.

This declaration of principle is even more topical today than it was when the Charter was adopted. The barbarous aggression against and invasion of Angola by the racist hordes of the current Botha-Malan regime makes the need for the implementation of the Freedom Charter even more urgent. The double crime of the illegal occupation and misuse of Namibia for these purposes has once more "vindicated the assertion that the international responsibility of our movement is closely interconnected with our national mission whose essence is the liquidation of the racist fascist regime."

The formulation that "South Africa shall be a fully independent state" is an expression of the realization by our movement that racist South Africa is not a "fully independent state" - something which needs to be heeded by some African states which are seeking a *rapprochment* with racist South Africa. *Mayibuye,* an ANC Bulletin, commented:[12]

> This demand was not included purely for the sake of form, for the emphasis is clearly on the words "fully independent". It must be remembered that the Freedom Charter was adopted by the Congress as far back as 1955, and it is noteworthy that even at that time when most of Africa was still under the colonial heel, the Congress of the People was aware of the dangers of neocolonialism - hence the emphasis on the words "fully independent". Recent events in Africa have tragically demonstrated the need for such programmatic clarity. There is no need to emphasise that a democratic South Africa which desires to be fully independent shall by the same token respect the rights and sovereignty of all nations.[13]

There were no illusions amongst those who drafted the Freedom Charter. They were aware that these demands would not come about on their own, they would have to be fought for: "We pledge ourselves to strive together sparing neither strength nor courage, until the democratic changes here set out have been won." And the Charter repeats for emphasis: "let all who love their people and their country now say, as we say here: *These freedoms we will fight for, side by side, throughout our lives, until we have won our liberty."* In other words, the Freedom Charter "demands that South Africa must come out of the imperialist camp and join the community of freedom and peace-loving peoples of the world."[14]

These were the demands of the people. The ANC ratified the Freedom Charter in March 1956. Chief Lutuli said:

> It was, I may say, necessary that this should happen, since there were principles embodied in the Charter policy. I sent a note to the Conference which ratified the Charter urging delegates to discuss very fully such things as, for instance, the principle of nationalisation.[15]

By adopting the Freedom Charter the ANC committed itself in precise terms to what it stood for. This envisaged new society was conceived not in vague terms but specifically on the principle of common access to and benefit from the wealth of the country. Writing about this aspect of the Freedom Charter, Mandela has stated:

> It is true that in demanding the nationalisation of the banks, the gold mines and the land, the Charter strikes a fatal blow at the financial and gold-mining monopolies and farming interests that have for centuries plundered the country ... but such a step is absolutely imperative and necessary because the realisation of the Charter is inconceivable, in fact impossible, unless and until these monopolies are first smashed up and the national wealth of the country turned over to the people.[16]

In case some people think that the Freedom Charter is a socialist document, Mandela warned against such erroneous notions:

> Under socialism the workers hold state power. They and the peasants own the means of production, the land, the factories, and the mills. All production is for use and not for profit. The Charter does not contemplate such profound economic and political changes. Its declaration "The People shall Govern" visualises the transfer of power not to any single social class but to all the people of this country, be they workers, peasants, professional men, or petty bourgeoisie.[17]

The Treason Trial

The racist government responded to the demands of the Freedom Charter by arresting the entire leadership of the Congress movement - 156 of them - and charging them with High Treason in December 1956. The basic contention of the state was that the Charter was a blueprint for a violent revolution and the unconstitutional and therefore illegal overthrow by force of the state and its replacement with a communist society.

The trial of the Congress leaders, which came to be known as the "Treason Trial", lasted four and a half long, tiring years, tying down the leadership to interminable hearings and causing grave problems for the maintenance of the direction and pace of the struggle.

Then, in 1961, all the accused were acquitted and discharged. The presiding Judge, Mr Justice Rumpff, admitted in his judgement that the state had failed to establish that the Freedom Charter was, in any possible interpretation, a communist document and that no convincing evidence had been led to show that the accused had conspired by illegal, unconstitutional and violent means to overthrow the state.

This was a defeat for the government which had clearly hoped to decapitate the movement and thus deprive the people of leadership and direction. It was yet another indication of the lengths to which the racist regime was prepared to go to smash the national liberation movement. This victory was acclaimed throughout South Africa as a victory for democracy although it was obtained at great personal cost for the defendants. Many had lost their jobs during the long trial, others had their businesses ruined and others could no longer resume their legal practices.

The failure of the court to find communism in the Freedom Charter was a great vindication for the fact that the Freedom Charter is a document for national democratic revolution in South Africa. However, another important fact to emerge from the trial was the undoubted popularity of the people's leaders. Ironically, also, the trial brought together Congress leaders from all different areas of South Africa. They sat, talked, ate and lived together for some years while the trial proceeded. This created a really united leadership out of what had been a geographically divided, and often politically separated, series of local leaderships. It also forced the movement, in its own defence, to clearly spell out its ideology.

Mass direct action

Throughout the 1950s, the ANC began in earnest to sharpen the weapon of mass direct action, which took the forms of boycotts, mass demonstrations of women and political strikes through the unique form of the stay-at-homes. There were also peasant revolts all over the country.

The boycott campaign

The 1953 Natal Congress raised the issue of protest action embracing an economic dimension. Congress was mandated to embark immediately on the boycott of selected business undertakings with a view of forcing them to accord civil treatment to their black customers; to improve the conditions of work of their black employees and to provide opportunities for their training and technical advancement; and most important, for the payment of higher wages to their black staff. Subsequent boycott campaigns which were launched included those against the PUTCO bus service, when fares were increased (the 1957 Alexandra bus boycott); the potato boycott - a protest against the inhuman work and living conditions of agricultural workers on the farms; the campaign for a national minimum wage for black workers; and the boycott of all cigarettes produced by the Rupert Group whose brands included such popular cigarettes as Rothmans and Pieter Stuyvesent.

With reference to the potato boycott, the Department of Native Affairs and Ministry of Justice together with the South African Police had devised a scheme whereby unemployed Africans or petty offenders were induced to work on farms. These people were sent to notorious farmers who could not get any labourers because of their cruelty. The farm labourers were forced to dig potatoes with their bare hands. The "boss boys" would beat them until they died. They were locked up at night to "protect" them from escaping; kept in overcrowded, badly ventilated huts; forced to sleep on filthy sacks, riddled with lice and so on. That is why the ANC conference of 1957 decided on a potato boycott and demanded an investigation into the conditions of farm labourers. Gert Nsibande and the Revd Michael Scott revealed details of the ill-treatment of African farm labourers on potato and maize farms in the Transvaal. And Ruth First and Joe Gqabi published the results of an undercover investigation into conditions on the farms in *New Age*. They were both later assassinated by the racist South African regime while working in exile for the ANC (in 1982 and 1983 respectively).

Many of the boycotts were so successful that companies were forced to negotiate with the ANC and the South African Congress of Trade Unions (SACTU), formed on 6 March 1955. Most important from the point of view of the freedom movement was the organizing aspect of these campaigns; the degree to which they answered the most immediate demands of the people; the drawing of people into the mainstream of political action on issues to which they could relate directly; and the demonstration to the people, the regime and the capitalist class, of the immense power which the organized force of the oppressed and exploited could wield.

In the late 1950s, the boycott campaign developed into mass "stay-at-homes" (so-called because strikes by black workers were illegal), when thousands of workers refused to go to work. In March 1958 a week-long stay-at-home was organized. Police reaction was brutal - they entered homes, confiscated and destroyed provisions and intimidated strikers to return to work. In addition, the white-owned press, even so-called liberal dailies like the *Rand Daily Mail*, pumped out a veritable barrage of half-truths and lies to demoralize the strikers. Nevertheless, the stay-at-home lasted for two days, threatening the entire exploitative system and demonstrating the strength of the workers. SACTU, although only formed in 1955, soon had a membership of over 100 000. It based its policy on the principles of non-racial and political trade unionism and soon began to effectively organize black workers into disciplined, democratic and militant trade unions capable of confronting the apartheid state as well as an economic system which lives off cheap black labour. SACTU understood that to campaign for workers' rights it had to fight both state and employers.

SACTU was involved from the start in the boycotts and stay-at-homes. Another early campaign was against the Industrial Amendment Act of 1956, which prohibited "mixed" (non-racial) unions from registered status, as well as against the statutory Job Reservation imposed by the Act. In 1957, SACTU led a national "Pound a Day" campaign for a minimum wage. Petitions, memoranda, conferences, strikes and stay-at-homes in this campaign involved thousands of workers, unionized and ununionized, employed and unemployed.

The Women's demonstrations

The struggle of the women continued throughout and found its climax in the 1950s. The ANC Women's League (formed in 1943 and inaugurated at the 1948 ANC Annual General Conference - see chapter 4) set itself the following tasks:

Apart from their duties as members of the ANC, women members of the Congress have special additional duties and responsibilities:

(a) to arouse the interest of African women in the struggle for freedom and equality; and assist the widespread organisation of women;
(b) to take up social problems and issues affecting women; and
(c) to carry on propaganda against apartheid and discriminatory laws among African women. [18]

Another significant organizational development, which played a fundamental role in increasing the mass participation of women, was the formation of the Federation of South African Women in April 1954. This was in response to a growing need for an organization which would:

● embrace all women irrespective of race, colour or nationality;
● help to strengthen, build and bring together in joint activity the various women's sections in the liberatory movements and other women's organizations;
● ● express the needs and aspirations of the house-wives, wage earners, peasants and professional women of South Africa; and
● ● bring about the emancipation of women from the special disabilities suffered by them under laws, customs and conventions and strive for a genuine South African democracy based on complete equality and friendship between men and women, and between each section. [19]

The Federation united women of different nationalities and cultures

131

on the basis of an unequivocal commitment to the liberation struggle. The women saw the struggle for their emancipation as an inseparable aspect of the struggle for national liberation; that is, the oppression of women was seen as a product of a system which had to be destroyed in order to end the three-fold burden of their suffering - as blacks, workers and as women.

The ANC Women's League worked closely with, and its members played a leading role in the Federation. This expressed an organizational unity which, in many respects, anticipated the broader unity of the Congress movement at the historic Congress of the People in 1955. The major campaign issue for women in the 1950s was the racist regime's proposal to force women as well as men to carry passes. The ANC issued directives to all its branches to take up and fiercely resist this. The ANC Women's League in particular, in collaboration with the Federation of South African Women, began organizing a massive protest campaign. The Annual Conference of the ANC held in December 1955 paid a great deal of attention to the women's anti-pass struggle. The report of the National Executive Committee stressed that the pass laws were the most burning grievance of the people. The statement went on:

> We who know the suffering the pass laws have brought to us over the decades will not tolerate the extension of this hated system to our women-folk. We warn the government: making women carry passes will be like trampling on the tail of a puff adder.[20]

The next few years' fierce anti-pass resistance proved this comment quite right!

On 11 March 1956, the Transvaal Region of the ANC Women's League organized a meeting to commemorate International Women's Day (8 March). Prominent on the agenda of that meeting was the issue of passes. It was from the same meeting that a resolution to march to Pretoria was unanimously adopted by the over 2 000 delegates present.

Despite difficulties created by the regime to prevent the women from staging their demonstration which had been declared illegal, 20 000 women filled the amphitheatre of the Union Buildings, Pretoria, on 9 August 1956. They quietly stood there, while the leaders of the demonstration went up to the offices of the three ministers responsible, but none of them were to be found. The Union Buildings had always been a hive of activity and it is remarkable that on that day the state machinery had been brought to a halt. In spite of the "non-admission" sign that had been put up on the door leading to Prime Minister Strijdom's office, the gallant leaders - Lilian Ngoyi, Helen Joseph,

Lily Diedericks, Rahima Moosa and Sophie Williams - marched in and left the bulk of the petition forms with his secretary. In all there were more than 100 000 signatures. Outside, the women's gathering sang in one voice:

Strydom, wathint'abafazi	Strydom, You have touched the women
Wathint'imbokodo	You have struck a rock
Uzakufa	You have dislodged a boulder,
	You will die.

The regime could not enforce passes for women until 1963. The fact that it took the racists 50 years to extend their hated pass laws to African women testifies to the calibre of our women, their organizational talents and courage.

Peasant Revolts

There have always been dynamic contacts between the rural black population in South Africa and black workers in the towns:

> Campaigns in the large towns not only had echoes in the rural areas, but were at times superseded by the struggles in one or other Reserve. This was a natural consequence of the interconnection of land and labour issues and the continuous movement, at least of menfolk, from the country to town and back. More than this, the reaction was so often against legislation which aimed to tighten the control on labour, and on its movement, that the same problem appeared at both ends of the labour market - in the Reserves and in the towns.[21]

In 1957 there was a peasant uprising in Zeerust in the Transvaal, precipitated by the issue of passes to African women in many villages in the Groot Marico - Zeerust District, i.e. Leeufontein, Braklaagte, Gopane, Motswedi and Witkleigat. The regime's aim was to avoid big cities and to start with the "ignorant Africans",[22] "slipping in passes through the back door." But they misjudged the situation: the rural people had contacts with the urban population and knew about the anti-pass campaign.

The regime started at Linokana and neighbouring areas. The Native Commissioner, a certain Richter, called on Chief Abraham Moiloa to order and if necessary compel, the women to take out the "reference books". The chief was not prepared to do this, however, even though he was threatened by Richter. When he was asked to address the people on the issue he did so but he made his position clear. On 1 April 1957, a handful of African women in the area came to take out passes but the majority refused.

Gallichan, a white shopkeeper who had lent his premises for the purposes of issuing passes, was boycotted and "according to his own evidence his takings for April dropped to practically nothing."[23] Chief Moiloa was instructed to convene a meeting on 4 April 1957 at which the Chief Native Commissioner for the area would address the people of Linokana. This he did. At this meeting, Chief Moiloa "was told to get off the chair as he was no longer Chief. He was also told that he was to leave the area within 14 days to go to Venterspost and that he was not to return without the permission of the Commissioner."[24]

It should be stated that "complaints" from the authorities about Chief Moiloa went as far back as 1952 (and were inquired into officially in November 1956). One of the charges was that he asked on one occasion, "Wie die hel is Verwoerd?" ("Who on earth is Verwoerd?" - he was then the Minister of Native Affairs). Moreover, it appears that in January 1957 the order for Moiloa's deposition and deportation had already been signed.

The Zeerust people working in Johannesburg chartered two buses and "went home" on 12 April. They called a meeting in the Kgotla (the public meeting) on 14 April. This became a court at which those who were believed to have betrayed the chief were "tried" and sentenced to death. The police intervened. That evening, whilst on their way back to Johannesburg, about 100 people were arrested; 25 were detained and charged with "incitement to murder and attempted murder" and "a most rare charge - *crimen laesio majestatis* - usurping the functions of the state."[25]

Five of the accused were convicted of attempted murder and sentenced to imprisonment ranging from three to five years; some were given a nominal fine for holding unlawful gatherings and the rest were discharged. The post office at Linokana was closed; the school was boycotted and subsequently forced to close down because the teachers' wives had taken out passes; the railway bus was discontinued and more arrests for "holding unlawful meetings" or burning passes were made. The pass-issuing unit was reinforced by a special squad of police from Pretoria, under the command of Sergeant Van Rooyen, notorious for his brutality. The squad did not fall under the local command, but remained a law unto itself; this was a period of terror for the people.

Shortly after the conclusion of the trial of those arrested on 14 April and with indecent haste, it was announced that the regime intended holding a commission of enquiry into the causes of unrest in the Groot Marico Zeerust District. The people were not notified about the commission but the chiefs who supported the government did know about it, and were ready to proceed with their evidence on the day it opened.

The people then responded by organizing a petition calling on the commission to recommend, amongst other things, the return of the deposed chief Moiloa; the re-opening of the school and post office at Linokana and the suspension of the issue of passes to women. Thousands of signatures to the petition were obtained in the space of a few days.

Despite the short notice given, the lack of publicity and the lack of transport, large crowds of people managed to attend the opening session of the commission. There was no room in the Native Commissioner's court for them all to be accommodated and special arrangements had to be made for an outside arena.

After a week, the police were out in full force to prevent people coming to the so-called public enquiry. Harvard aeroplanes swooped down on the area to intimidate the people, and police road blocks prevented the people from entering Zeerust. Women coming from Gopane were baton-charged and beaten up by the police. Some of those injured were unable to get to Zeerust for medical treatment and a large number of them went to Bechuanaland where they were treated at Lobatsi Hospital.

This commission was just one man, a certain H. Balk - a Native Appeal Court Judge, and as such an employee of the Native Affairs Department, the department most involved in the troubles! There was no agenda, no one to lead evidence and no cross-examination of witnesses was allowed. The evidence was therefore practically useless: anyone could say anything.

The government, the supporting chiefs and their protagonists unanimously blamed the ANC for all their troubles, the reason being that the people gave the "Afrika" salute. The false impression was created that outside "agitators" incited the people and the regime went even further, to claim that its legal advisers were attacked. This was sinister enough but the regime found it more "distressing" and "disheartening" that most of the people accused at the trail were defended in such a manner that they were acquitted![26]

Things came to a climax in September: the women of Gopane who had had their "reference books" for nearly a year and were now thoroughly disillusioned, decided to burn them. There were no benefits derived from them: they were either useless or would be used as instruments of oppression. The police then came to arrest a handful of women who had done so, who had been pointed out by the local chief. Other women in the area joined them. "If they are guilty, we are also. You must arrest us all." Well over 200 of them were taken to Zeerust. Chaos prevailed at the charge office. Women and children overflowed into the yard at the police station and the police practically had to beg the women to leave.[27]

What is noteworthy about these incidents in Zeerust is that where there was no chief (in Linokana) or where the chief had taken a "neutral attitude" to the government, (in Braklaagte) and not tried to impose himself on the will of the people, there was no trouble. The trouble arose in those areas where the police incited the chiefs to intimidate the people. This was evidenced during the Christmas disturbances in the Groot Marico - Zeerust District. Those chiefs who opposed the government and represented the will of their people were either summarily deposed or the government "usurped the powers of the Chief". In Zeerust what began as demonstrations against passes for women and the deposing of a chief turned into more widespread resistance to the whole scheme.

There were similar incidents in other areas as well - in Sekhukhuneland (now Lebowa), Natal, Witzieshoek and Pondoland. The immediate causes of the violence that erupted in these areas were local grievances about the government's attempts to impose tribal authorities which were either willing, or could be persuaded to carry out government policies limiting and controlling the number and size of land allocation to peasant families.

The powers and the role of chiefs were changing under the conditions of the 1950s. In the olden days, the chiefs were ultimately responsible to their people and retained their powers only so long as they were considered satisfactory for the people. The racist regime, on the other hand, has never been accountable to the African people, whom it represses, and its power over them rests on the strength of the police and military, while the chiefs have become responsible not to "their subjects" but to the racist regime which appoints them.

In compliance with the Bantu Authorities Act, the Promotion of Self-Government Act (1959) aimed at turning all chiefs in the reserves into despotic ruthless agents and dividing the Africans into small "manageable" ethnic groups. This division was not only among African people as a whole but within African ethnic groups themselves. The head of a "Bantu authority" was the chief or headman; two or more "tribes" could combine to form a "Bantu authority". The government decided the minimum or maximum of councillors to serve in these "authorities". Government officials or Bantu commissioners had a right to attend all the meetings or even to cancel any appointments of headman or chief; they could cancel any appointment of a councillor with whom they were dissatisfied for various reasons. Many chiefs were banished to remote areas in the 1950s for refusal to be party to these schemes.[28]

This was all part of apartheid's grand plan of confining Africans in reserves or bantustans which were overcrowded and infertile, and from which African men and some women were forced to go to the so-called white industrial areas to look for work. Part of the implementation of this bantustan scheme entailed the reallocation of land, the removal of families from existing holdings and cattle culling. In short, the peasants were being dispossessed of their arable allotments.

The emergence of the Pan African Congress (PAC) (1959-60)

The PAC has made a lot of noise internationally but very little inside South Africa. I would like to put the record straight, to tell the story of what the PAC is, what they wanted to achieve and the methods they have used.

From the mid-1950s, discontent grew among a small minority within the ANC, especially after the adoption of the Freedom Charter and the establishment of the Congress Alliance. In the end, these people withdrew to form a new organization and thus, in April 1959, the PAC was born. What were their "grievances" and demands?

The PAC claimed "to be the direct heir and legitimate successor to the original Congress which was founded in 1912." This they justified by claiming that the ANC had been undermined by the birth of the multi-racial Congress Alliance in the 1950s, and was finally destroyed when it adopted the Freedom Charter into its new constitution in 1958.[29] They accused the Congress Alliance of being "a union of exploiters and the exploited" and the ANC was supposed to have "betrayed the material interests of the African people. They have sacrificed these interests upon the political altar of an ungodly alliance, an alliance of slave-owner, slave driver and slave". The African members of the Congress Alliance were "self-confessed lackeys and flunkeys of the white ruling class and the Indian merchant class". The ANC was led, they said, by a "white pseudo-leftist directorate", and, by adopting the Freedom Charter, it had repudiated the 1949 Programme of Action. The PAC rejected cooperation with other sections of the country's population because they preferred to be a "mouthpiece of the African people" and not of the "people of South Africa".

To answer this approach let me first state the obvious fact that African nationalism has always been a contradictory phenomenon with different, and at times antagonistic and divergent trends and tendencies. These differences of opinion were not a new phenomenon in our movement.

137

The PAC was not the first nor the only such trend to emerge in the 1950s. There was Bhengu's Bantu National Congress - the "National Minded" bloc, which called for a "purified Bantu" organization and no co-operation with Indian and other population groups. Even Dr Xuma, who was instrumental in the late 1940s in laying a foundation for unity between Africans and Indians, alleged that the ANC had "lost its identity as a national liberation movement with a policy of its own and a distinctly African leadership".[30]

Analysing the policy of the PAC as propounded by P. Nkutsoeu Raboroko, the Secretary-General of the ANC, Duma Nokwe, stated in 1960:

A striking feature of their policy is its silence on the fundamental political and economic rights of the people. Do they accept the principle of adult universal suffrage? Would they distribute the land and wealth of South Africa to all? Or do they believe that only the Africans, as indigenous, are entitled to fundamental political rights? Do they avoid any concrete policy on these questions precisely because they refuse to be committed one way or the other?[31]

Besides this "silence on the fundamental political and economic rights of the people" there was another aspect to the policy of the PAC that one can call a "semantic revolution". Robert Sobukwe, the first President of the PAC, found it difficult to resist the temptation to "manipulate" language. At the inaugural convention of the PAC, he told his followers that "multi-racialism" is "racialism multiplied which probably is what the term connotes", and, by implication, that was what the ANC and its allies stood for.[32] He then went further:

Politically we stand for a government of the Africans for the Africans by the Africans, with everybody who owes his loyalty only to Africa and accepts the democratic rule of an African majority, being regarded as an African.[33]

There are problems with this statement. Here, the word "African" means all things to all people. It is subjective: you need to owe loyalty to only Africa and "accept democratic rule of an African majority", then you are an African! But why did they close their doors to "Africans of Dutch, English or even Indian" or other extraction? Perhaps the answer lies in a statement by Josias Madzunya, one of the leaders, a populist who allied himself with Selope Thema's National-Minded bloc in opposition to the general trend within the ANC. He once said: "No white man is sincere."[34]

The dangers with the PAC policy were that this "majority nationalism" which did not take into consideration the interests and aspirations of "minorities" could lead to "minority nationalism" - exclusivism - breaking the broad democratic front of patriotic forces which the ANC was painstakingly building. They were making it easy for the enemy to rule and ruin the people. There was no class analysis; the interests of the masses were completely ignored; all that they said was that they would "guarantee individual liberties" which were regarded as "the highest guarantee necessary and possible". As for the struggles of all oppressed people in Latin America, Asia, the Middle East, and even Europe, they were regarded as irrelevant because Sobukwe emphasized "loyalty only to Africa".

In a penetrating article in 1959, Sisulu pointed out that the PAC sought to impose the experience of other African countries on a totally different situation in South Africa. Due to differences of historical development and actual conditions, African liberation movements in many other parts of the African continent did not find allies in their struggle among other population groups. The PAC unfortunately mistook this or "misunderstood" or distorted this to mean that Africans should oppose such an alliance on principle. They were negating our experiences and our contribution to the African revolution and therefore moving against the tide of history and the African revolution. The PAC, Sisulu said, used Africanism as a sort of escape from discipline, the hard slogging day-to-day work, and the personal dangers which faced the ordinary Congress member. On a warning note, Sisulu concluded:

Yet, these truths should not blind us to the fact that there are men and women amongst them who genuinely believe that the salvation of our people lies in a fanatical African racialism and denunciation of everything that is not African. And such a policy is not without its potential mass appeal. It would be unrealistic to pretend that a policy of extreme nationalism must, in the nature of things, always be unpopular. The people are quick to detect the insincerity of the mere demagogue, and they have confidence in the courage and wisdom of their tried and trusted leaders. But in a country like South Africa, where the Whites dominate everything, and where ruthless laws are ruthlessly administered and enforced, the natural tendency is one of growing hostility towards Europeans. In fact most Africans come into political activity because of their indignation against the Whites, and it is only through their education in Congress and their experience of the genuine comradeship in the struggle of such organisations as the Congress of Democrats, that they rise to the broad, non-racial humanism of our Congress movement.

With a State policy of increasingly barbaric repression of the African people; with the deliberate destruction of every form of normal human contact between people from different population groups; and with the systematic banning and isolation of the convinced and fervent anti-racialists among the Africans from political activity, there is no knowing what the future will hold. [35]

Sisulu went on to say that the PAC had thus far failed:

But their mere appearance is an urgent warning to all democratic South Africans.

The Africans have set a wonderful example of political wisdom and maturity to the rest of the country, but they are not perfect, any more than any other community of men and women sorely beset. In certain circumstances, an emotional mass-appeal to destructive and exclusive nationalism can be a dynamic and irresistible force in history . . . It would be foolish to imagine that a wave of black chauvinism, provoked by the savagery of the Nationalist Party (and perhaps secretly encouraged and financed by it too) may not some day sweep through our country. And if it does, the agony will know no colour-bar at all.[36]

I have quoted at length from this article because it goes to the core of the matter; it indicates that this phenomenon is not accidental but endemic in current South African society. It will disappear with the disappearance of colonialism and apartheid in South Africa.

The turning point (1960-61)

In 1959-60, the ANC prepared plans for a nationwide campaign of resistance against the racist regime. This was to take the form of a national stoppage of work, burning of passes, and so on. "By March 1960, the ANC's massive campaign was already underway throughout the length and breadth of South Africa. Thus the masses of the oppressed people were successfully mobilized for the March 31st Anti Pass National stoppage of work."[37] However, on 21 March, 10 days before the start of the campaign, the PAC issued a call to the people to go and stand in protest outside police stations. Jack Simons has stated that "only at Sharpeville and Langa was there a big response to Sobukwe's appeal". What happened there is well known: 69 people were shot dead by the police and many more were injured. Most were shot in the back and the victims included women and children. Simons goes on to comment on the aftermath:

It was the shooting that made March 21st a red letter day. The shots echoed round the globe, caused a panic in ruling circles, sent the share market rocketing downwards, unleashed a storm of criticism of racial policies, produced the State of Emergency, precipitated the banning of the ANC and PAC, and changed life for many people.[38]

As news of the Sharpeville massacre spread within South Africa, several riots broke out in towns throughout the country. The regime declared a state of emergency and detained over 20 000 people. In mid-1960 the ANC and PAC were banned under the Suppression of Communism Act: a new reign of repression was unleashed.

In October 1960 the racist regime held a white referendum on whether to break away from Britain and become a Republic. A

140

majority voted in favour and the date for the proclamation of the Republic was set for the fifty-first anniversary of the Union - 31 May 1961. The ANC, operating underground, called for a three-day strike or "stay-at-home" to coincide with Republic Day. "The issue that sharply divided white South Africans during the referendum for a Republic did not interest us," said Mandela.[39]

> It formed no part in our campaign. Continued association with the British monarchy on the one hand, or the establishment of a Boer Republic on the other - this was the crucial issue in so far as the white population was concerned and as it was put to them in the referendum. We are neither monarchists nor admirers of the Voortrekker type of republic.[40]

The Africans were inspired by aspirations more worthy than those of people who took part in the referendum; they were inspired by the idea of bringing into being a democratic, people's republic - where all South Africans would enjoy human rights without the slightest discrimination, where they would be able to live together in peace, sharing a common citizenship which would lead to a common nationality and a common loyalty to South Africa, their motherland.

The Africans were opposed to the type of republic proposed by the racist regime, just as they were opposed to the 1910 Act of Union establishing the constitutional basis for South Africa as part of the British Empire. If there were to be any constitutional changes in South Africa, the ANC felt, these should abolish the real basis of the South African constitution, white supremacy and white domination.

In organizing the May 1961 general strike - which included travel throughout the country, living now in African townships, then in country villages and again the cities - Mandela was guided by the All-In African Conference which took place in Pietermaritzburg on 25-26 March 1961. This conference was attended by 1 500 delegates from town and country, representing 145 religious, social, cultural, sporting and political bodies. The conference established an All-In African Action Council, with Mandela as its secretary. It resolved that, to avert the dangerous situation developing in South Africa, a "sovereign national convention" representative of all South Africans should be called to draw up a new non-racial and democratic constitution. This convention was to discuss the national problems of South Africa and work out solutions which would seek to preserve and safeguard the interests of all sections of the population. It was to be called before 31 May and, failing this, country-wide demonstrations would be held on the eve of the Republic, that is from the 29 to 31 May. The Africans were also to be called upon to refuse to co-operate with the proposed "Republic".

Mandela as secretary of the National Action Council wrote letters to the Prime Minister H.F. Verwoerd on 20 April and on 30 April. No reply, no acknowledgement was received. So the strike went ahead. Mandela has assessed its success:

> The response was much less than we expected but we made solid and substantial achievement. Hundreds of thousands of workers stayed away from work and the country's industries and commerce was seriously damaged. Hundreds of thousands of students and school children stayed away from the school for the duration of the strike.[41]

Born in Umtata in the Transkei, Cape Province, on 18 July 1918, Nelson Rolihlahla Mandela grew up like many young African men who lived in the rural areas and later went to the cities. His father died in 1934 and David Dalindyebo, an acting paramount chief, became his guardian. He is related to both Sabata Dalindeyebo, the former paramount chief of Thembuland and to Kaiser Matanzima, the Transkei bantustan stooge. Both, are according to custom, Mandela's nephews.

In 1941, Mandela left the Transkei (after a spell at Fort Hare University College) for Johannesburg, where he applied for a job at Crown Mines as a clerk. Later, he worked for a year as an estate agent for £2 a month plus commission. In 1951, he was articled to a Johannesburg firm of attorneys, Witkin, Sidelsky and Eidelman. He obtained a BA degree by correspondence from the University of South Africa and became a qualified solicitor. The influence of Sisulu on Mandela cannot be minimized: "It was Walter Sisulu, in fact, who acted as guide and mentor to Nelson Mandela when he first came to Johannesburg, who worked with Mandela, Oliver Tambo and others in the African National Congress Youth League."[42]

Mandela practised in Johannesburg for a number of years in partnership with Tambo, now president of the ANC. He had this to say about this period:

> Right at the beginning of my career as an attorney, I encountered difficulties imposed on me because of the colour of my skin and further difficulty surrounding me because of my membership and support of the African National Congress. I discovered, for example, that unlike a white attorney, I could not occupy business premises in the city unless I first obtained ministerial consent in the terms of the Urban Areas Act. I applied for that consent, but it was never granted. Although I subsequently obtained a permit, for a limited period, in terms of the Group Areas Act, that soon expired, and the authorities refused to renew it. They insisted that my partner, Oliver Tambo, and I should leave the city and practise in an African location at the back of beyond, miles away from where clients could reach us during working hours. This was tantamount to asking us to abandon our legal practice, to give up the legal service of our people, for which we had spent many years training . . . For some years we continued to occupy the premises in the city illegally . . . It was an act of

142

defiance of the law. We were aware what it was, but nevertheless, that act had been forced on us against our wishes, and we could do no other than to choose between compliance with the law and compliance with our consciences. [43]

In 1944 Mandela joined the ANC Youth League and became its secretary. By 1952 he was elected President of the Transvaal Branch of the ANC and also became Deputy National President. From 1952 to June 1953 he was confined to the magisterial district of Johannesburg by the authorities and also prohibited from attending gatherings. Both these restrictions were later renewed for two more years. Then to those bans a third was added: "I was ordered by the Minister of Justice to resign altogether from the African National Congress and never again to become a member or to participate in its activities."[44]

In 1953, Mandela was given a suspended sentence of nine months' imprisonment for his part in organizing the 1952 Defiance Campaign in which he was the leading volunteer. In February 1956, the bans were again renewed - this time for five years. In December 1956, he was arrested with 155 members of the Congress movement on charges of "high treason". He was jailed during the state of emergency declared after Sharpeville, when 2 000 Congress members were locked up, and was only discharged in 1961, after the Treason Trial acquittals. Then "early in April 1961, I went underground to organize the May strike and have never been home since".[45]

The usual tactics of violence were used by the racist regime to try to avert the resistance around Republic Day in May 1961. All meetings were banned throughout South Africa and ANC field workers were trailed and hounded by members of the security police. More than 10 000 Africans were arrested under the pass laws. A general mobilization was ordered across the country and every available white man and woman was placed under arms.

In fact, the regime was then already engaged in deploying police and regular troops, backed up by helicopters and armoured cars, in Pondoland, in the Transkei. This was in reaction to the peasant uprising there which began in 1960.

The leaders of the Pondo rebellion had organized a mass demonstration of 50 000 people in Bizana, the capital of Pondoland, at the same time presenting a list of their grievances and demands, which echoed the Freedom Charter and rested on the declaration that the peasants would stop at nothing short of representation in parliament. The intensity of the regime's attempts to repress this resistance, and the determination of the people to continue, led to their adopting the tactics of guerrilla struggle. Entire areas came to be controlled and administered by the peasant resistance movement - Intaba (the Mountain). At the same time, the leadership of that resistance, in an effort to

143

prevent their isolation, established contact with the ANC for aid and solidarity. The Ganyile brothers, Anderson and Mthethunzima, were among the prominent leaders of the resistance. ANC leaders, especially from Port Elizabeth, Govan Mbeki being the most prominent, held many meetings with the resisters in the dark forests of Pondoland. Even the ANC headquarters in Johannesburg sent emissaries. T.T. Nkobi, now Treasurer-General of the ANC, remembers those midnight meetings when you saw nothing but a cigarette or zoll (rolled tobacco) light and people speaking almost simultaneously: *"Xelela undlunkulu, sifuna izixhobo"* (Tell headquarters, we want weapons).[46]

Massive repression by the regime, an inability to sustain the high level of struggle and organization required, and a lack of the means to confront and withstand the enemy assault, led to the defeat of the Pondoland revolt. Nevertheless, here had been the beginnings of an armed resistance movement, and this profoundly influenced the orientation of the ANC leadership and led them to seriously confront the whole question of armed struggle. Mbeki summed up the new ANC thinking in this way: "the success of the struggle against white rule could only be achieved if a strategy was adopted that would mobilize and organize both city and country dwellers.'[47]

6
ANC Strategy and Armed Resistance (1961 - 69)

The formation of Umkhonto we Sizwe

On 16 December 1961, the first organized acts of sabotage against South African government installations took place, marking the emergence of Umkhonto we Sizwe (the Spear of the Nation), which was later to become the armed wing of the ANC. The date chosen for these initial sabotage acts was of historical significance. It is a public holiday in South Africa, commemorating the military victory of the Afrikaner Voortrekkers over the African warriors on the banks of the Ncome River (rechristened by the settlers as Blood River) in Natal in 1838 and is thus symbolic of the ascendancy of white power over the blacks.

To the Africans, this day symbolizes resistance and the indomitable quest for freedom. It was also on this day that Johannes Nkosi, a communist activist, was killed in Durban in 1930 and, since that time, 16 December has been connected with many and various campaigns organized by the ANC and the Congress Alliance. Thus it was logical that it was on 16 December 1961 that a leaflet issued by the High Command of Umkhonto we Sizwe was widely distributed throughout South Africa. The leaflet stated that:

> Umkhonto we Sizwe will carry on the struggle for freedom and democracy by new methods, which are necessary to complement the actions of the established national liberation organisations. Umkhonto we Sizwe fully supports the national liberation movement and our members jointly and individually, place themselves under the overall political guidance of the movement.

It declared that:

> The people's patience is not endless. The time comes in the life of any nation when there remain only two choices: submit or fight. That time has now come to South Africa. We shall not submit and we have no choice but to hit back by all means

within our power in defence of our people, our future and our freedom ... We are striking out along a new road for the liberation of the people of this country. The Government policy of force, repression and violence will no longer be met with non-violent resistance alone!

The document then determined the place and role of Umkhonto we Sizwe in the overall strategy of the movement:

Umkhonto we Sizwe will be at the front line of the people's defence. It will be the fighting arm of the people against the Government and its policies of race oppression. It will be the striking force of the people for liberty, for rights and for their final liberation...In these actions, we are working in the best interests of all the people of this country - black, brown and white - whose future happiness and well-being cannot be attained without the overthrow of the Nationalist Government, the abolition of white supremacy and the winning of liberty, democracy and full national rights and equality for all the people of this country. [1]

This document spelt out the policy of armed struggle as conceived by our movement. It signalled the dawn of a new era - that of armed struggle in its proper perspective, under the overall political guidance of our movement.

The question then arises of who formed Umkhonto we Sizwe and under whose political direction and guidance it was to operate. Although it was made up of members of the Congress Alliance and the CP - a fact which became quite clear with the number of trials that later took place - none of the constituent organizations of the Alliance had formally adopted the policy of armed struggle. Nelson Mandela provided the answer:

At the beginning of June 1961, after a long and anxious assessment of the South African situation, I and *some of my colleagues*, came to the conclusion that as violence in this country was inevitable, it would be wrong and unrealistic for African leaders to continue preaching peace and non-violence at a time when the government met our demands with force. [2]

Mandela has further explained that the problem was not really whether to fight with arms but how to continue the fight in general. That is, the main issue to resolve was not a technical one - the military training of cadres to advance the struggle along this new path - but was essentially political and concerned the strategy and future conduct of the struggle.

The decision to form Umkhonto we Sizwe was not an organizational decision, but one taken by individual members of the liberation movement. This is clear in the opening statement of Umkhonto we Sizwe's manifesto: "Umkhonto we Sizwe is a new *independent* body, formed by Africans" and in such formulations as ["We] complement the actions of the established national liberation organizations", or "Umkhonto we

146

Sizwe fully supports the national liberation movement".[3]

Nowhere in the manifesto of Umkhonto we Sizwe is the ANC mentioned; allegiance to it is, rather, implied. After the banning of the ANC in 1960 and the declaration of the state of emergency (see chapter 5), it became virtually impossible for the ANC to meet and discuss matters relating to its underground activity: special care had to be taken and questions of security were infinitely more important than during the days of its legal existence. Yet people had to be informed about Umkhonto we Sizwe. This was the key political problem facing Mandela and his comrades - to convince people of the need for an armed struggle and establish the proper political relationship between the liberation movement and Umkhonto we Sizwe.

The formation of Umkhonto we Sizwe was facilitated by the fact that even before 1961, during the Defiance Campaign in 1952, a "volunteer section" of the ANC was formed and the term "Amadelakufa" (those who defy death) was first used to describe them. They were dedicated workers and activists who were prepared to lead campaigns initiated by the ANC to distribute leaflets, to organize strikes or to do whatever the particular campaign required. They were called "volunteers" precisely because they volunteered to face the penalties of imprisonment and torture. They were the forerunners of Umkhonto we Sizwe. That explains why Mandela said when Umkhonto we Sizwe was formed that the problem that faced the ANC was not whether to fight but how to continue to fight.

Umkhonto we Sizwe had its own structure. Its affairs were controlled and directed by a National High Command which had powers of co-option, and which could (and did) appoint Regional Commands. The High Command determined tactics and targets and was in charge of training and finance. The Regional Commands were responsible for the direction of local sabotage groups in their areas.

What was the thinking behind the formation of Umkhonto we Sizwe? The leaders of the liberation movement believed *that as a result of the racist regime's policy* of violence, a reciprocal "violence" by the black people had become inevitable and that unless there was responsible leadership to channel the feelings of the people into organized resistance, there would be outbreaks of terrorism which would produce intense bitterness and hostility between the various national groups in South Africa. The racist regime had closed all channels and lawful means of expressing opposition to its policies. There was no way *without violence* open to the black people to succeed against white supremacy. The Movement was placed in a position in which it had either to accept a permanent state of inferiority or to defy the Government. It chose defiance.

Those who formed Umkhonto we Sizwe were all members of the ANC and the Communist Party and had behind them the tradition of non-violence and negotiation as a means of solving problems. Mandela, a founder member and the first Commander-in-chief, has said, "It is a fact that for a long time the people had been talking of violence ... and we, the leaders of the ANC had nevertheless always prevailed upon them to avoid violence and to pursue peaceful methods.'[4] But at the beginning of June 1961, this attitude of the leaders was to change.

The reasons for a change of policy leading to the acceptance of armed struggle have been further expounded by Tambo, President of the ANC.

> For decades we did not think violence had a role to play in the ANC's struggle: not until the National Party came into power in 1948 and was physically violent. The obvious thing was to respond with violence, but then we thought that perhaps that was what they wanted - that they would use our violence to rally whites around them.
>
> We decided we would not be provoked into violence. If the regime had not been violent, we would not have thought of violence. It was our policy to be consciously, deliberately, non-violent and we persisted with this during the 1950s. There has never been a more violent regime in South Africa, but we stuck to our non-violence.
>
> But as the years went by, violence increased. We saw more armed police - with pistols at first, then sten guns. Then the tanks came. Women's demonstrations were put down with tanks. As we approached the 1960s our people asked - where do we go from here? In 1960, when the ANC leadership were still insisting on non-violence, on discipline, that we must get the support of the white electorate - the white electorate continued to support the regime. Then we had the Sharpeville shootings (67 Blacks killed, 187 wounded). Even after that we decided to continue with non-violence.
>
> In 1961, we called a strike to protest against the formation of a republic in South Africa, because the government had failed to respond to our call for a national convention. But the army was mobilised on a scale not seen since the Second World War - against a peaceful strike. We knew then that the army had left its barracks and that we had reached the end of the road of non-violence. Once the army was involved we could not take it any further than that. The police were no longer sufficient. It was a new situation.
>
> We decided then to embrace violence as a method of struggle.

Tambo went on to stress, however, that the use of violence was always strictly controlled:

> We were still cautious. The strict rule was that sabotage should involve no injury to life. We carried out numerous sabotage actions, but no one was injured. We always selected targets away from the likelihood of anyone being hurt. That was in December 1961. I recall that the office of a Cabinet Minister in Pretoria could not be attacked because he was there. Ultimately, it was hit; but he was not there - we had taken care of that. That has been the pattern.[5]

148

The humanity and consideration shown by Umkhonto we Sizwe contrasts sharply with the barbaric brutality of the enemy who has tortured, maimed and mercilessly interrogated captured freedom fighters, extracting false statements and on the basis of these false statements, imposing long terms of imprisonment or death. Of those freedom fighters who have escaped murder, many have become demented after severe torture, some becoming complete mental wrecks.

Mandela's tour of Africa

During the ANC's early period of underground mobilization (1961 - 62), the organization received an invitation to a conference of the Pan African Freedom Movement for East and Central Africa (PAFMECA) (this later became PAFMECSA, including Southern Africa, and was the predecessor of the OAU). Mandela attended this conference in Addis Ababa in 1962, and addressed it on behalf of the ANC. Part of his mission was to tour Africa and to make direct contact with African leaders on the continent. "The tour of the continent made a forceful impression on me," he later remarked.[6]

Mandela met and had discussions with many leading African politicians: Julius Nyerere and Rashidi Kawawa (Tanganyika); Emperor Haile Selassie (Ethiopia); General Abboud (Sudan); Habid Bourguiba (Tunisia); Modiba Keita (Mali); Leopold Senghor (Senegal); Sekou Toure (Guinea); William Tubman (Liberia); Ben Bella and Colonel Boumedienne (Algeria); Milton Obote (Uganda); Kenneth Kaunda (Northern Rhodesia, now Zambia); Oginga Odinga (Kenya, then still a British colony); Joshua Nkomo (Southern Rhodesia) and many others. It is important to note that some of these leaders were then freedom fighters - their countries were not yet independent. "In all these countries we were showered with hospitality, and assured of solid support for our cause," remembered Mandela.[7]

I had discussions with leaders of political movements in Africa and discovered that almost every single one of them, in areas which had still not attained independence, had received all forms of assistance from the socialist countries, as well as from the West, including that of financial support. I also discovered that some well-known African States, all of them non-communists, and even anti-communists, had received similar assistance ... I made a strong recommendation to the ANC that we should not confine ourselves to Africa and the Western countries, but that we should also send a mission to the socialist countries to raise the funds which were so urgently needed.[8]

Mandela also went on to visit Britain, where he was received by Hugh

Gaitskell, leader of the Labour Party and Jo Grimond, leader of the Liberal Party, among others.

This African trip was very important for the strategy of our movement and the nascent Umkhonto we Sizwe. Mandela stated:

> I started to make a study of the art of war and revolution and ... underwent a course of military training. If there was to be guerrilla warfare, I wanted to be able to stand and fight with my people and to share the hazards of war with them ... I acknowledge that I made these studies to equip myself for the role which I might have to play if the struggle drifted into guerrilla warfare.[9]

Mandela did not stop at that. He also made arrangements "for our recruits to undergo military training ... The first batch of recruits actually arrived in Tanganyika when I was passing through that country on my way back to South Africa".[10]

Mandela returned to South Africa in July 1962 and worked underground until he was arrested in Natal on 5 August 1962. He was convicted on 7 November and sentenced to three years' imprisonment on the charge of incitement, plus two years for leaving the country without valid documents. At the close of the trial the crowd ignored a special prohibition on all demonstrations relating to trials and marched through the streets singing *"Tshotsholoza Mandela"* (Struggle Mandela).

The Lobatse conference of 1962

The banning of the ANC in March 1960 posed what amounted to insurmountable problems for the organization. Besides the onerous task of readjustment to meet the rigours of underground activity, the discipline involved, problems of "conspiracy" and communication, security and recruitment, there was the question of a need for the movement to meet, assess and review the situation. But where could the ANC leaders meet? Certainly, not in South Africa. Moreover, South Africa was almost completely surrounded by British and Portuguese colonies. Lobatse in the then British colony of Bechuanaland was therefore selected as a venue.

There are some people who believe that this conference was convened and set up by the External Mission of the ANC which, on the instructions of the ANC National Executive Committee, was set up by the then Deputy President, Oliver Tambo, in 1960. Nothing can be further from the truth. It is true that on 15 August 1962, a special conference of the External Mission was held in Dar es Salaam. This resolved, among other things, to seek the earliest opportunity to confer with the leadership at home for an exchange of reports and ideas, something which could be accomplished only through direct and personal contact with them. But the External Mission of the ANC only learnt about the preparations for the Lobatse conference at about that time, some two months before the event. Details of the meeting, such as the actual venue, were unknown to the External Mission; they only knew that the conference would be held in Bechuanaland. The Lobatse Conference, therefore, offered them the opportunity they wanted for such an exchange of reports and ideas.

The external representatives of the ANC who attended the conference were O.R. Tambo, T.X. Makiwane, Mziwandile (Mzwai) Piliso and Moses Mabhida. They had no problems going to Bechuanaland "except the sudden appearance of the press as the plane touched down in Francistown."[11]

The Lobatse conference was convened in October 1962. It was run more or less along the same lines as any ANC conference. It was representative of all the main areas of the country. This was, however, an underground conference and the attendance was obviously small - about 50 delegates, although more from the Transvaal soon arrived. To capture the spirit of the meeting, let us quote from the report:

> No words can be found to describe the moving scenes in Lobatse when the reunion took place of the delegates of the external mission and those from inside the country, of friends and comrades-in-arms who had not met or seen each other for many, many years. There, gathered in Lobatsi, were Congressites who had not participated in formal Congress activities for the last ten years due to bans imposed on them by the Nationalist Party Government. Men who last met each other in the Treason Trial or in the various jails during the state of emergency, embraced each other, shook hands. Many described the whole thing as a dream. Such was the atmosphere when the conference began. However, time for exchange of felicitations and greetings soon passed and conference business stated.[12]

The conference deliberations were, indeed, businesslike. Govan Mbeki presided and the steering committee consisted of Moses Kotane, Dan Tloome (acting as secretary), and Oliver Tambo. Messages from the President-General, Chief Lutuli, and Nelson Mandela - who had been arrested and was in jail in South Africa - were given verbally to the conference. The agenda was as follows:
(a) Chairman's opening remarks (delivered by Govan Mbeki).
(b) Executive report divided into three parts:
  1. Report of external work given by Tambo.
  2. Report of the National External Committee given by Tloome.
  3. Report on work in the rural areas given by various heads of area committees in the Transkei, Ciskei, Transvaal and Natal.

151

(c)　Organizational report given by Kotane.

(d)　Report on the trade unions given by Mark Shope.

In addition, there was a closed session of the conference. Comrade Yengwa proposed a vote of thanks to the External Mission.

The report on the situation in the rural areas indicated that the ANC was finally establishing an effective presence amongst the peasants. Everywhere people were in revolt against government measures such as the introduction of the Bantu authorities, stock culling and rehabilitation schemes. Even in areas such as Western Pondoland where the people were still "licking their wounds" after the racist regime's terrible reprisals following widespread anti-government resistance in 1960 - 61 (see chapter 5), the spirit of the people had not died down. On the bantustans the conference denounced the regime's intended granting of so-called "self-government" to the Transkei and the setting up of "tribal authorities" in other rural areas as fraudulent and clearly designed to perpetuate white minority rule in South Africa.

The conference declared that the illusion of Transkei "independence" was being used to divert the attention of the world from the ugly realities in the Transkei and elsewhere in South Africa. This was referring to the notorious Proclamation 400 in terms of which a State of Emergency still exists in the Transkei today; the ban on meetings of more than 10 persons throughout the rural areas; the use of thuggery by so-called "home guards" to terrorize the people; the onerous and crushing burden of taxes; the forced recruitment of female labour and the housing of unmarried women with men in the farm labour compounds where they lived under humiliating and intolerable conditions. The chronic shortage of land for the African peasants; forced removals of people from their homes; and the famine and starvation which had become endemic were also deplored.

The conference therefore urged that the African peasants be further organized and their struggles be fully supported and integrated into the united struggle of the African people for the transfer of power to the people, to ensure the creation of a free democratic South Africa as envisaged in the Freedom Charter. It was further noted that not enough work was being done to mobilize African labourers working on white farms.

Kotane dealt with organization. The new situation, he said, demanded that members of the organization should love the movement, be loyal to it, be disciplined, and be daring in order to implement tasks assigned to them. He mentioned what he called "negative features" such as "loose talk" and "gossip" about the activities of the movement: "these features must be banished from the movement", he said. A lot of people had got into trouble with the police because ANC documents had been found in their possession; there was, therefore, a need for greater vigilance. Kotane also touched upon the "negative feature of traditionalism" when certain officials clung tenaciously to positions and refused to give way to others: "Such people who only remained active when they were themselves in positions of leadership had to be done away with." There was a vital need to give scope to new talent. [13] Kotane's ideas were reflected in the final resolutions, which stated that:

> Conference fully endorses the organisation report and instructs all organs and units of our organisation, as a matter of urgency:
>
> (a) to inculcate among the people a spirit of sacrifice and loyalty to the cause of freedom;
> (b) to raise the organisation of the freedom volunteers to full strength in all areas;
> (c) to enforce strict discipline; ensure observance of the security rules by our members and take steps to discourage loose talk, gossip-mongering and unnecessary curiosity among our people;
> (d) in the organisation of the youth to pay particular attention to their demands for cultural facilities and the special needs of rural youth;
> (e) to make punctuality and efficiency the hallmark of their work;
> (f) to carry out the national programme of political education for our members and people to ensure a high standard of political consciousness and understanding;
> (g) to ensure the full implementation of the "M" plan (the "Mandela Plan" of house to house, street to street cell organisation) and its rapid extension to every area in South Africa; for this purpose to appoint special organisers to guide and supervise its operation. [14]

Shope, in his report on trade unions, appealed for more co-ordination between the ANC and SACTU; stressing that SACTU should be regarded as a "department of our movement rather than a separate movement."[15]

The resolutions adopted by this conference included the need for more anti-racist and anti-apartheid propaganda and publicity; intensification of the struggle against the ultra-racist system of Bantu Education for Africans; and called for a national and international campaign to demand the:

> (a) lifting of the ban on the African National Congress and other outlawed organisations;
> (b) lifting of the State of Emergency in the Transkei;
> (c) release of all political leaders and freedom fighters imprisoned, banned, banished or otherwise subjected to restrictions for political reasons.

The conference saluted "the victorious march of Africa to freedom and independence as evidenced by the fact that some thirty-two flags of independence are now flying in Africa" and at the same time the conference pledged its solidarity with the independent states in their struggle to consolidate independence and oppose neo-colonialism. It did not forget

> To pledge its full and unqualified solidarity with those countries in Africa which are still groaning under the colonial yoke such as Angola, Mozambique, Kenya, Portuguese Guinea, Zanzibar, Sao Tome, Cape Verde Islands, Spanish Morocco, Nyasaland, Northern and Southern Rhodesia, South West Africa, and the three high Commission Territories of Bechuanaland, Basutoland and Swaziland.[16]

All these countries mentioned here - with the exception of Namibia - have now attained their independence. This foresight of the ANC reflected its commitment to African solidarity and unity, and was a manifestation of the ANC's anti-colonialist and anti-imperialist position.

The 1962 Lobatse Conference of the ANC was both inspiring and successful; discussions were serious and constructive and the promising factor was the fact that "the majority of the delegates were young people [and this] gave the unmistakable impression that our movement has a bright future."[17] As the delegates went back home they found that the police had blockaded the borders between Bechuanaland and South Africa, but there were no incidents.

The Rivonia Trial

Throughout 1962 and the first half of 1963, Umkhonto we Sizwe continued the armed struggle it had initiated, planning, recruiting, sending recruits abroad for training and continuing acts of sabotage. Then on 11 July 1963 the police raided a farm, Liliesfarm, at Rivonia near Johannesburg and arrested eight leaders of the liberation movement. They also captured a lot of documentary evidence which was later used against those who were detained. Walter Sisulu, Govan Mbeki, Ahmed Kathrada, Raymond Mhlaba, Rusty Bernstein, Denis Goldberg, Elias Motosoaledi and Andrew Mlangeni appeared in court on 9 October 1963 on charges of 193 acts of sabotage committed between 27 June 1962 and the date of the Rivonia raid. Mandela was brought from Robben Island prison to become Accused Number One.

These acts of sabotage were allegedly carried out by people recruited by the accused in their capacity as members of the High Command of Umkhonto we Sizwe. Denis Goldberg, it was alleged, had been negotiating for the purchase of components which would have been sufficient for the manufacture of some 200 000 handgrenades. Umkhonto we Sizwe had certainly gone past the negotiating stage in its efforts to acquire tons of high explosives and boxes had been ordered in vast quantities for the manufacture of land mines. The aim was to start guerrilla warfare coupled with an "armed invasion and a violent revolution of uprising".[18]

The trial itself was heard in Pretoria Supreme Court. After a long and tedious procedure which involved more than 173 prosecution witnesses - including Bruno Mtolo and Patrick Abel Mthembu who had inside knowledge of ANC and Umkhonto we Sizwe - the defence case opened on 20 April 1964 with Mandela's statement from the dock. His speech made use of the courtroom to indict the racist regime led by the then Prime Minister Verwoerd. He turned the court into an ANC political platform; addressed the people and informed them about the policy of the ANC; and even after conviction by the court, refused to plead for mercy from the oppressors.

Mandela explained the policy and politics of Umkhonto we Sizwe. He refuted the suggestion made by the state prosecutor that the struggle in South Africa was "under the influence of foreigners and communists" ... "I have done what I did, both as an individual and as a leader of my people, because of my experience in South Africa and my proudly felt African background and not because of what any outsider might have said."[19] The interconnection between tradition and revolution is clear. Mandela's "proudly felt African background" included his upbringing in the Transkei "where the tales they related to me were those of wars fought by our ancestors in defence of the fatherland": The names of Dingane and Bambata, Hintsa, Makanda, Dalasile, Moshoeshoe, Sekhukhuni and others were praised as the glory of the African people. Making the link between history and politics, Mandela said:

> I hoped then that life might offer me the opportunity to serve my people and make my own humble contribution to their freedom struggle. This is what motivated me in all that I have done in relation to the charges against me in this case.

Mandela did not refute that he planned sabotage:

> I did not plan it in a spirit of recklessness, nor because I have any love of violence. I planned it as a result of a calm and sober assessment of the political situation that had arisen after many years of tyranny, exploitation, and oppression of my people by the Whites.[20]

Sisulu followed Mandela as the next defence witness, refusing to implicate others who were still not arrested. In some earlier trials of members of the PAC, the defendants had attempted to exonerate themselves by naming or implicating dozens of others who had participated in their activities and so spread the persecution even wider.

By not answering the prosecutor's questions in this way, therefore, the defendants in the Rivonia trial broke new ground in the South African Courts.

The Rivonia defendants were political people. They hoped to set a new standard which would be followed by others in political trials in South Africa's future. In fact, the example they set there has become a precedent, and in subsequent political trials many of the accused have followed it; many unwilling witnesses have refused to testify and have faced months of imprisonment for doing so.

As an illustration of the calibre, courage and conviction of the Rivonia defendants (in the face of a threatened death sentence), let us take the case of Ahmed Kathrada.

Vernon Berrange led Kathrada's evidence. He was concerned to get the judge to see the man who was the defendant as well as seeing the actual case at hand. Berrange led Kathrada through the story of his life, how he had come to dedicate himself to political struggle and what led him to devote his life and activity to the national liberation struggle of the black people. Kathrada described his reaction when the ANC was declared illegal in 1960: "I was greatly disturbed," he declared.

For many years, the African and Indian Congresses had cooperated on numerous issues which affected both races. I believed that the disappearance of the ANC from the political scene in South Africa would deprive the African people, or should I say all the oppressed people in the whole of South Africa, of a most responsible leadership.[21]

Berrange asked: "And as a member of a minority group where do you think your future lies?" to which Kathrada replied, "I have long come to the conclusion, and so have the Indian people, that our future lies with the policies of the African National Congress."[22]

Kathrada described how he had been placed under house arrest in 1962. This prohibited him from entering factories, though his work at that time required his daily entry into printing works for whom he was a canvasser. It prohibited him from communicating with any other banned or listed people, from attending social gatherings, or from being out of doors during the hours of darkness or over the week ends. Up to 1963, he said, he had been arrested "something like seventeen times since 1946 ... I am not including charges for just putting up posters or distributing leaflets or that sort of thing. In fact I was acquitted on nearly every charge except five." The story went on up to the time of the Rivonia raid when they were arrested.

Then Percy Yutar, the state prosecutor, started his cross-examination. It was really a battle of unmatched weights. Politically, Dr Yutar was in the flyweight class; while Kathrada was a heavyweight, with a devastating upper cut and unexpected left. The contest brought much amusement to the accused and the public. They enjoyed seeing Kathrada strike out to the discomfort of Dr Yutar, who spoke in a voice several octaves higher than his normal tones, a real sing-song voice, rising to a crescendo. Let us take a few excerpts from the courtroom battle to illustrate this:

Yutar: You have called them [the cabinet ministers] amongst other things, criminal?
Kathrada: That's what they are.

Yutar found it hard to keep his temper, especially when Kathrada refused to answer questions about other people and their activities.

Yutar: Sisulu adopted that attitude in the box and you are doing the same."
Kathrada: Is there anything wrong with that?
Yutar: Don't ask me ... I am telling you that you are adopting the same attitude as Sisulu.
Kathrada: That's obvious.
Yutar: And this political organisation to which you owe this loyalty; does it also include the African National Congress?
Kathrada: Yes.
Yutar: It also includes the Umkhonto?
Kathrada: If I knew anything about the Umkhonto I would not tell you. If the fact of it was to implicate anybody, I would not tell you.
Yutar: Then how am I to test your story and what you are telling us?
Kathrada: I feel very sorry for you Dr, but I am unable to help you there.
Yutar: How is his Lordship to test the accuracy of your evidence?
Kathrada: I am afraid I have no suggestions. [23]

So it went on. In his irritation Yutar picked upon one of Mandela's captured diaries in which there had been some entries referring to a certain "K". Yutar was rather anxious to prove that the "K" referred to was Kathrada.

Yutar: Are you sometimes referred to as K?
Kathrada: I am not referred to as K.
Yutar: Never?
Kathrada: I don't know anybody who refers to me as K.
Yutar: Do you know anybody else who goes under the initial K?
Kathrada: Yes.
Yutar: Who?
Kathrada: Mr Krushchev.

There was laughter in the court. Yutar bellowed, "So you are trying to be funny at my expense," and Kathrada replied that Yutar had asked him of a K he knew of and he had replied. [24]

On Friday 12 June 1964, eleven months after the Rivonia arrests,

Judge Quartus de Wet passed the sentence of life imprisonment on all the defendants except Rusty Bernstein, who was acquitted. All except Denis Goldberg were flown secretly to Robben Island. Apartheid in South Africa extends even to prisons, Goldberg was the only white defendant found guilty. Imprisoned in Pretoria, apart from his black comrades, Goldberg missed their support and political guidance. In 1985 he accepted an offer of amnesty by the regime in return for renouncing violence, and flew to exile in Israel and then on to Britain.

Bram Fischer, who was leading defence counsel in the Rivonia trial, wrote a letter to a young comrade in exile on 24 June 1964 saying:

> I must tell you one important event. Some days before the end of the argument in court, Govan, Walter and Nelson came to an early morning consultation to tell us of a decision they had taken with regard to the sentence if it turned out to be capital punishment. They had made up their minds that in that event there was to be no appeal. Their line was that, should a death sentence be passed on them, the political campaign around such a sentence should not be hampered by any appeal for mercy ... or by raising any vain hopes ... We lawyers were staggered at first, but soon realised the decision was politically unassailable. *But I tell you the story not because of its political wisdom. I want you to know to what incredibly brave men you and others will have to be successors.* [25]

Bram Fischer was himself arrested in September 1964 and charged under the Suppression of Communism Act. In 1966 he was sentenced to life imprisonment and he died in prison in Pretoria in 1975. The regime refused to release his ashes to his family.

All the Rivonia accused spoke up in defence of their actions; in defence of the movement; in defence of the aspirations of our people and they gave an explanation of why they had taken such actions. Their inspiring words will be remembered for centuries to come wherever and whenever men and women talk of freedom. Besides their invaluable contribution to our struggle for decades before the Rivonia arrests, what they achieved in 1963 - 64 was to implant Umkhonto we Sizwe in the political history of our country. Chief Lutuli, restricted as he was at Groutville, made a statement as President-General of the ANC on the same day of the pronouncement of the sentences:

> The African National Congress never abandoned its method of a militant, non-violent struggle, and of creating in the process a spirit of militancy in the people. However, in the face of the uncompromising white refusal to abandon a policy which denies the African and other oppressed South Africans their rightful heritage - freedom - no one can blame brave and just men for seeking justice by the use of violent methods; nor can they be blamed if they tried to create an organised force in order to ultimately establish peace and racial harmony ... They represent the highest in morality and ethics in the South African struggle; this morality and ethics have

been sentenced to an imprisonment it may never survive.[26]

Those fighters of the liberation movement who were sentenced to life imprisonment at the Rivonia Trial and in subsequent trials were simple men, mostly of working-class origin with a peasant background, that is, born in the rural areas. Throughout their lives they knew deprivation and police harrassment because of their political beliefs and actions as members of the ANC and/or the CP.[27]

The injustice of the racist courts of law has been very apparent through all the political trials in South Africa. Let us take the case of Raymond Mhlaba to illustrate this. Mhlaba was a member of one of the first groups to leave South Africa for military training in the early 1960s. This group included Wilton Mkwayi (also sentenced to life imprisonment in 1964), and others. Mhlaba had left the country illegally around August/September 1961 - before the formation of Umkhonto we Sizwe. He, like the other members of the group, completed his training and returned clandestinely to the country in February/March 1962.

The important point is that Mhlaba was not in South Africa when Umkhonto we Sizwe publicly announced its existence on 16 December 1961 through a series of sabotage acts in all the main centres of South Africa, including Mhlaba's home town, Port Elizabeth. He was eventually captured at Rivonia in 1963 but at the time the police could find no evidence, outside the fact of his presence at the Rivonia farm during the raid, of the degree of his involvement in the underground movement, nor of what he had been doing since he had disappeared from public life in Port Elizabeth in 1961. The police and state, nevertheless, included Mhlaba in the Rivonia Trial and cooked up charges against him. The main burden of these charges rested on the testimony of false witnesses including a notorious Port Elizabeth sell-out, Kholisile Mdwayi, whose false evidence sent Vuyisile Mini, Wilton Khayingo and Zinakile Mkhaba (all from Port Elizabeth) to the gallows on 6 November 1964. These false witnesses testified that Mhlaba personally supervised and participated in the Port Elizabeth blasts of 16 December 1961.

Yutar, the state prosecutor, was very much aware that the evidence against Mhlaba was false and the Special Branch was desperately keen to know of his involvement in the underground. They had failed to extract this information from Mhlaba when he was in detention, so they framed him for acts of sabotage purportedly carried out at a time when he was not in the country, when they could not establish where he was! This is racist South Africa's justice!

They hoped that Mhlaba would either "defend" himself (and in the process reveal where he was at the time of the sabotage acts of 16 December 1961) or that he would break down under an intense barrage of cross-examination by Yutar. In the trial, Mhlaba denied that he was guilty of the charges against him. Yutar, doing the job of the police, demanded that Mhlaba establish an alibi by revealing where he had been during that crucial period. Mhlaba's response to Yutar's relentless pressure was his infectious, high-pitched laugh and firm retort, "I am not going to tell you that".

The ANC after Rivonia

After the Rivonia Trial, the External Mission became the leadership of the ANC. In 1965, a consultative meeting of the National Executive Committee (NEC) was held in Dar es Salaam to assess the Rivonia Trial and the damage it had caused the ANC's internal underground organization. This was an enlarged meeting of the NEC, as then constituted abroad, following the imprisonment of much of the leadership at Rivonia and in subsequent detentions by the racist regime. It followed the pattern of External Mission consultative meetings previously held when representatives from various offices were called to Dar es Salaam to discuss and decide on issues. In addition to senior leading personnel of Umkhonto we Sizwe, representatives of the South African Indian Congress, the Coloured People's Congress, the CP and SACTU also joined in this ANC meeting.

The purpose of the meeting was to review the political situation, set new tasks, and improve our machinery for vigorously pursuing the objectives of our armed struggle, including in particular, the movement of Umkhonto we Sizwe units to the home front. Though the decisions of this meeting were recommendations to the NEC, they laid the basis for a steady recovery of the initiative of our movement.

It was around this time that the working co-operation between the ANC and CP became a more open alliance and began to be officially acknowledged. In November 1966, another consultative meeting was held in Dar es Salaam. This was also attended by NEC members and the members of the same fraternal organizations which were represented at the 1965 meeting. This time the main item on the agenda was the role and status of the members of these organizations in the ANC's External Mission, especially in its dual task of mobilizing the masses at home in preparation for the armed struggle and building up international solidarity in support of our cause.

After Rivonia, the underground machinery of the liberation movement was almost completely destroyed, with ANC and other political leaders in jail, exiled, banned or under one form of restriction or another. The External Mission of the ANC, hitherto engaged in vital international solidarity work, began, therefore, to take over the onerous task of training people, infiltrating trained cadres, weapons and ammunition, resuscitating underground units - in short the whole process of preparation for armed struggle.

At this time, the ANC was faced with what seemed to be insurmountable problems. Apart from the need to reorganize, there was the objective fact that we were confronting a strong enemy with powerful imperialist allies in the West - especially the US and Britain. The enemy possessed a relatively stable economy, sophisticated communications systems and a repressive state machinery. The geopolitics of the whole region added another stumbling block to the prosecution of the armed struggle, for South Africa had no borders with independent Africa.

The ANC was aware that, because of all these factors, the struggle for liberation would be arduous, bitter and protracted and would impose more onerous tasks on the movement than other liberation movements in Africa had been called upon to shoulder. It therefore concentrated on heightening the political consciousness of its cadres and keeping up their morale. It became evident that, in order to prosecute the struggle in a revolutionary way, the ANC needed a thorough understanding and appreciation of the forces at its disposal, i.e. their economic, social and political background, their attitudes, moral conduct and other aspects of their social behaviour, to be able to channel their energy towards the attainment of our cherished goal.

The ANC believed that this could be done by constantly keeping in touch with the cadres; by making persistent efforts to cultivate in them a strong sense of belonging to the organization of which they were such an important part; by making them feel that their contribution to the struggle was recognized and their role honourable; and by seeking at all times to understand their moods, prejudices and grievances without idealization or patronization, thereby winning their confidence and through that their steadfast loyalty to the organization and the cause for which they were prepared to give their lives.

The ANC - ZAPU alliance

At this time, the armed struggle was being adopted throughout Southern Africa by the liberation movements as a method of struggle. In Mozambique and Angola, the guerrilla movement was spreading; in Namibia it was just beginning. In Rhodesia (now Zimbabwe) Smith had declared his "Unilateral Declaration of Independence" (UDI) in 1965 and this brought the alliance between the white minority regimes in Rhodesia and South Africa into the open.

It was as a result of these developments, and recognizing the need to co-operate and co-ordinate their efforts, that the ANC forged an alliance with ZAPU in 1967. The ANC cadres who had received military training outside South Africa were sent to Zambia with the intention of proceeding home. In April 1967, a plan for the prosecution of the armed struggle was put forward. After lengthy debates and consultations, an order was issued to the effect that our men and women were to cross the Zambezi towards home. It was at this time that the President-General of the ANC, Chief A.J. Lutuli, died on 21 July 1967. Thus the first detachment to cross the Zambezi was christened "The Lutuli Detachment" in his honour. The ANC-ZAPU alliance had become a reality.

It is not my task here to relate the battles that took place in Rhodesia nor to evaluate their success or failure, but one thing is important to state. That is that, for the first time since the nineteenth century, armed clashes took place between the white rulers and the oppressed black people in our region. ANC men inflicted losses and casualties on the enemy; they saw the white soldiers run in panic. This was of great psychological and political significance.

The acts of heroism and bravery shown by ANC men in the battles in Rhodesia will always be a shining example and an inspiration in the battles to come. There was devotion and dedication to the cause, selflessness, unity and solidarity. These ANC men and women were filled with hatred for the enemy and were prepared to fight him wherever he was, even outside the borders of their own country. This was internationalism in action, or what today is called African unity - that identity of interests and aspirations of all those who are fighting against colonialism and imperialism in Africa. The ANC armed involvement in Rhodesia against the white minority regime laid the basis for a broader alliance of the liberation movements in Southern Africa.

Despite the fact that the ANC gained a lot of experience in Rhodesia, its External Mission still had to cope with the problems of assuming responsibility for the fate of the entire movement both outside and inside the country. This was no longer a theoretical question but a hard, cold, and at times unpleasant, fact of life. New plans for prosecuting the revolution had to be worked out.

The 1969 Morogoro Conference

On 25 April 1969, an ANC conference was held in Tanzania; this was the Morogoro Conference. Its main task was to bring about organizational changes, a "new framework and structure" as some people said. Commenting on this conference, *Mayibuye*, the Zambian-based organ of the ANC, remarked:

Comrades and supporters may well wonder why it has only been possible now to give expression to an organisational necessity which arose some years ago. The answer lies in the scientific fact that there is always a time lag between the demands of history and the development of social forces except at that precise moment of revolutionary change when both factors coincide perfectly to advance society to a new, and qualitatively different, higher plane.[28]

Some sceptics call this moment a "crisis". At the Morogoro Conference there was no "crisis", - but lots of problems.

The main task before the conference was to map and chart the way to victory. But this could only be done through a democratic process. This explains why the ANC involved all its members in large-scale pre-conference discussions at all levels in all the centres where ANC people were to be found. These pre-conference preparations took the form of expert papers, objective analyses and discussions of issues, and criticisms of our work. The formulation of proposals aimed at removing shortcomings and ensuring improvements were a guarantee not only of fruitful results at the conference but also of a solid basis for future operations - that is, total mobilization of the millions of our people and radical changes in the ANC machinery and style of work to enable it to accomplish the tasks that lay ahead. The question of collective responsibility and a pooling of experiences and ideas was very important, especially for a movement like ours which was then largely based externally.

In the pre-conference discussions one comrade warned that a "new structure" alone might not solve the problem because a "good structure" could also act as a yoke of slavery round the necks of those it was supposed to serve, thus exciting the desire to break it up into pieces. The "new" and "good structure" had to be accompanied by a human element, i.e. better politically and militarily trained cadres.[29] Another comrade made a clarion call, "A change is required; a change of heart and a change of attitude; a change of outlook towards the forces of the revolution and the revolution itself."[30]

Central to all the problems discussed and partly solved at the Morogoro Conference, was the problem of reaching the fighting front and the means of communication between external centres and the home front. Some of the questions that arose were: Was the order of priorities correct? Were we concentrating revolutionary manpower, talent and material resources where they were most urgently required? Did our existing organizational structures make for efficient and effective implementation of these plans? We needed answers to these questions because although history was on our side, strategically time was not. The South African racist regime was constantly strengthening its defences and extending its horizons of economic domination and political influence well beyond the borders of South Africa. It was also desperately striving to demoralize, divide and weaken our people; to intimidate and corrupt them into submission, while trying to stamp out and prevent the growth of a revolutionary movement in the country by every means at its disposal.

The enemy's basic vulnerability was the reason for this aggression. The discovery at Rivonia of large-scale and advanced preparations for armed struggle and the racist regime's disastrous contact with ANC - ZAPU fighters in Rhodesia in 1967, were a frightening revelation of the danger it faced. Both events stung the regime into panic-stricken preparations for war on all fronts and at all levels. The enemy was afraid of the revolution; he had seen the writing on the wall.

History, including contemporary history, has demonstrated that the overriding determinant in a people's war of liberation is not the military, economic or manpower resources of imperialism (important though these may be) but the intensity and protracted nature of the conflict. This meant that the ANC should prepare itself for hardships and setbacks. This also served as a pointer to the scale on which the ANC should operate and emphasized the vital importance to the success of a powerful and truly revolutionary movement.

The outcome of the discussion at the Morogoro Conference on the nature and character of the movement was the (now famous) "Strategy and Tactics of the ANC", which I shall discuss later. The machinery was created to deal professionally and adequately with internal reconstruction and propaganda, planning of the commencement of sustained guerrilla operations and the injection back home of our trained personnel to form the core of the armed force. This was also meant to correct the imbalance between the work of the movement externally and internally; to correct our priorities and to bring home the idea of the primacy of internal needs and the fact that the only possible justification for the existence and activity of the ANC outside the country was as an adjunct of the needs of the situation at home. The body responsible was later called the Revolutionary Council, the majority of whose members were relieved of all external work and administration except in so far as this had a bearing on the military side.

One of the major decisions of the Morogoro Conference was that non-African political activists and cadres should be integrated into the ANC's External Mission. The alliance between the ANC and other organizations, notably the South African Indian Congress, the Coloured People's Congress, the Congress of Democrats and SACTU had evolved and changed in a constant process of search and renewal. This alliance, as the political opposition in South Africa, offered the only real alternative policy to that of the white supremacists and, indeed, the only realistic alternative government. It stirred the masses from political apathy and fatalism, awakening consciousness not only of the need for radical change, but also awareness of the shape, direction and possibility of change. Through hard work and sacrifice it created a solid and unshakeable foundation among the social forces whose mission it was to accomplish the South African revolution. That was the imperishable contribution of the Congress Alliance to the liberation struggle in the 1950s.

Every step along the road to unity had had to be fought for bitterly, not only in direct struggle of the movement against the racist regime, but also against the forces of conservatism, prejudice, anti-communism, racism, suspicion, and hostility which centuries of colonialism had sown among the various social, religious, class and racial divisions of the South African population.

Despite the banning of the ANC in 1960 (and subsequently the dissolution of the Congress of Democrats, whose activities were crippled after 1960 and the arrest of its leaders), this Alliance had continued for a while to operate and meetings were held from time to time, with the participation of the banned ANC. There was a dangerous illogicality and weakness in this position. What were they to discuss - the illegal activities and sabotage campaign? Was the ANC not exposing its leaders to meetings with representatives of public organizations which could not, by their very nature, operate proper security precautions and were open to penetration by enemy agents? Were these organizations, legal as they were, in a position to endorse armed struggle without subjecting their leadership and entire membership to prosecution and persecution?

I pose these questions not to minimize the significance of legality - spurious as it was - because a legal existence for radical organizations is a precious right to be fought for and rightly clung to as long as possible. The point I am making is that with the banning of the ANC, a new chapter in the history of our struggle had begun - a chapter which necessitated new forms of struggle, organization and alliances.

All this was at the back of the minds of people at the Morogoro Conference, where the nature of relations between the ANC - an

African organization - and non-African comrades abroad (Coloured, Indian and whites) was questioned. The ANC was then also learning from other organizations on the continent. In some African countries, liberation movements that had been exclusively African in composition had, since independence, i.e. when a new situation arose, opened their doors to non-Africans as members. Was the ANC to wait until independence before it introduced this process of opening its doors to other nationalities? Had it not become undesirable, especially under the conditions of exile, to confine the membership of the ANC exclusively to members of the "majority group" since this effectively denied the members of "minority groups" an opportunity to participate in the democratic process within the ANC? This was all the more important because "participation in the democratic process" meant *how* to mobilize the different national groups, how to *draw them into* the struggle for the attainment of our goal.

It goes without saying that the brunt of the struggle in South Africa will be borne by the African majority. Their effective mobilization is the first consideration of the movement and this means that the struggle must be led by their representatives. But, given this basic pre-requisite, it is clearly to the advantage of the people's movement and its victory that the oppressed Coloured and Indian people be *won* over to the side of the revolution and *mobilized* for the fight. For that matter, it is also important that as many of the privileged white group as possible be detached from the racist regime, "compelled" to recognize the inevitable defeat of white minority rule and, if possible, recruited to the camp of revolutionary democracy, human liberty and equality.

This policy should not be misinterpreted or misunderstood as "liquidationism" or "nihilism". The ANC never for a minute believed that there is no need or room for the South African Indian Congress, Coloured People's Congress, SACTU or CP. Where national groups are concerned, the revolutionary potential of groups as such is influenced, among other factors, by the extent of exploitation and oppression. The size of the national group and its political consciousness are relevant to its effectiveness. But to be effective to any degree, and for its individual members to be fully involved, the group must be organized. In other words, we need to speak to the African people, to the Coloured people, to the Indian community, the workers, the intellectuals, the youth, the Christians, and so on.

This decision to integrate all revolutionaries - irrespective of colour and nationality - into the External Mission of the ANC - had another important dimension: a moral value. Here were members of the same movement faced with the same problems, striving for the same objectives of building an internal organization in which each revolutionary was a potential organizer in any community with direct benefit to the entire movement, and where he or she ran an equal risk of maximum penalty if captured by the enemy. In such a situation all revolutionaries and activists were of equal worth, and equally entitled to participate in discussions and decisions affecting the prosecution of a cause for which they offered their lives.

The spirit and mood of the Morogoro Conference was captured by Joe Slovo in a speech he made 14 years later (in 1983) at a SACTU seminar in Morogoro on the life and times of J. B. Marks, held to commemorate the eightieth anniversary of Marks' birth:

> In 1969, he [J. B. Marks] presided over one of the most important conferences in the history of the ANC - the Morogoro Conference. It was an extremely critical moment. As chairman, J. B. was confronted by a democratically elected but at the same time very angry assembly of men and women who had lost confidence in many members of the National Executive Committee. We do not believe that history depends on one individual, but in the case of this particular conference it is true to say that it was Uncle J. B. who saved the day.

> I want to say a few words about the Morogoro conference. People tend to think about it loosely and for every person Morogoro seems to have a different meaning. Most people who talk about the Morogoro Conference tend to concentrate mainly on the integration of non-African revolutionaries into the external mission of the ANC. It is true that this was one of the key demands of the rank and file of MK (Umkhonto we Sizwe) and it was very hotly debated. Quite a few of the then leaders of the NEC who have since shown their true colours were opposed to this move ...

> But Morogoro was more than this question alone. In the first place, Morogoro asserted the right of the rank and file to have a say as to who would lead them ...

> Morogoro also proclaimed that we must devote the bulk of our resources and efforts to work inside the country. At the time the ANC's underground structures were virtually non-existent and MK had not fired a single shot on South African soil ...

> Looking back on it comrades, it could be said that there were moments at that Morogoro Conference when the very future of our whole movement seemed to be in jeopardy. But it was J. B.'s skill as chairman and the greatness of Comrade President Tambo [who was then Acting President] which pulled us through and laid the basis for what we are today. [31]

The Morogoro Conference adopted the following resolutions:

(1) The Consultative Conference of the ANC approves the new administrative structure of the organization and:
(a) Affirms the necessity to integrate all oppressed national groups and revolutionary forces and individuals under the banner of the ANC;
(b) Instructs the NEC to take urgent steps to work out the means by which this can be done so as to mobilise all revolutionaries in functioning units of the ANC.
(2) Conference expresses its unanimous approval of the political report of the NEC:

167

the Strategy and Tactics and the programme of the revolution - the Freedom Charter;

(3) Conference considers that insufficient attention has been paid to the proper organisation of the Youth and Students, and Women's Section of the ANC. That proper provision must be made in the ANC for personnel and resources to be allocated to this vital task;

(4) That the working class and its organizations constitute a fundamental foundation for the success of the revolution. That the SACTU and Trade Union organisation should be strengthened at home and abroad. The NEC is instructed to give all necessary help to SACTU and to release personnel required for this purpose;

(5) That the ZAPU-ANC Alliance must be strengthened and steps taken to form alliances with other liberation movements in Southern Africa; namely FRELIMO, MPLA, SWAPO and PAIGC of Guinea-Bissau.

(6) Conference vehemently condemns the continued imprisonment, detention and persecution of thousands of our gallant Freedom Fighters by the Vorster regime;

(7) Conference salutes our gallant leaders languishing in Robben Island and other prisons, such as Walter Sisulu, Nelson Mandela, Ahmed Kathrada, Elias Motsoaledi, Denis Goldberg, Andrew Mlangeni, Raymond Mhlaba, Wilton Mkwayi, Abraham Fischer as well as numerous ANC and Umkonto we Sizwe men and women;

(8) Conference pledges never to rest until these comrades are released;

(9) Conference instructs the NEC to convey its gratitude to TANU the Government of Tanzania, and the people of Morogoro for the warm hospitality extended to the Conference;

(10) Conference expresses its thanks to the OAU Co-ordinating Committee for the Liberation of Africa for the facilities and support given to the ANC (SA) in the organisation of the Consultative Conference;

(11) This Consultative Conference of the African National Congress extends revolutionary greetings to brother Fighters for Freedom in Africa, Vietnam, the Middle East and elsewhere who, arms in hand, are fighting our common enemy - imperialism in all its forms;

(12) We greet our brothers of Southern Africa and the Portuguese colonies, who have scored and are scoring brilliant victories over the enemy. We shall win! We South African revolutionaries pay unstinted tribute to the National Liberation Front of South Vietnam, who have added glorious pages to the history of liberation. We fully support their just demands for the unconditional withdrawal of the U.S. and mercenary troops from Vietnam and the reunification of their motherland;

(13) We greet the peoples of the Arab countries resisting imperialist backed Zionist aggression, and support the right of the dispossessed Arabs of Palestine to fight for their return to their homeland;

(14) Conference salutes our valiant comrades who are carrying on the struggle in South Africa in the face of the most vicious police and military terrorism. Their courage and determination continues to be a source of inspiration to all in the struggle for freedom;

(15) Conference urges the NEC to give priority to:

(a) the provision of intensive political education for all sectors of the movement;

(b) the adoption of a code and oath which all revolutionaries in the ANC and Umkhonto we Sizwe should be governed and bound by;

(c) the appointment of an Ombudsman or Commission to receive, investigate and act upon any complaints and receive grievances in all sectors of the movement;

(d) the provision of military training for all sectors of the movement both in and outside of Umkhonto we Sizwe. [32]

168

The theory of armed struggle in the context of our struggle was also further developed. The "Strategy and Tactics" document precisely formulated and articulated the ANC military theory and doctrine.[33] This document sees the objective factors for the emergence of guerrilla warfare as dependent on:

(a) disillusionment with the prospect of achieving liberation by traditional peaceful processes because the objective conditions bar the way of change;
(b) readiness to respond to the strategy of armed struggle with all the enormous sacrifices which this involves;
(c) the existence of a political leadership capable of gaining the organized allegiance of the people for armed struggle and which has both the experience and the ability to carry out the painstaking process of planning, preparation and overall conduct of the operations; and
(d) that there exists favourable objective conditions in the international and local planes.

It goes without saying that these conditions are created not by subjective conditions or:

Heroic revolutionaries who give a monopoly to subjective factors and confuse their own readiness with the readiness of others: but are brought about by developing political, economic and social conditions - and not to undermine the subjective factor - by the long hard grind of revolutionary work, the response of the enemy, the extent to which he unmasks himself and the experience gained by the people themselves in actual political struggle.[34]

These politico-military aspects of the struggle were viewed in the context of historical experience and political reality which was characterized as follows:

The main content of the present stage of the South African revolution is the national liberation of the largest and most oppressed group - the African people. This strategic aim must govern every aspect of the conduct of our struggle whether it be the formulation of policy or the creation of structures. Amongst other things, it demands in the first place the maximum mobilisation of the African people as a dispossessed and racially oppressed nation. This is the mainspring and it must not be weakened. It involves a stimulation and a deepening of national confidence, national pride and national assertiveness. Properly channelled and properly led, these qualities do not stand in conflict with the principles of internationalism. Indeed, they become the basis for more lasting and more meaningful cooperation; a cooperation which is self-imposed and equal and one which is neither based on dependence nor gives the appearance of being so. The national character of the struggle must dominate our approach ... Thus, our nationalism must not be confused with chauvinism or narrow nationalism of a previous epoch. It must not be confused with the classical drive by an elitist group among the oppressed people to gain ascendancy so that they can replace the oppressor in the exploitation of the masses ... the national sense of grievance is the most potent revolutionary force which must be harnessed. To blunt it in the interests of abstract concepts of internationalism is, in the long run, doing neither a service to revolution nor to internationalism.

169

This was no abstract theory. It was applied concretely to the situation in South Africa and affected even the organizational structures:

Whatever instruments are created to give expression to the unity of the liberation drive, they must accommodate two fundamental propositions: Firstly, they must not be ambiguous on the question of the primary role of the most oppressed African masses; and secondly, those belonging to the other oppressed groups and those few white revolutionaries who show themselves ready to make common cause with our aspirations, must be fully integrated on the basis of individual equality. Approached in the right spirit these two propositions do not stand in conflict but reinforce one another. Equality of participation in our national front does not mean a mechanical parity between the various national groups. Not only would this in practice amount to inequality (again at the expense of the majority) but it would lend flavour to the slander which our enemies are ever ready to spread of a multiracial alliance dominated by minority groups. This has never been so and will never be so.

The document also stated that this approach was not pandering on chauvinism or other backward attitudes:

We are revolutionaries not narrow nationalists, committed revolutionaries are our brothers to whatever group they belong. There can be no second class participants in our movement. It is for the enemy that we reserve our assertiveness and our justified sense of grievance. [35]

The Morogoro Conference worked out the art and science of political and military (armed) liberation struggle in the modern epoch, specifically related to South Africa. It emphasized the dominance in our thinking of achievement over drama, adjusting our experiences to the new situation, creating a new apparatus actually capable of clandestinely hitting the enemy and making preparations for a more advanced stage, invoking tradition and combining tradition with revolution, and history with politics.

7
The Re-emergence of the ANC (1969-85)

In a report to the ANC National Executive Committee in 1985, President Tambo described the years 1969-74 as a "period of regrouping and recovery". This was a period of intense battles between the forces of liberation in Southern Africa and the white minority regimes. The Vorster regime was at the pinnacle of its power and Pretoria tried to further secure itself by helping to suppress the armed liberation struggle in Rhodesia and by holding on to Namibia despite the fact that the International Court of Justice had described its presence in Namibia as an "illegal occupation".

Internationally, the apartheid regime still had its friends. US National Security Study Memorandum 39, of 1969, stated that:

> For the foreseeable future South Africa will be able to maintain internal stability and effectively counter insurgent activity....

> The Whites are here to stay and the only way that constructive change can come about is through them. There is no hope for the Blacks to gain the political rights they seek through violence, which will only lead to chaos and increased opportunities for the communists....

> We can, through selective relaxation of our stance towards the white regimes, encourage some modification of their current racial and colonial policies....

> At the same time, we would take diplomatic steps to convince the black states of the area that their current liberation and majority rule aspirations in the south are not attainable by violence and that their only hope for a peaceful and prosperous future lies in closer relations with the white-dominated states. [1]

This was an outrageous statement, displaying arrogance and insensitivity, neglect of African aspirations - which were subordinated to US imperialist designs - and exposing the racist approach of the US administration.

This was also the period when the racist South African regime was involved in early attempts to so-called "dialogue" with some independent African states, but these tactics were thwarted by the ANC, together with the OAU, in 1971.

The balance of forces gradually shifted in favour of the struggling oppressed people of Southern Africa. The liberation wars in Rhodesia, Mozambique, Angola and Namibia all intensified during this period. The collapse of the Portuguese empire in 1974 and the independence of Mozambique and Angola in 1975 transformed the whole region. The ANC normalized its relations with the governments of Botswana and Lesotho. Chief Leabua Jonathan, then Prime Minister of Lesotho, reasoned thus, "If the Portuguese empire could collapse as it did, apartheid in South Africa could do so as well and the future of Lesotho demanded an alignment with anti-apartheid forces, namely the ANC...[he] developed an astonishing personal rapport with ANC President Oliver Tambo."[2]

At the same time, there was the growth of the anti-Vietnam-war campaign in the US and increasing international support for national liberation movements. When the heroic people of Vietnam finally achieved their victory against US imperialism in 1975, oppressed peoples throughout the world were triumphant.

During this period, the ANC revived its contact with the people. Radio Freedom, beamed from Tanzanian and Zambian broadcasting stations, strengthened the voice of the ANC inside South Africa. Cadres of Umkhonto we Sizwe were sent into the country through the machinery of the Revolutionary Council which had been established at the Morogoro Conference (see chapter 6). This raised the confidence of the masses of the people in their own ability to confront the apartheid regime and, as President Tambo has put it, "Our people were once more beginning to feel the organised presence of our movement among them and draw courage from this, to break out of the state of dormancy that the enemy had sought to impose on us through a policy of terror."[3]

Resistance grew within South Africa through the student movement, workers' action and a radicalization of some of the churches. Many will also remember this period for the rise of the Black Consciousness Movement.

Steve Biko and the Black Consciousness Movement (BCM)

Nineteen sixty-seven saw a ferment of a revival of the people's initiative. It started with students. This was when the University Christian Movement (UCM) was formed - the initial beginnings of what was later to develop into the Black Consciousness Movement (BCM).

African student organizations of the early 1960's reflected the political divisions and ideological loyalties of the time. The African Students' Association (ASA) belonged to the ANC tradition. PAC adherents then felt it necessary to form the African Students' Union of South Africa (ASUSA). The National Union of the South African students (NUSAS), a basically white, liberal student body on the English-speaking white universities of Witwatersrand, Rhodes, Cape Town and Natal, also had some presence on black campuses such as Fort Hare. But black students could not attain leadership positions in NUSAS, and NUSAS could not speak for black campuses, although at times it tried to do so.

The UCM had better possibilities of functioning on black campuses than NUSAS. In July 1968, at the UCM Conference in Stutterheim, Cape Province, about 40 black students, from all the main black centres of higher education in South Africa, formed themselves into a caucus and agreed on the need for a nationally representative black student organization. The University of Natal Black Group (UNB), which included Steve Biko, was asked to continue preparations for such a body and, as a result, a representative conference was held at Marianhill, Natal, in December 1968. The South African Students' Organisation (SASO) was formed there. It was inaugurated in July 1969 at Turfloop University and Biko was elected president.

Steve Biko has at times been called the "father" of the Black Consciousness Movement in South Africa. There is some justification for this. Born in King William's Town, Cape Province - a town which played a significant role in the emergence of African Nationalism at the turn of the century - on 18 December 1946, Steve Bantu Biko went to the Roman Catholic Marianhill School in Natal (after a short spell at Lovedale), where he matriculated at the end of 1965. He entered the medical school of the University of Natal, Non-White Section (as it was called) in Durban at the beginning of 1966. It is said that Biko attended a NUSAS conference while still at Marianhill and about 1966, while a student at Wentworth (University of Natal, Non-European) he joined NUSAS and became "active and indeed prominent in that organisation".[4] He broke with them in 1968 and was instrumental in

173

forming SASO.

1968 was the year in which the students in the Western world "stormed the barricades". In South Africa NUSAS was challenged. In black campuses there was a "miraculous renaissance".[5] In the 1960s the student movement throughout the world had become stronger and in South Africa the student population had increased. There were also other factors connected with the general crisis of capitalism. In the United States, the anti-Vietnam-war campaign had grown tremendously and the civil-rights movement saw the emergence of "Black Power". The student revolts in France in 1968 had brought the De Gaulle government almost to its knees. And students also rebelled in West Germany and West Berlin as well as in other European countries.

There was also the influence and impact of the attainment of independence by most African countries, and of the liberation struggles in Angola and Mozambique and, even closer to home, of Swapo guerrillas fighting South African troops in Namibia and ANC - ZAPU units fighting the illegal Smith regime in Rhodesia.

This explains the atmosphere and climate for the emergence of black consciousness in the late 1960s and early 1970s. But this was not a new phenomenon in the history of South Africa. I have shown in earlier chapters that, since the end of the nineteenth century, African nationalism (sometimes called black nationalism) emerged at various times, manifesting itself in different forms: cultural, social, religious and political as well as trade unions. The whole history of the ANC is full of such incidents and examples. Hilda Bernstein confirms:

> Whatever their differences with some of the principles of their forerunners, the Black Consciousness movement was descended from the organisations that the government banned in 1960 ... the African National Congress and the Pan Africanist Congress.[6]

The reasons for the emergence of black consciousness are obvious: the brutal, racist, colonial system of apartheid, which is a vicious form of oppression and economic exploitation of blacks, and the total exclusion of blacks from the political, economic and cultural life of the country. The notorious Bantu Education system was a particular factor behind the numerous youth, workers' and journalists' organizations that emerged in the early 1970s. These included the Black People's Convention (BPC), set up in 1972; the Black Allied Workers' Union (BAWU), also established in 1972; the National Youth Organisation (NAYO), 1973; and many regional and provincial youth and cultural organizations, including the Union of Black Journalists.

There have been many black leaders well-known to black people inside South Africa, who have died at the hands of and in the prisons of

174

the racist South African regime, but they were seldom known to the outside world. So why did Biko attract so much attention inside the country and internationally? Three factors stand out clearly, which helped the spread of black consciousness and Biko's prominence.

Firstly, there was the racist regime's utter ignorance and disregard of black aspirations and black thinking. They were so obsessed with "racial politics" and "separate development" that they confused themselves. Aelred Stubbs gives us an insight into their thinking when he says:

> Ironically, the Organisation [SASO] was immediately accorded official recognition by the Fort Hare Administration, who liked its segregated appearance! Although SASO's strategy in confining its membership to blacks was one of "withdrawal" in order to regroup, build up confidence, a sense of identity and a power base, and then to re-emerge to confront the white power structure, the latter saw it initially (as indeed SASO was clever enough to portray itself) as conforming to the segregationist "separate development" policy of the Nationalists.[7]

This shows that the gap between the oppressor and the oppressed in South Africa is so great that it is unbridgeable - the two live in two different worlds and move in different, or rather opposite, directions.

Secondly, Biko became better known internationally than many of his contemporaries partly because of his contact with some influential whites. Besides meeting senators and embassy officials, he had a friend in the newspaper editor, Donald Woods. Bernstein has stated that "Biko's importance was developed as a leader of black people; but it was through the white press and white friends that people outside South Africa first heard of him".[8]

Some of these white friends nevertheless had a different approach to the struggle in South Africa and after Biko's murder, many obituaries and articles were written about him. Woods wrote:

> The government quite clearly never understood the extent to which Steve Biko was a man of peace. He was militant in standing up for his principles yes, but his abiding goal was a peaceful reconciliation of all South Africans, and in this I happen to know he was a moderating influence.[9]

Surely young blacks followed him more for his militancy "in standing up for his principles" than his "moderating influence".

Thirdly, Biko had another quality, what Stubbs calls "compelling eloquence" and an "extraordinary gift of leadership": "He had at that time extraordinary magnetism. His hold on his all-black audiences was almost frightening; it was if they were listening to a new "messiah."[10]

These three factors - the regime's "confusion" about what black consciousness was all about, some sympathetic friends within the white press, and Biko's personal dynamism - laid a basis for black consciousness to advance.

From 1971, Biko became increasingly involved in political activity and in 1972, his course at Wentworth was terminated. He then helped to set up the Black Community Programme (BCP) in Durban but in March 1973, together with seven other SASO leaders, he was banned. He was restricted to his home town, King William's Town. He founded the Eastern Cape Branch of the BCP and worked as branch executive secretary. This did not last long. In 1975, an extra clause was inserted in his banning order prohibiting him from working for BCP. The same year he formed the Zimele Trust Fund ("Zimele") meaning "stand on your own") to help political prisoners, especially those coming back from Robben Island, and their families. He became the Secretary-General of the Trust Fund. He also formed the Ginsberg Educational Trust for the purpose of assisting black students (Ginsberg is the name of the township where he was born, grew up and lived, in King William's Town). In 1977, he was appointed Honorary President of BCP (in absentia because he was banned).

Banning means a life full of restrictions and tensions and requires constant alertness by the banned person to avoid further police action against him or her. For Biko this meant:

Confinement to King William's Town; he could not enter an educational institute; he could write nothing for publication; he could not speak in public; he could attend no gathering of any kind except a bona fide church service; he could not be quoted in the press or in any publication (this ban included all he had written before); no one could visit him at his home where he had to reside, except a doctor; he could never be in the company of more than one person at a time; even a chance meeting in the street would constitute a "gathering" if protracted beyond the most formal exchanges.[11]

This did not, however, only happen to Biko. His colleagues in the Black Consciousness Movement - a whole generation of activists - also faced this persecution. I depict the life of Steve Biko so as to portray through an individual the life of a generation. Those who worked with him were many, spread throughout the four provinces of South Africa and, interestingly enough, - they were black and white. Two whites immediately come to mind, besides Woods: One was the Revd David Russell "a young Anglican priest only a few years older than himself, fluent in Xhosa and dedicated to the service of the poor and the oppressed",[12] the other one was Father Aelred Stubbs. C.R., whose personal memoir of Biko helps us to understand the man.

Biko had problems with the Ciskei authorities, especially their obstructive hostility to the Zanempilo Community Health Centre, one of the projects of the BCM. According to Lennox Sebe, then Chief

Minister and now President for Life of the Ciskei, the "problem" with the Zanempilo Clinic was that the staff "talked politics" to the patients! Sebe's younger brother, Charles, then working for BOSS, the racist South African state security organization, had the job of watching over Biko.

Biko was arrested, and detained many times under Section 6 of the Terrorism Act:

- in 1975 he was arrested and detained for 137 days without trial or charge;
- in August 1976, that is during the height of the Soweto uprisings, (see later in this chapter) he was arrested and held in solitary confinement for 101 days;
- in March 1977, he was arrested, detained and then released;
- in July 1977, arrested, charged and released on bail;
- and, finally, in August 1977; he never came back alive from jail.

Biko was murdered on 12 September, that is 25 days after his last arrest. Those were 25 days in hell. On the last day, the dying Biko was driven, unattended, naked in the back of a Land Rover from Port Elizabeth to Pretoria, a distance of 1 184 kilometres (740 miles).

The details about the torture he went through and the circumstances of his death are well known. The response of the racist regime can be seen in these comments by Jimmy Kruger, then Minister of Police, at a Nationalist Party Congress: "I am not glad and I am not sorry about Mr Biko. It leaves me cold (*Dit laat my koud*)."[13] He went on to endorse what a certain Mr Venter, a congress delegate, had said, namely that prisoners in South Africa have the "democratic right" to starve themselves to death, because South Africa is a "democratic land". Steve Biko is supposed to have "died" of "hunger strike"! Yet the autopsy showed he died from head wounds.

Kruger's remarks bluntly express the mentality of racism, of fascism, in South Africa. Table 1 shows the number of deaths in detention from 1963 - 85, and the official "explanations" given.

Table 1
Deaths In Detention 1963 - 85

	Name	Date of death	Official explanation of death
1.	Bellington Mampe	1.9.63	Causes undisclosed
2.	"Looksmart" S. Ngudle	5.9.63	Suicide by hanging
3.	James Tyitya	24.1.64	Suicide by hanging
4.	Suliman Saloojee	9.9.64	Fell out of seventh floor window

5.	Nengeni Gaga	7.5.65	Natural causes
6.	Pongolosha Hoye	8.5.65	Natural causes
7.	James Hamakwayo	8.66	Suicide by hanging
8.	Hangula Shonyeka	9.10.66	Suicide
9.	Leong Yun Pin	19.11.66	Suicide by hanging
10.	Ah Yan	30.11.66	Suicide by hanging
11.	Alpheus Maliba	9.9.67	Suicide by hanging
12.	J B Tubakwe	11.9.68	Suicide by hanging
13.	An unidentified man died at an undisclosed time of an undisclosed cause at an undisclosed place. (Disclosed in Parliament on 28.1.69)		
14.	Nichodimus Kgoathe	5.2.69	Bronchopneumonia following head injuries sustained in a shower
15.	Solomon Modipane	28.2.69	Natural causes
16.	James Lenkoe	10.3.69	Suicide by hanging
17.	Caleb Mayekiso	1.6.69	Natural causes
18.	Michael Shivute	16.6.69	Suicide
19.	Jacob Monakgotla	10.9.69	Thrombosis
20.	Imam Abdullah Haron	27.9.69	Fell down a flight of stairs
21.	Mthayeni Cutshela	22.1.71	Natural causes
22.	Ahmed Timol	27.10.71	Fell out of tenth floor window
23.	Joseph Mdluli	19.3.76	Application of force to neck
24.	William Tshwane	25.6.76	Gunshot wounds
25.	Mapetla Mohapi	15.7.76	Suicide by hanging
26.	Luke Mazwembe	2.9.76	Suicide by hanging
27.	Dumisani Mbatha	25.9.76	Unknown illness
28.	Fenuel Mogatusi	28.9.76	Suffocation
29.	Jacob Mashabane	5.10.76	Suicide by hanging
30.	Edward Mzolo	9.10.76	Causes undisclosed
31.	Ernest Mamasila	18.11.76	Suicide by hanging
32.	Thabo Mosala	25.11.76	Internal bleeding
33.	Twalimfene Joyi	undisclosed	Undisclosed
34.	Wellington Tshazibane	11.12.76	Suicide by hanging
35.	George Botha	15.12.76	Fell six floors down stairwell
36.	Naboath Ntshuntsha	9.1.77	Suicide by hanging
37.	Lawrence Ndzanga	9.1.77	Natural causes
38.	Elmon Malele	20.1.77	Heart failure
39.	Mathews Mabelane	15.2.77	Fell out of tenth floor window

40.	Samuel Malinga	22.2.77	Heart or respiratory failure
41.	Aaron Khoza	26.3.77	Hanged himself
42.	Phakamile Mabija	7.7.77	Fell from window
43.	Elijah Loza	2.8.77	Natural causes
44.	Hoosen Haffejee	3.8.77	Hanged himself
45.	Bayempin Mzizi	15.8.77	Hanged himself
46.	Steve Biko	12.9.77	Brain injury
47.	Bonaventura Malaza	7.11.77	Hanged himself
48.	Mbulelo Rocky James	9.11.77	Shot while escaping
49.	Mzukisi Nobhadula	20.12.77	Natural causes
50.	Lungile Tabalaza	10.7.78	Fell out of fifth floor window
51.	Saul Ndzumo	9.9.80	Natural causes
52.	Sifundile Matalasi	10.12.80	Self-strangulation
53.	Manana Mgqweto	17.9.81	Undisclosed
54.	Tshifhiwa Muofhe	12.11.81	Beaten to death
55.	Neil Aggett	5.2.82	Hanged himself
56.	Ernest Dipale	8.7.82	Hanged himself
57.	Tembuyise Simon Mndawe	8.5.83	Found hanged in cell
58.	Molifi Paris Malatji	4.7.83	Bullet at point-blank range through his head
59.	Samuel Mugiohela Tshikhudo	20.1.84	No reasons disclosed
60.	Ephraim Thamsanqa Mthethwa	25.8.84	Hanged himself
61.	Mxolisi Sipele	4.7.84	No reasons disclosed
62.	Tatleheho Korotsoane	25.3.85	No reasons disclosed
63.	Johannes Ngalo	15.7.84	Internal injuries
64.	Jacob Moleleke	29.9.84	Shot in police van
65.	Anthony Masunyane	7.9.84	No explanation
66.	Samson Maseko	19.9.84	Died of injuries
67.	Bheki Mvulane	29.3.85	Tortured to death
68.	Sipho Mutsi	5.5.85	Died of head injuries in custody
69.	Andries Raditsela	6.5.85	Died of head injuries in custody
70.	Mzwandile Muggels	3.7.85	Bleeding from gunshot wounds while in custody
71.	Johannes Spogter	5.7.85	Death due to head injuries
72.	Sonnyboy Mokoena	16.8.85	Found hanging in his cell
73.	Thembaleke George	16.8.85	Tortured to death
74.	Loyiso Ndzandze	19.8.85	Tortured to death

An evaluation of BCM

An evaluation and appreciation of the theory and philosophy of black consciousness is impossible without taking into account the practical problems and politics of the BCM.

From its inception in 1968, up until 1971, SASO was confined to the campuses and then decided to "go out into the community". But this could not be realized fully because black consciousness did not have a clear programme of action nor a clearly defined philosophy for social transformation such as the Freedom Charter, for example. There was no strategy for mobilizing the working class; it was not a homogeneous movement capable of acting in a co-ordinated fashion. It failed to develop roots in the masses - especially the working class - and did not (could not) muster all the social forces (black and white) that need to come together to bring about change in South Africa.

There was also the question of racist onslaught: many of the leaders were arrested, harassed and banned. The wholesale bannings of 19 organizations on 19 October, 1977, covering student and youth movements, welfare organizations, charitable and church groups, associations of writers, journalists, and women, cultural organizations and two black newspapers, showed clearly that Vorster's racist regime was not prepared to tolerate anything, even the peaceful voices and forms of cultural and national expression voluntarily chosen by the people. This gave rise to problems of continuity of leadership and financial problems in BCM; the amount of money and time spent on the defence of leaders and activists affected the smooth running of the organization.

The BCM asserted the need for self-determination and national liberation of blacks. It stressed black unity and leadership in the struggle, but this was done in a romantic manner. The oppression of the blacks was treated primarily on the psychological, cultural and ideological level and this, in turn, was linked to an emphasis on consciousness-raising mainly amongst students and intellectuals, rather than mass activity.

According to Father Stubbs, one of the weaknesses of BCM was that "it was too much the movement of an idea, too little a ruthless, organised force", but again this was its ultimate strength because it was "extraordinarily infectious".[14] The strength of BCM in the field of ideology became more discernible when contrasted with the ideological bankruptcy of apartheid: "What BOSS and its government lack are creative ideas, and it is in this area that the strength of black consciousness lies."[15]

But the BCM philosophy was full of contradictions. One of these was the assertion that the whites in South Africa must be made aware that they are either part of the problem or part of the solution. At the same time, BCM called for the exclusion of all whites in all matters relating to the struggle of the oppressed blacks. Yet there is a contradiction between making the whites aware that they are "either part of the solution" or "part of the problem" which, by implication, means that their consciousness and awareness should be raised so that they can have a role to play in the struggle, and the call for their exclusion from the liberation struggle.[16]

The question of the role of whites in the liberation struggle was crucial to the rise of BCM. Raymond Suttner refers to what he calls the "rupture in the tradition of non-racial democratic resistance to apartheid" caused by the repression of the ANC and black political activity in general in the 1960s: "Because state repression was primarily directed at black political activities this was a period when (mainly whites) liberal and university political activities achieved considerable prominence, more or less in isolation from blacks, but also in a sense as surrogates for black opposition."[17] The formation of SASO and its breakaway from NUSAS was, therefore, in part, a reaction to the roughshod chauvinism of white liberal students in NUSAS.[18]

It was this rupture in democratic non-racial resistance that led to a distortion of reality and a confusion of issues. The BCM barred its doors to white democrats. Those white democrats, in turn, reoriented themselves towards the labour movement and began to insist that the way forward was purely through class struggle, downgrading the significance of racial discrimination and the national oppression of blacks.

The battle of ideas is never easily won. These issues are still very much alive today and are being resolved in day-to-day struggle. In 1971 a faction emerged within the ANC which sought to pose itself as the defender of "African heritage."[19] They described themselves as "ANC-African Nationalist" but, within the ANC, were known as the "Gang of 8". Their ideas were based on anti-communism and "racist chauvinism" (African exclusivity) and they campaigned against what they saw as white communist influences within the ANC, trying to change the orientation of the ANC towards their point of view. After many discussions with them, this group was expelled from the ANC in 1976. The emergence of the United Democratic Front and National Forum in the 1980s has added a new dimension and has somewhat changed the premises of the debate but, basically, the issues remain the same, namely working out the relationship and interconnection between national liberation and class struggle, and the priorities and stages of the South African revolution.

Steve Biko was against racism and white liberalism, and "the liberal establishment, including racial and leftist groups",[20] by which he was

181

referring to the white intelligentsia which tended towards the labour movement. On the question of "unity" of the "liberation groups" (his own term) Biko had this to say: "I personally would like few groups. I would like to see groups like ANC, PAC and the Black Consciousness Movement deciding to form one liberation group." [21]

There are problems here. It is true that we are "all oppressed as Blacks" but there are other factors to be considered when it comes to the question of "unity of all democratic forces". Colour alone is not sufficient criterion. Indeed, the struggles of the Vietnamese, Angolans, Mozambicans, Guineans, and Namibians, teach us, among other things, one lesson: they have challenged the validity of the argument of an "all-embracing national unity" covering all movements and classes. They suggest the inevitability at some stage of an open confrontation between the narrowly "nationalistic petty bourgeois elements" - who are always allied and collaborate with imperialism and its surrogates - and those who favour the further advance of the revolution from opposition to colonialism to a broader anti-imperialist struggle. [22]

There is a lot more that can be said about Biko and black consciousness. Suffice it to say that here was a man who was in the thick of the struggle - sacrificing his life to liberate himself and his people from white racism and white liberalism; a man who tried hard to understand his environment and a solution to the crisis in South Africa. Here was a young African intellectual trying to emancipate himself and his people "through peaceful means" [23] from the violent system of apartheid which he calls "an island of Europe in Africa". [24]

The BCM was part of the broad forces fighting together with, and not in competition with, the ANC, against colonialism, racism and exploitation in South Africa. Indeed, by 1976, the ANC felt that the time had come to meet the leading representative of the BCM - Steve Biko. This was because Biko and his colleagues had arrived at the following position:

(1) that the ANC is the leader of the South African revolution;
(2) that the Black People's Convention (BPC) should concentrate on mass mobilization;
(3) that the BPC should function within the context of the broad strategy of the liberation movement; and
(4) that a meeting between the leadership of the BPC and the ANC was necessary. [25]

Arrangements were made in 1976 and 1977 for the ANC leadership to meet Biko, but in both cases it was impossible to get him out of the country. Then Biko's murder put paid to such plans.

Workers' action

The ANC believes that class struggle is not in competition with, but is complementary to, the national liberation struggle. This does not mean that working-class problems and struggles are "subordinate" to the struggle for national liberation; they are central to it. Hence the demand by the ANC that the working class should lead the struggle for national liberation.

The workers' organization that has closely allied itself with this approach has been SACTU. It has combined economic struggles with political demands, understanding that the emancipation of the working class will ultimately be achieved after the national liberation of the oppressed blacks, especially the Africans. But this does not mean that the class struggle against employers and the state has had to wait; it must, and does, continue.

SACTU was formed in March 1953 as a federation of black and white trade unions. It soon had a large membership and became a signatory to the Freedom Charter and, hence, a component of the Congress Alliance (see chapter 5). After the banning of the ANC in 1960, "SACTU fearlessly continued its mobilising and organising role among the masses."[26] There were massive detentions of SACTU leaders between 1960 and 1966; over 160 of them were banned and some served long sentences of imprisonment on Robben Island,[27] while three SACTU leaders - Vuyisile Mini, Wilson Khayingo and Zinakile Mkhaba - were executed. SACTU was never officially banned as an organization but, by 1965, it had been effectively silenced.

It was in the early 1970s that the black trade union movement began to re-emerge. It all started at the end of 1971, when 20 000 Namibian contract workers went on strike. This brought the mining industry to a halt and interrupted communication and transport systems as well as commercial operations and rural production.[28] The South African Defence Force was brought in to suppress the strike and six people were reported killed.

This was a signal that the class struggle against apartheid exploitation was once again on the move. Black workers in South Africa were inspired by the developments in Namibia. During 1972, there was an increase in strikes, but the strike wave spread in earnest in 1973. In January, about 2 000 black workers at the Coronation brick works outside Durban went on strike. They chanted, "Man is dead, but his spirit lives." That year, more than 90 000 black workers were involved in strikes, compared with 9 224 in 1972. The strikes continued into 1974. This was the time when unions mushroomed and "the strikes were to bring in their wake a sharp increase in black real wages through the mid-1970s." [29] Employers began talking about skills training and job advancement for black workers. They even admitted that the colour bar was increasingly creating a skilled-manpower shortage - there were not enough white skilled workers. We saw in the section above on the Black Consciousness Movement that some white intellectuals turned towards the labour movement "partly in reaction to black consciousness and partly in response to wider intellectual trends". [30] Many regarded themselves as Marxists, hence, their preoccupation with class issues. These people were sympathetic to black trade unions even though they did not have working-class backgrounds, and many of them associated themselves with the black trade union movement, and the strikes of the 1970s and 1980s.

Friedman has written that "In Durban, Cape Town and Johannesburg, Whites sympathetic to black trade unions began to organise worker bureaux which were to become the nucleus of the union movement." He goes on to add that "the real fillip to the re-emergence of the unions was provided by workers themselves." [31] What he does not see, however, is that the whites who assisted the black trade unions were not helping others, but were fighting for their own social emancipation - whites in South Africa who do not own the means of production also suffer from economic and social oppression, although they are not nationally oppressed. The African workers seem to have understood this. Friedman, however, exaggerates the role of whites in black trade unionism and says that "the banning of union leaders - all white intellectuals - began a decline which was to see paid-up membership in the Durban area slump to something in the region of 2 000 by the mid-1970s." [32]

The real reasons for a slump in union activity in the mid-1970s were, however, that the unions were denied official bargaining rights - black workers were only allowed to air their grievances through plant-level works' committees; strikes were illegal; and the threat of action against strikers by the police or army was always present.

In 1974, it was reported that 59 000 workers, "almost all of them Africans", went on strike and the figures "declined sharply thereafter" to 23 000 workers in 1975. This drop however, was, still relative because "at its lowest point in the mid-Seventies, the strike figure was more than three times that in the Sixties", and although "the period from 1974 to 1979 was undoubtedly a lean time for the unions, they continued to operate and slowly began to grow again." [33]

The 1973 strikes did mark a watershed in South African society - and the Wiehahn Commission recommendations [legalizing but controlling democratic black trade unions] which were to come six years later could well be seen as a delayed reaction to them... But the strikes were the first occasion in which the authorities and employers

184

saw reform - or, indeed, control - through reform - as an option. rather than the repression which had met earlier strikes or waves of organisation.[34]

The late 1970s once again saw militant worker action, and the emergence of radical, black and non-racial trade unions. The working class was becoming the pace-setter of the struggle against apartheid. Because the workers, in general, and trade unions, in particular, had been radicalized, and had become more militant, they became the prime targets of the police and Special Branch.

The black trade unions also became targets of another form of onslaught: the active intervention of US trade unions, especially the American Federation of Labour and the Congress of Industrial Organisations (AFL-CIO). The aim of these US unions was to gain influence in and to co-opt the South African trade-union movement. They wanted to "step up aid" to local emerging unions and to sponsor union training programmes, union education, worker education, training of union staff and much more. What particularly concerned the black trade unionists in South Africa was the CIA connection and involvement in these US trade unions. Such assistance, with all the huge sums of money that accompanied it, was suspect to say the least.

The Soweto uprising

In 1974-75 Southern Africa was transformed by the intensification of the liberation struggles that led to the collapse of the Portuguese empire, the independence of Mozambique and Angola and the South African invasion of Angola.

The independence of Mozambique and Angola offered hope and inspiration to black South Africans: here were two neighbouring countries which had attained their freedom through armed struggle. The psychological impact of this cannot be over-emphasized. But what was more important was the real change of the balance of forces in the region, in the interests of the oppressed blacks in South Africa. There emerged in Southern Africa a new kind of state power, fundamentally new types of property relations and new social relations: "For the peoples of Southern Africa, Mozambique and Angola were the latest examples demonstrating that exploitative relations are a transitional phase in the development of human society."[35]

Within South Africa, the revolutionary fervour unleashed by these examples of black liberation exploded in the Soweto uprising of 1976. What triggered it off was the instruction by the Minister of Bantu Education that half the subjects in schools at Standards 5 and 6 be taught in Afrikaans - the language of oppression:

From a strictly educational point of view a switch to Afrikaans would have been disastrous. Nearly all African teachers had received their own training in English and
could not possibly have conducted a course of instruction in Afrikaans. English was
moreover the main language of industry and commerce, an international language,
and the medium through which contact could be maintained with the rest of Africa.
The language issue provided a point of unity for the community and offered a clear
theme around which an anti-Bantu Education campaign could be built. The reaction
against this particular government decree however, reflected a general mood of resistance to an undemocratic and discriminatory education system.36

During the first half of 1976, tension built up in the junior schools of
Soweto. "School boards opposed the policy and clashed with school
inspectors. Board members resigned. Parents' meetings were unanimous in rejecting Afrikaans, and students clashed with principals who
attempted to enforce the Department's ruling."37

Students boycotted Afrikaans-medium lessons and refused to write
their examinations in Afrikaans. The recently formed South African
Students' Movement (SASM), which represented high school students,
was independent of SASO, and involved itself in community work,
played a central role in the whole conflict: it decided on 13 June to hold
a mass demonstration against the imposition of Afrikaans and formed
an "action committee" consisting of two delegates from each school in
Soweto. This body was to become the Soweto Students' Representative
Council. On 16 June, 20 000 students converged on Orlando Stadium
in a peaceful demonstration - but the police opened fire, killing Hector
Peterson, a 13-year-old student who became the first of many victims of
that uprising. Peter Walshe states that "By the end of October 1977,
continuing disturbances had claimed at least 700 officially recorded
deaths - a total which in reality probably exceeded 1 000."38

This figure excluded the several thousands of those wounded, injured or maimed. The shock, anger and bitterness are indescribable
and the repercussions of the Soweto uprising are still with us today.
However, the immediate reaction was the exodus of thousands of
young people, who left the country to join the ANC, some through
Swaziland and Mozambique. Over 500 teachers resigned and the
Soweto Urban Bantu Council (UBC), a collaborationist institution, col-
lapsed. The uprising also spread beyond Soweto:

In August [1976] the Bophuthatswana legislative assembly was burnt down and over
sixty instances of arson were reported in the Bantustans - in most cases, school buildings. School boycotts spread too, a major example being the demonstrations which
erupted on 11 August in the African townships of Cape Town when thirty persons
were killed. The Cape upheavals continued into September when thirty more individuals died as African and Coloured students, armed with their placards, marched

186

against Bantu Education and called for the release of detainees. Within two months of the first Soweto shootings, eighty black communities erupted, and by the end of October a further eighty. What the government found even more alarming was the prospect that student protests might mesh with a general strike of black workers in Johannesburg, including migrant labourers housed in Soweto's single-sex hostels. Approximately 60 per cent of the African labour force stayed home from work for two days in early August, an impressive if short-lived show of solidarity the like of which had not been seen since the Defiance Campaign of the 1950s. A few weeks later, a comparable two-day stay-at-home occurred in Cape Town.[39]

In 1979, the students formed the Congress of South African Students (COSAS) and the Azanian Students' Organisation (AZASO); which continued the fight at school and university level. Commenting on the struggle at the students' front, *Dawn*, the journal of Umkhonto we Sizwe stated:

Blacks have never wanted the same education as Whites - in its present form. What Blacks want is the improvement of the content of education, a reflection of Black thinking and achievement in the syllabus, a direct say in what is being taught, how much money is being spent and what it is being spent on.

Bantu Education is a system designed not by Black educationists and Black parents, but by a white government in which they have no say. Verwoerd's philosophy and motivation - which he enunciated so bluntly - has poisoned the entire system, probably beyond repair. Bantu Education is closely linked with Black poverty, jobs colour bar - and now "total strategy".

An oppressed people cannot gain control over its own education without first gaining control over the economy of the country, and this depends on the political arrangements within the country. Therefore it becomes clear that any talk about struggle against Bantu Education is essentially about political power. . .

A say in the educational decision-making ultimately means a say in the political decision-making.

And concretely, on the Soweto uprising, the article states:

This is why the Soweto uprising started off as a reaction to the imposition of the Afrikaans language and developed to be a rejection of the whole system of apartheid.[40]

The Soweto uprising was also accompanied by an increase in "deaths in detentions" as Table 1 shows.

The churches

Church figures have always featured strongly in the South African freedom struggle. Men such as Ambrose Reeves, Trevor Huddleston,

Michael Scott, Joost de Blank, the Revd Calata, the Revd Mahabane, Desmond Tutu, Allan Boesak, Dr Manas Buthelezi, Beyers Naude, and others, have emerged at different times as outspoken champions of the oppressed, many of them suffering expulsion or restrictions imposed by the racist regime. Some of the churches have themselves also come into conflict with the state in South Africa, as they have had to decide where they stood on issues such as the 1960 Sharpeville massacre, the banning of the ANC and imposition of a state of emergency that same year, international isolation of South Africa and, and more recently, the emergent black consciousness and black/liberation theology.

There has been a long-standing tension between the English-speaking churches and the pro-apartheid Dutch Reformed churches. In December 1960, after a World Council of Churches (WCC) meeting in South Africa to consider the worsening situation in the country, the Dutch Reformed churches withdrew from the WCC in protest over a mild declaration which stated that:

> The church, as the Body of Christ, as a unity within the natural diversity among men was not annulled but sanctified; believers should not be excluded from any church on grounds of race or colour; there were no scriptural grounds for the prohibition of mixed marriages; migrant labour was decimating family life...wage structures were below the poverty line for millions of non-whites; men had a right to own land wherever they were domiciled and to participate in the government of their country.[41]

Leaders of the other churches in South Africa felt it vital to meet to try to work out the "implications of the Kingdom of God" for the people of South Africa and, therefore, called a meeting in Johannesburg in 1963 to consider the establishment of a new ecumenical body, to be known as the Christian Institute of Southern Africa.

The first director of the Christian Institute was Beyers Naude, an old Afrikaner and former member of the Broederbond, the hard-core secret society that permeates and controls Afrikaner cultural, economic, church and political life. Naude had renounced apartheid and broken his vow of secrecy concerning the Broederbond. For this, he was vilified and hounded by the Special Branch (headed by Van den Berghe), the Broederbond itself (Piet Koornhof was then its secretary) and by the South African Broadcasting Corporation (SABC) - Dr P. J. Meyer was then head of both the Broederbond and the SABC. *Sechaba* has stated that Naude's political evolution "shows that people can change. By sheer force of example he has shown that it is possible to break with the forces of darkness".[42]

The Christian Institute oriented itself towards the struggles of the blacks, which gave it life and strength. *Sechaba* has commented: "The history and evolution of the Christian Institute teaches us that revolutionaries make a mistake when they think that revolutionary changes can be made by revolutionaries alone. We, as a liberation movement, must work in alliance with all patriotic forces in the most diverse spheres of activity. That is even if we do not agree with them on everything."[43]

The Christian Institute was banned on 19 October 1977, together with 18 other organizations that actively opposed apartheid. This was the racist regime's clamp-down on opposition groups after the 1976 Soweto uprising and the murder, on 12 September 1977, of Steve Biko. Some 540 black leaders were detained at the same time; and seven whites were placed under banning orders for five years, most of them associated with the Christian Institute and the South African Council of Churches, (SACC).

The massacres of schoolchildren during the Soweto uprising, and the arrests, detentions, and bannings of individuals and organizations had, however, a further radicalizing effect on the churches as well as on the black population in general. To illustrate this, let us take the example of Bishop Desmond Tutu, who rose to prominence following the Soweto uprising as a fighter against police brutality. He became Bishop of Lesotho, then Secretary-General of the SACC, (he is now Anglican Archbishop of South Africa), and he used this platform to speak out on behalf of the oppressed black people of South Africa. The SACC has 13 million non-Dutch Reformed church members, 80 per cent of whom are black. In 1978, the Dutch Reformed church withdrew from the SACC because of its stand against apartheid. Until 1987 the SACC Secretary-General has been none other than Beyers Naude, whose banning order, imposed in 1977 and renewed in 1982, was lifted in 1984.

There is a marked continuity in this tradition of radical churchmen. Archbishop Tutu is a successor to Ambrose Reeves and Trevor Huddleston, the two Anglican priests who had earlier challenged the system of apartheid. Huddleston is reported to have said in the 1950s that "the church sleeps on though sometimes it talks in its sleep".[44] Today, he says there is no time for talking, this is time for action.

The ANC: consolidation and further advance (1975-85)

After 1975, the ANC strove to secure independent Africa as a rear base. It was able to establish an official presence in Swaziland but Malawi, because of its links with apartheid, could not have relations

189

with the ANC. (The sinister intentions of the apartheid regime in entrenching itself in Malawi need further special research.)

The heroic struggles of Soweto had a profound impact on the ANC. They resulted in the accelerated expansion of the movement both inside and outside the country, increasing the relative proportion of youth and students within ANC ranks. This brought into the ANC many young people who had had very little, if any, previous contact with the organization. Young, militant, cadres who were ready and yearning to carry out even the most difficult missions the ANC wished to give them, were put at the immediate disposal of the movement and this was particularly important since the resumption of the armed struggle was an extremely urgent matter.

The message of Soweto was that the liberation struggle in South Africa had entered a new phase that would be marked by an ever-sharpening confrontation between the masses and the apartheid regime and in which the mass offensive would, to all intents and purposes, be continuous and uninterrupted. This was all the more so since the regime was using, and would continue to use, maximum force against the risen but unarmed people.

Talking about repression in a colonial situation, Alf Stadler remarks:

Firstly we should remember that there is a limit to state repression ... In a situation where the poor have evolved out of a conquered people, these limits are likely to be very high...

In societies based on colonial conquest and domination the limit to repression is likely to be drawn at a point dictated by its disutility to dominant interests...

Secondly, colonial conquest historically provided the base from which industrial capital recruits its labour force, the conception of disutility is likely to be linked with the bare survival of the work force. Both conceptions of disutility are consistent with very high levels of repression.[45]

The ANC introduced a new element after the Soweto uprising namely the combination of armed struggle with unarmed demonstrations. The incidents involving and surrounding the arrest in 1977 of Solomon Kalushi Mahlangu for ANC activities, and his execution on 6 April 1979, were directly connected with the resumption of the armed struggle. Solomon Mahlangu - a hero of the revolution - represented this young generation who had moved to the forefront of the revolution and was ready to pay the supreme sacrifice for liberation. He wrote his own epitaph when he said: "My blood will nourish the tree which will bear the fruits of freedom. Tell my people that I love them and that they must continue the struggle."[46]

190

These were the beginnings of the escalation of armed struggle in South Africa.

The difficulty one faces when it comes to detailing the armed activities of the ANC is the lack of record of them, because of official concealment of these activities. Nevertheless, we know that, between 1977 and 1982, Umkhonto we Sizwe attacks concentrated on the sabotage of railway communications, industrial installations, attacks on government offices, that is, buildings belonging to the regional Administration Boards responsible for African township administration. There were also assassinations and attacks on African security policemen, community councillors and former ANC members who had turned state witness in political trials or who had in some way or other betrayed the organization: "The ANC, like any African elephant, has demonstrated a long historical memory in such cases."[47] It was in this period that there were also incidents of clashes between ANC guerillas and paramilitary police or army units and, in June 1979, in the Northern Transvaal and Bophuthatswana, Chief Mangope's army helped to track down and kill some ANC guerrillas.

Police stations became a focus of guerilla assault, where sophisticated weaponry such as grenade launchers (RPG7s) were used by ANC guerillas. Since then police stations have been fortified with sandbags and bullet-proof screens, especially in the countryside. The rocket attack on the Voortrekkerhoogte military base near Pretoria in 1981 convincingly demonstrated the increasing technological expertise of the ANC guerillas and the quality of their organization.

These attacks - often accompanied by pamphlet bombs scattered in the city centres - demonstrated considerable sensitivity to local conditions: an attack on a police station in Soekmekaar in the northern Transvaal was intended to combine or identify armed struggle with the resistance of the Batlokwa people who were fighting against forced removals or enforced resettlement. The bombing of the Langa commissioners' court in Cape Town had as its objectives the hampering of influx control through the destruction of records. The "Railway warfare" was linked with the day-to-day grievances of the people: the bomb which the police succeeded in defusing and which had been left on a railway bridge across the Orange River near Upington in 1980 was meant to disrupt troop movements from South Africa to Namibia, since this line links the two countries.

What about the fuel storage tanks? The most well-known attack on these was when Umkhonto we Sizwe struck at Sasolburg in 1980, an act of sabotage which *Sechaba* called "a sea of flames, the fires of freedom, the most beautiful fire which symbolised the largest act of sabotage ever in South Africa."[48]

191

These attacks were also a warning to those who violate sanctions against South Africa that they will be "caught in the crossfire" and South Africa's dependence on oil imports was emphasized.

All this pointed to a change in the weapons used; a determined attempt to equal the armed strength of the racist regime and a shift in the relationship of contending forces, in favour of the oppressed people of South Africa. The very fact that ANC guerilla units became active inside South Africa for longer periods of time also indicated a shift in the forms and methods of operation - a higher stage in the armed operations of the ANC.

Throughout 1980 - the year in which Rhodesia became a free Zimbabwe - the people responded to this revived presence of the ANC by burning the racist flag and hoisting the ANC flag; the Coloured and Indian youth were up in arms against apartheid and the Freedom Charter was "revived" and popularized. Many people from different walks of life came to associate themselves with the ANC - the people were, effectively unbanning the ANC.

An integral part of this mass upsurge was a call for the release of Nelson Mandela and all other political prisoners; a campaign which was influenced by the independence of Zimbabwe:

The present campaign for the release of Nelson Mandela was initially a reaction to a call for a convention by two "influential" Afrikaans newspapers following the overwhelming victory in the recent Zimbabwe independence elections of the Patriotic Front alliance. But these Afrikaans papers blundered. They misread the mood of the people.

This is exactly what the Zimbabwean Whites did. They misread black attitudes. And not only that. The Zimbabwean elections, against most white expectations, have shown that black "leaders" who are picked out by Whites as suitable people to lead, will be politically destroyed by precisely that recognition and replaced by a people's choice. Zimbabwe has also shown the folly of believing that a white minority can enjoy power and privilege indefinitely at the cost of a black majority. These reasons perhaps explain why recently in the South African press there has been a consistent use of terms like "true leaders" or "real leaders", "recognised black leaders", "right leaders" or even "authentic black leaders", Nelson Rolihlahla Mandela is one. This is the unique leadership role accorded him by our people.[49]

The momentum of mass upsurge was maintained and developed to higher levels, resulting in the formation of the United Democratic Front (UDF) in Cape Town on 20 August 1983, at a gathering where more than 12 000 people converged. The formation of the UDF was a reaction to a call by Dr Allan Boesak made at the January congress of the Transvaal Indian Congress. It was not, however, simply a response to a call for unity: it was the culmination of local campaigns and the need to co-ordinate isolated struggles into a broader national campaign of resistance. It was an indication of a new level of organization.

One or two things need to be said about the UDF. It is composed of more than 700 affiliate organizations, comprising all sections and national groups - trade unions, churches, civic and community organizations, sports bodies, and political organizations. The UDF unites them in the struggle for a non-racial democratic South Africa, pools their resources, and their work to mobilize the people against the crime of apartheid.

The UDF is organized in urban and rural areas working outside the government-created structures and organized in a decentralized, federal structure with established regions in the Transvaal; Natal; Border (the East London area); eastern Cape (Port Elizabeth area); western Cape; northern Cape and the Orange Free State.

The UDF mobilizes all the people into one mass movement and co-ordinates community resistance, but it does not purport to be a substitute movement to the ANC. It articulates the viewpoint of the broad cross-section of the people - that discrimination falls on the poor - accordingly, the main thrust of the UDF is directed towards the participation of the people in the workplace and in their living areas.

The UDF is, as its name suggests, a united front in which all organizations keep their identity and independence but co-operate in opposing the regime. There is nothing sinister in that. But the UDF is not a front organization of the ANC manipulated by its invisible hand as the regime claims, for the simple reason that the ANC is not (and cannot) be an affiliate of the UDF.

There have been attempts in the West to promote Gatsha Buthelezi, Chief of KwaZulu, as a "moderate" black leader. Buthelezi is the leader of Inkatha, an ethnically based organization which is moderate towards the racists and very violent when it deals with those who oppose the regime - and this includes the UDF. Inkatha claims to be an "African organization", but is far from having an "independent" policy. Its practical political activity is sending UDF leaders and ANC activists to long terms of imprisonment, or even killing them. In this respect, Inkatha aids the racist regime and does its dirty work for it.

There has also been much confusion in the West and, in particular, in the Western press, about P. W. Botha's so-called "reforms" of the apartheid system. These have been portrayed either as belated "benevolence" towards the blacks or as the end of apartheid. But the other side of these "reforms" has been the ruthlessness and violence with which the racist regime's policies are enforced. "Reforms", violence and naked brutality are, in South Africa, not mutually exclusive. They are the twin reactions of the desperate regime that knows its days are numbered. The "reforms" are an attempt to ap-

193

pease international condemnation of apartheid and to undermine the liberation struggle within South Africa. The violence and brutality are the naked face of the regime - cornered and frightened - trying to hammer acceptance of the "reforms" and so-called "harmony" into the black population.

Their nightmares are our dreams

These apparently contrasting strategies are, however, not new to South Africa, nor to the subcontinent as a whole. The racist South African regime has long used the double-edged sword of "dialogue" and military attack as a weapon to keep independent Africa at bay and to try to undermine the solidarity between ANC forces and independent black states in Southern Africa.

South Africa regards independent black Africa as the "second mortal enemy" (the first being black South Africa). And in 1984 two major events took place which epitomized the connection between the regime's internal and regional policies. Firstly, there was the signing of the non-aggression pact - The Nkomati Accord - by the racist President (then Prime Minister) P. W. Botha and President Samora Machel of Mozambique on 16 March.[50] Secondly, elections took place in August and September 1984 to the tricameral parliament of Whites, with Indians and Coloured as junior partners.

The ANC considered "the situation in Southern Africa" in the light of these events and assessed the "frantic diplomatic political and propaganda counter-offensive" of the racist regime as having the following aims:

● To isolate the ANC throughout southern African and to compel the independent countries of our region to act as Pretoria's agents in emasculating the ANC, the vanguard movement of the South African struggle of national emancipation.
● To liquidate the armed struggle for the liberation of South Africa.
● To gain new bridgeheads for the Pretoria regime in its efforts to undermine the unity of the Frontline States, destroy the SADCC and replace it with a so-called constellation of states, and thus to transform the independent countries of southern Africa into its client states; and
● To use the prestige of the Frontline States in the campaign of the white minority regime to reduce the international isolation of apartheid South Africa and to lend legitimacy to itself and its colonial and fascist state.[51]

The Nkomati Accord pledged Mozambique not to provide bases for those fighting against the South African racist regime. In return, South Africa was supposed to stop supporting Renamo (MNR) - the counter-revolutionary force it had funded, trained and equipped to undermine

194

the Frelimo government in Mozambique. In the ANC's view, this accord, concluded with "a regime which has no moral or legal right to govern our country, cannot but help to perpetuate the illegitmate rule of the South African white settler minority". [52]

What about the tricameral parliament? A widespread campaign against this whole attempt to incorporate the Coloured and Indian communities into the structures of the racist regime led to the boycott of the elections for the tricameral parliament by the vast majority of Coloureds and Indians. The police responded, as ever, with brutality and terror, arresting UDF leaders (who were later charged with high treason).

This campaign opened a new chapter of resistance against the racist regime. The people's opposition to P. W. Botha's new strategies intensified. In November 1984, there was a mass stay-away from work in the Transvaal - the industrial heartland of South Africa - which seriously affected the economy. Since then, South Africa has known no peace. Strikes, boycotts, rent strikes, community action, the virtual take-over of many black residential areas by black activists, the campaign to free Nelson Mandela and other political prisoners - all these forms of resistance and more have kept up a relentless pressure on the racist regime. Alongside this political and economic pressure has been the continuing armed attacks of Umkhonto we Sizwe, striking closer and closer to the very heart of white power.

In response to this resistance, the regime unleashed a vicious form of state terrorism. Death squads emerged and gangs of policemen and their agents, with their faces concealed in balaclavas, began to harrass and attack people. The use of soldiers from the South African Defence Force (SADF) and heavy military equipment to occupy African residential areas became routine. This testified to the fact that the crisis in South Africa had reached a new peak. The South African police could not contain the people's resistance: the army had to move in. The racists had once more declared outright war on the African population.

Many UDF activists are on the regime's hit list. Such people - leaders in their communities - have been found dead, their bodies mutilated or burnt beyond recognition. Hundreds of people have simply disappeared, in a manner reminiscent of "disappearances" in parts of Latin America. Mass graves have also been discovered - of people secretly killed and buried by the army and police. It has been impossible to get the exact statistics about the number of people killed or those who have disappeared or what happened to them: "The state of terror and the occupation of black townships by the SADF and the SAP made it difficult to establish what happened to the many people

195

who had disappeared."[53]

A number of sworn affidavits give an indication of the extent of the atrocities perpetrated on innocent black South Africans by the police and army. They describe the kind of violence and intimidation in the eastern Cape that is being used against the people by the police and soldiers of the Pretoria regime, before and during the state of emergency declared in 1985. The following extracts are from some such affidavits.[54]

Mrs Willel Zinto of KwaNobuhle made a statement in February about events that had taken place on 29 January 1985:

My son, Thulani, was about to go to the shop to buy some cool-aid. I was standing at the kitchen door. I heard a bus coming. I could see Thulani at the gate of the back yard. Suddenly I heard screams and noise. I believe this was from a group of children when they realised that there were police inside the bus. This was followed by shooting. My neighbour came screaming and crying, saying: "Thulani - Thulani has been shot". I crossed to her yard and found him lying inside her yard.

I was very distressed. Another person put my son in a car and took him to Dr Maqhagi, who has his surgery in our street. As soon as I reached the surgery, I was taken to see my son, who was unconscious. While we waited for the ambulance to arrive for the three children, my son and two others, there came the police van. The policemen came into the surgery and asked for the children. These policemen were all white and wore blue uniforms. They came in three vans. The police made chaos in the surgery, asking various people there, "Are you the one who has been shot?"

... The youngest child was about eight years of age and had been shot in the arm. He was crying. Nobody from his family was with him. The other child, I think she is about 12, was lying unconscious. She too was alone...

The police did not have stretchers. The doctor's nurses carried the children outside to the police van. I realised that my son was no longer unconscious by this time, as I could hear his screams ... To my knowledge there were no mattresses in the back of the van ...

I sent my younger son to check if the police had taken Thulani to the KwaNobuhle day hospital. He returned, saying they were not there.

I hired a car and went to Provincial Hospital, where I was told that they had been transferred to Livingstone. It was about 7 p.m.

I hired another car to Livingstone. I was shown where Thulani was. My husband was with me and signed consent papers for an operation. The nurses showed us X-rays which showed birdshot above the eyes, both arms, neck and chest and both thighs .... Thulani was fully conscious and he told me that when he had been taken from the surgery and put in the police van, the police had placed their spare wheel on top of him. I did not question exactly how this was placed and he was crying.

Mrs Maria Qomoyi, aged 59, of Graaff Reinet made a statement in August, describing a police raid in July:

On Tuesday, 30 July, at 7 a.m. I was in bed. I had flu ...My ten-year-old grand-daughter called out that the police were coming (I found out afterwards that the police had used loud-hailers to call the people outside to clean the streets. I did not hear the call).

A white policeman unknown to me entered the room. He said to me, "Why didn't you come outside when called?" I said, "Who called me?" He said, "You ask," and hit me with a long sjambok across the back and then across the face.

I jumped up and grabbed the whip. We struggled. Another group of policemen came up, threw me on the floor and kicked me on the head and arms. They walked away...

Her pregnant daughter, 24-year-old Marina Qomoyi, took up the story in a statement made the same day as her mother's:

I was at home in my bedroom when suddenly I heard some children screaming. I got out of my room to investigate and found that some white policemen, about four in the bedroom, were assulting my mother. The police were in their ordinary blue uniform. They were beating my mother with black sjamboks and they were also kicking her. My mother was sprawled on the floor at the time ... I then intervened and asked why they were beating my mother. After I intervened they turned on me and beat me in the same way ... At this point they dragged my mother along the ground towards the back door, all the time beating. First of all, the police sjam-bokked me across my back - I still have the marks.

I followed them dragging my mother, and once I was outside the house they con-tinued to beat me - this time on my abdomen. I am pregnant and I have been told that I can expect to give birth to my child any day now ...

...I went to my mother and talked to her as she wanted to proceed immediately to the police station to lay a charge ... I ... went inside to attend to my little cousin ... who is three months old. I had seen the police trample on this baby when they entered the room. I believe this was done accidentally. The baby was unconscious for several hours after this happened.

Lena Rasmen of Lingelihle described in August her encounter with some soldiers earlier in the same month:

In the late evening I walked to a relative's home. I was alone. A Hippo drove up be-hind me and stopped. Two white soldiers jumped out. One said: "Hier loop 'n bitch, alleen in die nag, seker 'n man soek. Ons sal haar help" ("Here walks a bitch alone in the night, she must be looking for a man. We'll help her".) One soldier lifted me by my shoulders and another by my ankles. I struggled, and said, "Where are you taking me?" The same soldier said, "You'll see."

197

> . . . The Hippo drove to the National Road and went towards Port Elizabeth ... A few kilometres away the Hippo stopped. The one soldier jumped out and the other pushed me out. The two soldiers lifted me over the fence, and climbed over.

She then described how she had been raped by both soldiers, who afterwards drove off in the Hippo, while she set off on foot.

> I . . . went to my brother's house and told him ... It was 9 p.m. ... My brother gave me coffee and put me to bed with hot water bottles. I was in pain and still bleeding.

When she made her statement a week later, Lena Rasmen was still in pain.

Another aspect of the level of brutality now common in South Africa is the terrorism unleashed by Gatsha Buthelezi's Inkatha movement against anybody who differs with, let alone, opposes him and *his* Inkatha. He has used every trick in the book: tribalism, big tribe chauvinism - claiming to lead the biggest tribe, the Zulus - and anti-Indian propaganda. Buthelezi's Inkatha has its own death squads, terrorizing and killing the people the same way the racist regime does. This is particularly so in Natal. He claims to lead the Zulu-speaking people but he is terrorizing and killing them.

These are acts of desperation, and show the racist regime's fear of a people united in struggle and its inability to provide solutions to the problems facing the people. Apartheid is in deep crisis.

What about the National Forum Committee? This group exists in some parts of South Africa. It has adopted a programme which is called "The Manifesto of the Azanian People". This manifesto characterizes apartheid as "racial capitalism" and goes further to state that the National Forum is fighting for the establishment of a democratic anti-racist worker Republic in Azania" and that black workers "alone can end the system as it stands today because they alone have nothing at all to lose." [55]

This position differs radically from that of the ANC and was rejected in a jóint statement by the South African Allied Workers' Union (SAAWU), General and Allied Workers' Union (GAWU), Congress of South African Students (COSAS) and Azanian Students' Organisation (AZASO):

> We reiterate our uncompromising commitment to the historic Freedom Charter as the only democratic document drafted in the history of the liberation struggle.

> The Charter stands out from all other alternatives for change in South Africa, not only because of the manner in which it came into being, but also because of the demands reflected in it. It can therefore never be substituted without the will of the majority. Any attempt by an individual or group to discredit or undermine it can be seen as an act of betrayal to the aspirations of all the people of South Africa. [56]

These are not the only problems facing the ANC. There are also diplomatic pressures as well. The ANC is being told by Western governments to abandon the armed struggle, to "loosen" its ties with the CP with which it is in alliance, and also its ties with the Soviet Union. In short, they want the ANC to be part of the "reform process". Their aim is to disband the ANC and its military wing, Umkhonto we Sizwe. And if physical liquidation of the ANC, through open mass terror and its isolation from the masses it leads and the socialist countries fails, then "moral" pressure has to be applied through sowing political and ideological divisions and the creation of splits and pro-imperialist forces, looking for collaborators amongst the black people - a so-called "third force". The imperialist countries want to "twist" the arm of Botha so that he can do away with apartheid or the "hurtful aspects" of it, but leave capitalism intact. This has to be done with the "approval" of the ANC - hence the talks about talks. This is not because they like the ANC. They recognize its growing popularity and feel that it has to be "nipped in the bud" to be "neutralised".

The significance of the ANC in the present crisis derives from the fact that its popularity among the masses has grown tremendously. The ANC's democratic programme is accepted by the people and its leaders in jail are an inspiration to all freedom fighters and activists.

The ANC is the only organization in the country that engages the enemy militarily. Umkhonto we Sizwe has become the hope of millions of the oppressed. The policy of the ANC on armed struggle is based on the conviction that no victory is possible without mass participation, without the conscious and active involvement of the oppressed black masses. No group of revolutionaries acting on their own, however gallant, disciplined and self-sacrificing they may be, can succeed in overthrowing the government. The struggle has to be fought by the entire people, not only in strikes and demonstrations but in the field of armed struggle. In other words, the role of the masses as the prime combat force is growing. This means that political education of the masses is the principal task for the ANC, to enable it to lead the masses into struggle and this, in turn, facilitates unity in action by the black masses and the democratic forces as a whole. There can be no unity of the democratic forces or black unity as such without unifying the Africans under the banner of the ANC.

The armed operations of the ANC inside South Africa have a crucial psychological impact as well as a military one. They instil self-confidence in the people and transform the latent hostility of the people to the government into open mass confrontation; they intensify the sense of unease and insecurity among the enemy forces; they increase the conviction among the struggling people that victory is certain; and they popularize armed struggle - the term "armed propaganda" has gained popularity within the ANC circles. This, and much more, explains why the ANC flags, symbols, slogans and freedom songs are sung everywhere, especially at the funerals of those gunned down by the enemy.

Internationally, the prestige of the ANC is equally high. The ANC is regarded as the alternative to apartheid. The struggle and the sacrifices of the masses of the people inside the country have contributed to this. The policies of the ANC and its leadership, under the President O. R. Tambo, have brought admiration from many quarters.

Born at Bizana in eastern Pondoland, eastern Cape, in 1917, and of peasant origin, Oliver Tambo attended school at Ludebe, the Holy Cross Mission and, later, at St Peter's Secondary School, Johannesburg. Matriculating in 1938, he went on to Fort Hare University College where he graduated in 1941 with a BSC Degree. He was involved in students' strikes and was expelled from Fort Hare because of these activities. Then he obtained his Education Diploma and taught at St Peter's Secondary School from 1943 to 1947, where his students included the late Duma Nokwe (Secretary-General of the ANC from 1958 to 1969).

In 1948, Tambo began to study law. He started in legal practice with Nelson Mandela in December 1952, establishing an African legal partnership to defend Africans charged with "crimes" under the racist apartheid laws. He even travelled to Namibia to represent Namibians facing political charges.

Tambo was one of the founders of the ANC Youth League in 1944 and, successively, its National Secretary and National Vice-President. In 1949, he became a member of the National Executive of the ANC and Secretary-General of the organization in 1955, holding the position until 1958, when he was elected Deputy President-General.

In 1954, Tambo was banned, under the Suppression of Communism Act, from attending all gatherings for two years and he was restricted to the magisterial districts of Johannesburg and Benoni for the same period. In December 1956, he was charged with high treason together with 155 other members of the Congress Alliance. And in 1959, he was served with a further order prohibiting him from attending any gatherings for five years. The legal practice that Tambo and Mandela had set up was seriously affected by these restrictions.

A week after the Sharpeville shootings on 21 March 1960, and two days before the declaration of a state of emergency on 30 March, Tambo was directed by the ANC National Executive to leave the country in order to put the case against South Africa in world forums.

After the death of Chief Lutuli in 1967, Tambo became ANC Acting President. Then in 1977 the Robben Island leadership suggested he assume the full title of President-General.

Comrade Tambo's role in arousing world consciousness has had an immense impact on international opinion of South Africa. Since leaving the country in 1960, he has earned the respect of many world figures by his honesty, modesty, his incisive intelligence and his historic indictments against the South African regime at the United Nations and other world platforms. So ably has Tambo presented the case against South Africa that he has come to be regarded as a man whose authority cannot be challenged on such issues. He has travelled widely. The esteem with which he is regarded in Africa can be judged by the fact that the movement he leads - the ANC - is regarded as the authentic and representative voice of the black masses of South Africa. He knows personally almost all African leaders on the continent and they have great respect for his opinions. His speeches have been published and translated into many languages.

The ruling racists in South Africa say they will not deal with the ANC because it is a "communist-led" organization but, really, they fear the ANC because it is fighting for the national liberation of the oppressed black majority, especially the Africans, and for the social emancipation of all South Africans - black and white. The Freedom Charter does not envisage any transfer of power to one class; on the contrary it proposes a transfer of power to a coalition of classes that are against the status quo, forces that are for an implementation of the national democratic programme which has been - (and is still being) - elaborated in various ANC policy documents.

These are our dreams; these are the nightmares of the architects of apartheid.

The history of the ANC has become part of the folklore of the people of South Africa, who have come to identify their future with the ANC. Lindiwe Mabuza tells the whole story in her poem "Mangaung" (an African name for Bloemfontein).[57]

Mangaung
8 January, 1912

I was born on January the eighth
For my birth
My parents travelled
Days and long miles
To a place called
Mangaung
Which means
The meeting place of the leopards

Today,
The enemy calls my cradle
Bloemfontein
Mangaung was warm
Hospitable
A meeting place
Where now
Only poisonous crops
Of injustice
Bloom

Well,
Just for me
One January 8th
My parents came
From all corners heights and plains
Of our land
Stolen
And in pain ...
Our cattle gone
Our homes burnt
Our fields made green by us
But, especially not for us
And if they could only speak.
All those rivers of South Africa
Could tell of countless seasons
Of our blood, our tears

But that's when my parents
Were not married.
They walked alone,

Just like each fighting bulldozers alone
Alone, tried to brave
With bare hands
The mad stampede of elephants
When single-handed victories
Often leave each parent armless
If alive at all ...

But before that certain January 8th
After the enemy
Settled a little family he had
Over our *everything*
He united
And strengthened his fighting muscle
Against my people

Today
English French Dutch
German Italian Greek
Portuguese and other
Tongues of Europe
Pronounce themselves
Nation - indivisible
In my country!
And us -
Sotho Venda Xhosa
Tsopi Shangaan Zulu
The same European tongues
Pronounce
Nations - divisible
In my country!

Oh,
But just for my birth
Serious anxious and colourful parents
Were there,
They came
On foot on bicycle
Oxwagons horseback
Some by trains with cattle, like cattle,
Through rains and frying sun ...

The wind thorns and rock
Sand too they conquered,
They came
The flame-hearted ones,
The back-bent and bruised ones
Their unseen scars swelling anew
The whipped ones came
The down trodden
Violated again and again
Though unyielding
Whenever tried like reeds
In the cruel whirls and storms
Of Anglo-Boer love
They arrived,
These unconquerable custodians of justice

And rallied
Their visions fixed on a gigantic
A pregnant idea!
Down from the place
Of another birth
The birth of dispossession
Called Natal
They came with stories
Of how the valley of a thousand hills
Always green and swollen with hope
Seemed to swallow Tugela waters
Just to let freedom riders pass!
And those whose wagons and bicycles
Saw the Lekwa and Nciba waters
Rise
With African pride
Also impatient for return of stolen banks
Whispered in various tongues
That even creatures
Known to love human blood
Popped their head high
Up and down
Spirited by the call of
Mangaung
And bubbled
Deep in their water-home
Ndlelanhle!

Just to let freedom riders pass!
Titlela a ti basi
Tsela Tsweu
Just to let freedom riders pass!
Just to lighten the burden
Ndila tsena
Let the roads be white
They all sang
Just to let freedom riders pass!

They came
Burning deep inside
In the hidden brow
Watery in the hidden eye
Weighted on the mind
By what they called
The pains of labour

From pass-carrying mines
From pass-carrying farms
From pass churches, pass schools
Pass universities, pass stores, pass laws
From plenty heavy pass work
Our people did and still do
Speaking all the despised languages
Of our roots
And European ones too
They arrived
All their hearts pounding
All thoughts now extended, mingling
All embracing now
Awaiting
The beginning of the death of our
Splitting pain
The pain that separates us
Awaiting,
The birth of our nation
There at *Mangaung!*

I think my parents
Chose this place because
I was to be special
The first fruit of peace

From ourselves to ourselves
The living wedding gift
An unbreakable vow
That each is empowered
And raised higher
Only
And then only
In the tightening and linking
Of our clenched fists:
In short
A weapon against
Divide and destroy

Today,
The enemy greases the pockets
Of a few greedy ones
Who wear our leopard skins
And forget *Mangaung!*
The enemy dots our country
With smallpox and leprosy
Dumps
Called Bantustans
To hasten the death
Of our nation!

But I'm an extraordinary spirit
A power, a force, a home
A shield
A spear
A child
Yes, a child born with stubborn leopard spots
Of racism
All over
But born nonetheless
Breathing, kicking stretching
Into the future
Breathing heavily
With the hearts of leopards and lions
Plus all the known
And unknown courage and triumphs
Of Africa
For I was born
At a gathering of the brave!

Today,
The enemy tramples
On the burial place
Of our umbilical cord
With iron boots tanks
And bullet-belts

Oh no!
Please!
I'm not boasting
When I say
I have the most supreme family tree
For every vein in my body
Every artery was infused with blood
Rich
With the history of freedom fighters.
And just for my birth
They all came!
Thulimahashe was there
Remembering Soshangane
Sikhukhuni stood high
And kings standing taller
And more majestic
Than any Hollywood king of kings
Makhado with his elephants head
He remembered Thau ya Ndou
Khama Moshoeshoe
All shielding the lowly victims of
Capital and race
Victims of bloodsucking exploitation
Cetshwayo with unshakeable Shaka
On his mind
All took off
Their cloak of loneliness
Hintsa, Makhanda-Nxele
Their leopard flesh touching close
And all carrying
The spear of the nation!

And then
To think
All of them
All in me

This wealth, this vast greatness
Our country, our people
All in each of us
Whatever our birth
Wherever our birth
Wherever we carry the struggle

For I was born
Crying *Freedom!*
While our working people
The true midwives of our wealth
Midwives of vision, hope
Our future
Tenderly passed me
From hand to joining hand
Of leopard hearts
Blowing into me
The rising strains of
Nkosi Sikelel' "iAfrica"

And
What's my name?
The African National Congress
Of South Africa. Born January
8, 1912.
I gave birth to Umkhonto
We Sizwe on the 16th December
1961

Appendixes

Presidents-General of the ANC

1912-17	Dr J.L. Dube
1917-24	S.M. Makgatho
1924-27	Z.R. Mahabane (first term)
1927-30	J.T. Gumede
1930-36	Dr P. ka Isaka Seme
1937-40	Z.R. Mahabane (second term)
1940-49	Dr A.B. Xuma
1949-52	Dr J.S. Moroka
1952-67	Chief A.J. Lutuli
1967-	O.R. Tambo

Secretaries-General of the ANC

1912-17	Sol T. Plaatje*
1917-19	H.L. Bud Mbelle
1919-23	S. Msane
1923-27	T.D. Mweli Skota
1927-30	E.J. Khaile
1930-36	The Revd E. Mdolomba
1936-49	The Revd J. Calata
1949-55	W. Sisulu
1955-58	O.R. Tambo
1958-69	D. Nokwe
1969-	A. Nzo

* In the period 1914-17 Plaatje was in the United Kingdom, so R.V. Selope Thema took over in 1915.

The Freedom Charter

We, the people of South Africa, declare for all our country and the world to know:

- that South Africa belongs to all who live in it, black and white, and that no government can justly claim authority unless it is based on the will of all the people;
- that our people have been robbed of their birthright to land, liberty and peace by a form of government founded on injustice and inequality;
- that our country will never be prosperous or free until all our people live in brotherhood, enjoying equal rights and opportunities;
- that only a democratic state, based on the will of all the people, can secure to all their birthright without distinction of colour, race, sex or belief;

And therefore, we, the people of South Africa, black and white together - equals, countrymen and brothers - adopt this Freedom Charter. And we pledge ourselves to strive together, sparing neither strength nor courage, until the democratic changes here set out have been won.

The people shall govern!

Every man and woman shall have the right to vote for and to stand as a candidate for all bodies which make laws.

All people shall be entitled to take part in the administration of the country.

The rights of the people shall be the same, regardless of race, colour or sex.

All bodies of minority rule, advisory boards, councils and authorities shall be replaced by democratic organs of self-government.

All national groups shall have equal rights!

There shall be equal status in the bodies of state, in the courts and in the schools for all national groups and races.

All people shall have equal right to use their own languages, and to develop their own folk culture and customs.

All national groups shall be protected by law against insults to their race and national pride.

The preaching and practice of national, race or colour discrimination and contempt shall be a punishable crime.

All apartheid laws and practices shall be set aside.

The people shall share in the country's wealth!

The national wealth of our country, the heritage of all South Africans, shall be restored to the people.

The mineral wealth beneath the soil, the banks and monopoly industry shall be transferred to the ownership of the people as a whole.

All other industry and trade shall be controlled to assist the well-being of the people.

All people shall have equal rights to trade where they choose, to manufacture and to enter all trades, crafts and professions.

The land shall be shared among those who work it!

Restrictions of land ownership on a racial basis shall be ended, and all the land redivided amongst those who work it, to banish famine and land hunger.

The state shall help the peasants with implements, seed, tractors and dams to save the soil and assist the tillers.

Freedom of movement shall be guaranteed to all who work on the land.

All shall have the right to occupy land wherever they choose.

People shall not be robbed of their cattle, and forced labour and farm prisons shall be abolished.

All shall be equal before the law!

No one shall be imprisoned, deported or restricted without a fair trial.

No one shall be condemned by the order of any Government official.

The courts shall be representative of all the people.

Imprisonment shall be only for serious crimes against the people, and shall aim at re-education, not vengeance.

The police force and army shall be open to all on an equal basis and shall be the helpers and protectors of the people.

All laws which discriminate on grounds of race, colour or belief shall be repealed.

All shall enjoy equal human rights!

The law shall guarantee to all their right to speak, to organise, to meet together, to publish, to preach, to worship and to educate their children.

The privacy of the house from police raids shall be protected by law.

All shall be free to travel without restriction from countryside to

town, from province to province, and from South Africa abroad.
Pass Laws, permits and all other laws restricting these freedoms shall be abolished.

There shall be work and security!
All who work shall be free to form trade unions, to elect their officers and to make wage agreements with their employers.
The state shall recognise the right and duty of all to work, and to draw full unemployment benefits.
Men and women of all races shall receive equal pay for equal work.
There shall be a forty-hour working week, a national minimum wage, paid annual leave, and sick leave for all workers, and maternity leave on full pay for all working mothers.
Miners, domestic workers, farm workers and civil servants shall have the same rights as all others who work.
Child labour, compound labour, the tot system and contract labour shall be abolished.

The doors of learning and of culture shall be opened!
The Government shall discover, develop and encourage national talent for the enhancement of our cultural life.
All cultural treasures of mankind shall be open to all, by free exchange of books, ideas and contact with other lands.
The aim of education shall be to teach the youth to love their people and their culture, to honour human brotherhood, liberty and peace.
Education shall be free, compulsory, universal and equal for all children.
Higher education and technical training shall be opened to all by means of state allowances and scholarships awarded on the basis of merit.
Adult illiteracy shall be ended by a mass state education plan.
Teachers shall have all the rights of other citizens.
The colour bar in cultural life, in sport and in education shall be abolished.

There shall be houses, security and comfort!
All people shall have the right to live where they choose, to be decently housed, and to bring up their families in comfort and security.
Unused housing space to be made available to the people.
Rent and prices shall be lowered, food plentiful and no one shall go hungry.

A preventative health scheme shall be run by the state.

Free medical care and hospitalization shall be provided for all, with special care for mothers and young children.

Slums shall be demolished, and new suburbs built where all have transport, roads, lighting, playing fields, creches and social centres.

The aged, the orphans, the disabled and the sick shall be cared for by the state.

Rent, leisure and recreation shall be the right of all.

Fenced locations and ghettos shall be abolished, and laws which break up families shall be repealed.

There shall be peace and friendship!

South Africa shall be a fully independent state, which respects the rights and sovereignty of all nations.

South Africa shall strive to maintain world peace and the settlement of all international disputes by negotiation - not war.

Peace and friendship amongst all our people shall be secured by upholding the equal rights, opportunities and status of all.

The people of the protectorates - Basutoland, Bechuanaland and Swaziland - shall be free to decide for themselves their own future.

The right of all the peoples of Africa to independence and self-government shall be recognised, and shall be the basis of close co-operation.

Let all who love their people and their country now say, as we say here:

"These freedoms we will fight for, side by side, throughout our lives, until we have won our liberty."

Adopted at the Congress of the People, Kliptown, South Africa, on 26 June 1955.

Manifesto of Umkhonto we Sizwe, issued on 16 December 1961

Units of Umkhonto we Sizwe today carried out planned attacks against Government installations, particularly those connected with the policy of apartheid and race discrimination.

Umkhonto we Sizwe is a new independent body, formed by Africans. It includes in its ranks South Africans of all races. It is not connected in any way with a so-called "Committee for National Liberation" whose existence has been announced in the press. Umkhonto we Sizwe will carry on the struggle for freedom and democracy by new methods, which are necessary to complement the actions of the established national liberation movement, and our members, jointly and individually, place themselves under the overall political guidance of that movement.

It is, however, well known that the main national liberation organisations in this country have consistently followed a policy of non-violence. They have conducted themselves peaceably at all times, regardless of Government attacks and persecutions upon them, and despite all Government inspired attempts to provoke them to violence. They have done so because the people prefer peaceful methods of change to achieve their aspirations without the suffering and bitterness of civil war. But the people's patience is not endless.

The time comes in the life of any nation when there remains only two choices: submit or fight. That time has now come to South Africa. We shall not submit and we have no choice but to hit back by all means within our power in defence of our people, our future and our freedom.

The Government has interpreted the peacefulness of the movement as weakness; the people's non-violent policies have been taken as a green light for Government violence. Refusal to resort to force has been interpreted by the Government as an invitation to use armed force against the people without reprisals. The methods of Umkhonto we Sizwe mark a break with the past.

We are striking out along a new road for the liberation of the people of this country. The Government policy of force, repression and violence will no longer be met with non-violent resistance only! The choice is not ours; it has been made by the Nationalist Government which has rejected every peaceable demand by the people for rights and freedom and answered every such demand with force and yet more force! Twice in the past 18 months, virtual martial law has been imposed in order to beat down peaceful, non-violent strike action of the people in support of their rights. It is now preparing its forces - enlarg-

214

ing and rearming its armed forces and drawing the white civilian population into commandos and pistol clubs - for full-scale military actions against the people. The nationalist Government has chosen the course of force and massacre, now, deliberately, as it did in Sharpeville.

Umkhonto we Sizwe will be at the front line of the people's defence. It will be the fighting arm of the people against the Government and its policies of race oppression. It will be the striking force of the people for liberty, for rights and for their final liberation! Let the Government, its supporters who put it into power, and those whose passive toleration of reaction keeps it in power, take note of where the Nationalist Government is leading the country!

We of Umkhonto we Sizwe have always sought - as the liberation movement has sought - to achieve liberation, without bloodshed and civil clash. We do still. We hope - even at this late hour - that our first actions will awaken everyone to a realisation of the disastrous situation to which the Nationalist policy is leading. We hope that we will bring the Government and its supporters to their senses before it is too late, so that both Government and its policies can be changed before matters reach the desperate stage of civil war. We believe our actions to be a blow against the Nationalist preparations for civil war and military rule.

In these actions, we are working in the best interests of all the people of this country - black, brown and white - whose future happiness and well-being cannot be attained without the overthrow of the Nationalist Government, the abolition of white supremacy and the winning of liberty, democracy and full national rights and equality for all the people of this country.

We appeal for the support and encouragement of all those South Africans who seek the happiness and freedom of the people in this country.

Afrika Mayibuye!
Issued by Command of Umkhonto we Sizwe.

Chronology:
Important Dates in
South African History

Before 1487 South Africa was inhabited by different ethnic groups of African descent who had contact with each other, lived peacefully, tilled their land, looked after their cattle and involved themselves in other social activities.

1487	Bartholomew Dias (Portuguese) arrives at Mossel Bay, which he calls the Bay of Cowherds.
1497	*5 November:* Vasco de Gama (Portuguese) arrives at St Helena *en route* to India, lands on another coast on Christmas day, calling it Natal, sails to the mouth of a small stream he names Copper River, calling it the Land of the Good People as the local black inhabitants are hospitable.
1647	Haarlem trading ship of the Dutch East India Company is wrecked at Table Bay; crew who survive suggest the establishment of refreshment centre at the Cape of Good Hope. Recognition of the Khoi-Khoi as established and substantial cattle breeders makes this idea attractive.
1652	Jan van Riebeeck (Dutch) arrives to set up the refreshment station.
1657	First recording of slaves at the Cape. Settlement of so-called Free Burghers (independent colonial farmers) on Khoi land in the Liesbeek valley. Each are given a farm of 28 acres free of tax for 12 years by the settlers.
1659	Chief Autshumayo, leader of the Khoi-Khoi, leads the first battles against the seizure by van Riebeeck of the best pasture lands in the Cape Peninsula.
1662	War of resistance is fought by the Khoi in defence of their land.

1673-77	A further war of resistance is fought by the Khoi led by Chief Gonnama over the attempt to dispossess them of their land.
1687	Fever epidemic spreads through the Khoi people, killing many.
1702	First major military clash between trekboers and the Xhosa people near the banks of the Fish river.
1713	Smallpox - the white man's disease - wipes out thousands of Khoi people.
1770	The Gamtoos river is unilaterally declared the eastern boundary of the Cape by the Dutch governors.
1774	From the time of the trekboers' arrival, wars take place, and this period sees the San fighting wars of resistance against the policy of extermination. The San are regarded as outlaws. The Cape government offers rewards of £3 per head for San of any age and either sex captured alive and handed to serve life imprisonment on Robben Island, then, as now, an island prison.
1779-92	War of resistance is fought by the Xhosa against advancing Boers. They succeed in remaining in the area called Zuurveld.
1787	Birth of Shaka, pioneer nation-builder who united different ethnic groups who were later called the Zulus. Shaka's military expertise is legendary, and he is reported to have had up to 80 000 men in a standing army.
1793	Xhosa war of resistance in which the Xhosa manage to regain some land as far into the Cape Colony as the Swartkops river.
1803	In this Xhosa war of resistance the people manage to maintain their position in the Zuurveld.
1806	Britain takes over the Cape from the Dutch with a policy to provide military aid to the Boer commandos.
1808	Slave revolt attacks 5 000 Cape Town soldiers. One of many such revolts which results in the hanging of five leaders with 50 participants flogged and sentenced to life imprisonment in chains.
1811	Xhosa war of resistance and the people are again driven back across the Fish river.
1818-19	Xhosa war of resistance led by Makanda. Ten thousand warriors attack Grahamstown, but fail due to superior weaponry used by the colonizers. Makanda is sentenced to life imprisonment on Robben Island. After being in prison for one year, on Christmas Day, the prisoners

	rise up, overpower the guards and take away their guns. They seize a boat and head for Blaauwberg beach. The boat capsizes, but all manage to swim to shore. However, Makanda is swept off the rocks and drowned.
1824	Mosheoshoe, pioneer nation builder who united the Sotho-speaking people, fortifies Thaba Bosigu, his mountain stronghold, against constant aggression by the Boers.
1825	Slave uprising in Worcester which lasts until the slaves are defeated militarily.
1834	Xhosa war of resistance - the colonizers succeed in pushing the Xhosa back across the Kei river and enter the country of the people led by Hintsa.
1836	Resistance by the Tsonga people of the north-eastern Transvaal defeats the early expeditions led by Van Rensburg. Mzilikazi leads his people into battle against the advancing Boers, defeating them at the battle of Vegkop.
1837	Mzilikazi and his followers retreat across the Limpopo river after the Boers are reinforced from the Cape.
1838	*February:* Dingaan defends his land and his people against the invading Boers, striking back at Piet Retief and his troops when they come to Dingaan's headquarters at Mgungundlovu in Natal to demand his surrender. *16 December:* Battle of Blood river (Zulu name is Ncome), also known as Dingaan's Day on which a fierce battle is fought against invading Boers. Today we call it Heroes' Day.
1845-75	Sir Theophilius Shepstone, on behalf of Britain, introduces the system of segregation throughout Natal.
1845	Afrikaaners settle on the independent land of the Griquas, resulting in open warfare. Again Britain intervenes on the side of the Boers.
1846-48	Xhosa war of resistance, also known as the War of the Axe.
1849	Britain lays down the "Warden Line" in which a large area of the Orange Free State is "presented" to the Boers.
1850-52	Xhosa war of resistance - the War of Umlanjeni — resulting in more conquest of land by the colonizers.
1851	A British attack is led by Warden on Moletsane's villages on Viervoet mountain. With the help of Moshoeshoe, the British are crushingly defeated.

1852	The Pedi people of the eastern Transvaal, under the leadership of Sekwati, fight off sustained Boer attacks. Boer commandos attack the villages of Kwenga and Ngwaketse and ravage crops. Chief Sechele at Dimawe becomes the central figure of resistance to this aggression The Ngwaketse under Chief Gaseitsiwe and the Ngwato led by Chief Sikgoma and Macheng in the Shoshong region, also resist fiercely.
1856	Call for Xhosa people's rising by Nongqause and subsequent killing of the cattle, as a ritual act to help get rid of the colonizers, which creates famine over large areas of the eastern Cape.
1858	Moshoeshoe's forces resist, with the use of firearms. Boers attack Thaba Bosigu but are driven off.
1860	Import of indentured labour to work in the Natal sugar fields from India starts.
1865	Boers aggressively occupy part of Basutoland (now Lesotho) and launch further attacks on Thaba Bosigu, but are again driven off.
1867	The people of Venda defeat the Boers, forcing them to retreat from the Soutpansberg.
1868	Moshoeshoe agrees to annexation of Basutoland rather than suffer defeat by the Boers. Although Basutoland becomes part of the British empire, the people determinedly fight to retain their arms.
1873	Britain wages a savage war against the Hlubi people under the leadership of Langalibaleie in Natal.
1878	British and Boer once more combine to defeat the resistance of the people, this time in a war against Sekhukhuni in the Transvaal.
1879	Battle of Isandhlwana - the severest defeat of British imperial might recorded at the time when the British forces are routed by warriors of King Cetswayo. Cape Government again robs the people of their land by annexing parts of the Eastern Cape, Idutywa, Griqualand East, and African areas including Pondoland.
1880	Military defeat of the Zulu people by the British who move into Zululand in force and rob the people of their independence. The British attempt to disarm the Basuto people. Led by Moshupa and Lerodi, the people resist strongly and are more than a match for the British soldiers. They are allowed to keep their arms.

1882	African workers enter the field of class organization and struggle, coming out on strike for higher wages.
	Imbumba Yama Afrika is established in the eastern Cape. It is the first record of political organization set up by teachers, clergymen and others.
1884	Annexure of Namibia by Germany.
	Launching of the first African political newspaper in South Africa, *Imvo Zabantsundu*, edited by John Tengo Jabavu. Before that there were numerous religious papers owned by missionaries produced for their African converts.
1886	Intensification of the massive search for cheap labour, following the discovery of gold on the Witwatersrand.
1887	Annexation of Zululand to the British empire.
1889	Dinizulu arrested for organizing continued resistance and banished to St Helena Island.
1890	Invasion of Mashonaland (in present-day Zimbabwe) by settlers of Rhodes's British South Africa Company.
1893	Arrival of Mahatma Gandhi in South Africa.
1895	Britain annexes southern Botswana as "British Bechuanaland".
1896-97	Fierce wars of resistance fought by the people of present-day Zimbabwe.
1897	Britain hands Zululand over to Natal. Enoch Sontonga, gifted songwriter and teacher at a Methodist Mission School, writes the first stanza of our national anthem, Nkosi Sikelel'i Afrika. Two years later at an induction ceremony in Nancefield the anthem is sung in public for the first time. A few years later the famous Xhosa poet, S.E.K. Mqhayi, adds seven stanzas. The full text is published in 1927 in *Umthetheli wa Bantu*. During the same year, it is also published in the book *Imihobe nezi Bongo*.
1898	African wars of resistance culminate in the defeat of Venda people.
1899	*October:* Outbreak of the Anglo-Boer war.
1902	African People's Organization (APO) founded, the pioneer political movement among the coloured people. Dr Abdul Abdurahman was for many years its chief spokesman.
	31 May: Treaty of Vereeniging signed between the British Imperialists and the defeated Boers.
1904	Chinese labourers imported to the Rand mines.

1906	Pass laws for Indians introduced in the Transvaal. Gandhi leads the passive resistance campaign. The Bambata Rebellion in protest against the imposition of a hut and dog tax and against the furnishing of information for the census. Over 4 000 people die in the uprising which is ruthlessly suppressed.
1909	Delegation of African leaders goes to Britain in a vain attempt to prevent the British parliament approving the South Africa Act.
1910	The conceding of "independence" to South Africa in 1910 is designed in the interests of imperialism and power is transferred into the hands of the white minority to the exclusion of the black majority.
1912	*8 January:* Founding of the African National Congress.
1913	African women resist the imposition of residential passes by the Orange Free State municipality, organizing heroic passive resistance and thereby forcing the municipality to rescind its measures. Many women jailed. African miners strike at Jagersfontein diamond mine after one of their fellow workers is kicked to death by a white overseer. White employees suppress the strike called to protest at the brutality meted out to mineworkers. Eleven African mineworkers killed and 37 injured.
1915	The foundation of the International Socialist League (ISL) by the "anti war" internationalist section who broke away from the white Labour Party. It stood for full rights for all and for socialism, embracing all South Africans without distinction of colour or class. *21 December*: Strike of 2 800 African miners at the Van Rhyn Deep Mines in a bid to redress some of their grievances.
1917	The Industrial Workers of Africa founded by the ISL in Johannesburg - the first industrial African trade union to be formed.
1918	Antipass campaign by women ends in triumph. Led by the then Bantu Women's League of South Africa - the Women's Branch of the ANC, formed by Charlotte Maxeke. *May:* Bucket strike in which African sanitary workers in Johannesburg down buckets demanding a six pence rise. Strikers, 152 of them, are sentenced to two months hard labour for breach of contract under the Masters and Servants Act. The ANC launches a campaign for the

release of the prisoners which soon turns into a campaign for a general wage increase of one shilling a day and the threat of a general strike. The strikers are released.

1919 ANC organizes a campaign on the Rand against the pass laws.

African miners (70 000) strike against their whole status and impoverished existence. The strike is highly disciplined and organized and an alarmed government throws police cordons around each of the compounds preventing co-ordination of demands and actions. Troops break through the workers' barricades, with bayonets, killing three and wounding 40 people. Police and armed white civilians attack a meeting of solidarity with the striking miners, killing eight and wounding 80 people.

January: The Industrial Commercial Union of South Africa (ICU) is founded in Cape Town; at its height embracing workers nationwide.

1921 *24 May:* Bulhoek Massacre takes place near Queenstown when Colonel Theodore Truter, a police commissioner, leads six squadrons, a machine gun and an artillery detachment, against the Israelite religious sect collected at their annual gathering on the land of their leader and prophet, Enoch Mgijima, at Ntabalanga. The slaughter takes 10 minutes and costs 190 lives. Mgijima and his two brothers are sentenced to six years. Their crime was the refusal to demolish huts built on crown land and defiance of white authority.

30 July: Formation of the Communist Party (CP) of South Africa.

June: Non-European Convention held in Kimberley as a climax to a campaign of protest meetings and resolutions against the pass laws and the Hertzog Bills, first formulated in 1925, which propose to remove the limited franchise the Cape Africans enjoyed and define once and for all the area to be allocated to the Africans in the Native Land and Trust Bill. It is attended by more than 100 delegates representing the ANC, the APO, the Indian Congress, the Native Voters Association, the Bantu Union and religious and welfare societies from all over Southern Africa. Dr Abdurahman elected to the chair.

16 December: The CP calls for a united front campaign against the pass laws, culminating in the burning of passes throughout the country on 16 December, Dingaan's Day.

Johannes Nkosi and three other African workers attending a demonstration in Durban are shot, stabbed and beaten to death by police.

1935 The National Liberation League for Equality, Land and Freedom launched with Mrs Zaibuniasa (Cissy) Gool as President and James la Guma as General Secretary. Its foundation conference adopts a programme and constitution pledged to "unite all individuals organizations and other bodies in agreement with the programme of the League to struggle for complete social, political and economic equality of Non-Europeans with Europeans in South Africa", reflecting the need for unity against the white minority.

16 December: At the All-African National Convention, 400 delegates gather in Bloemfontein to oppose the Hertzog Bills.

15-16 December: Statement by ANC Conference in Bloemfontein: "Unless and until the government grants the Africans full democratic and citizenship rights, the ANC is not prepared to advise the Africans to participate in the present war [the Second World War] in any capacity."

1941 Council for Non-European Trade Unions founded with Gana Makabeni as President and D. Gosani as Secretary.

August: Policy and platform statement of the ANC issued by Dr Xuma in Inkululeko calling for racial unity, the ANC being the mouthpiece of the African people throughout South Africa.

1943 Foundation of ANC Women's League.

1945 *18 December:* ANC annual conference presents the African Claims in South Africa.

1943-44 Formation of the ANC Youth League, headed by Anton Lambede, Nelson Mandela, O.R. Tambo, Walter Sisulu, A. P. Mda and others.

1944-45 Anti-pass campaigns carry the struggle for national liberation forward.

1946 *13 June:* Indian Passive Resistance campaign led by Y. M. Dadoo and Dr G. M. Naicker against the Asiatic Land Tenure and Indian Representation Act (Ghetto Act) enacted by the Smuts government commences.

12-19 August: African miners (100 000) strike from the East to the West Rand. Police, with bayonets draw, charge and open fire, forcing the workers back underground. Hundreds of workers killed and injured.

No official figures of dead released and the strike is broken by the lawlessness and ruthlessness of the state. Kotane, Dadoo, Bunting, Fischer, J. B. Marks and Harmel and 46 others are accused of "conspiracy" to bring about the miners' strike.

1947   *March:* Xuma-Naicker-Dadoo Pact is signed on behalf of the ANC, and the Natal and Transvaal Indian Congress, and lays a firm foundation for the fighting Congress Alliance, the national liberation front of our country.

1948   The Nationalist Party comes to power, entrenching white minority fascist domination of our country.

1949   ANC conference adopts the Programme of Action - strikes, boycotts and resistance. Dr Moroko (President) and Walter Sisulu (Secretary) are elected to implement this plan, which outlines the methods to be used to achieve the right to self-determination of the African people.

1950   At Witzieshoek in the Orange Free State peasants come out in rebellion against the state policy of cattle culling, shortage of land and starvation. Many are killed by the racist police.
1 May: General strike against all discriminatory laws and for full franchise rights for all takes place. Trigger-happy police open fire in Alexandra township and other areas on the Reef, killing 18 and wounding 30. Later in May the Unlawful Organizations Bill is introduced banning the Communist Party of South Africa.
26 June: A massive campaign is called by the ANC as an act of national mourning and protest at the police killing of 1 May. Since then June 26 - a day of nationwide protests and strikes - has been observed annually as South Africa Freedom Day.

1951   Regime introduces legislation to remove the Coloured people of the Cape Province from the voters' roll.

1952   Suppression of Communism Act promulgated followed by a whole series of other repressive measures.
26 June: The ANC and the South African Indian Congress launch the nationwide campaign for the Defiance of Unjust Laws.
December: Chief A. J. Luthuli elected as President-General of the ANC.
July: Sisulu, Nokwe and others leave South Africa without passports to visit various overseas countries, including Romania, USSR and China.

September: Coloured Peoples' Organisation, later the Coloured Peoples' Congress, under the presidency of James la Guma, is formed in Cape Town as successor to the APO.

October: Congress of Democrats of white supporters is established, committed to upholding Congress policies.

December: Annual Conference of ANC adopts a proposal for summoning a congress of the people of South Africa.

1954 *17 April:* Birth of the Federation of South Africa Women.

1955 *February:* Over 60 000 people living in Johannesburg's Western Areas are removed at gunpoint in a massive military-style operation as part of the regime's policy of Group Areas. The area is declared "white" and given the name "Triumph".

Moses Kotane and Maulvi Cachalia leave the country without passports to attend the Asia-Africa Conference in Bandung, Indonesia, as representatives of the South African Liberation movement.

5 March: Formation of the South African Congress of Trade Unions (SACTU), the first non-racial trade union. It later adopts the Freedom Charter and becomes a member of the Congress Alliance.

April: ANC launches massive boycott of Bantu education and schools by both teachers and pupils, together with an attempt to organize an alternative system of education.

26 June: Congress of the People takes place at Kliptown after months of organizing. The Freedom Charter is adopted. At the Congress, Chief A. J. Lutuli, Dr Y. M. Dadoo and Father Trevor Huddleston are each awarded Isitwalandwe/Seaparankoe, the nation's highest honour, given by the ANC.

9 August: Over 20 000 women march on Pretoria in militant struggle against the extension of passes to African women.

The arrest of 156 leaders of the Congress movement throughout the country on a charge of High Treason.

1957 A Pound-a-Day national minimum wage campaign launched following the Alexandra Bus Boycott of 1957.

1958 Massive unrest erupts in Zeerust following the women's destruction of their pass books.

May: The people of Sekhukhuniland revolt against the imposition of "Bantu" authorities as part of the first step towards the creation of a Bantustan and the balkanization of our country. Sixteen peasants, including one woman, are executed by the regime in the course of brutal state repression. Similar battles fought in Zululand, Pondoland and Tembuland.

31 May: Beginning of the Potato Boycott directed against the savage exploitation of African farm labour.

October: The first issue of the African Communist, journal of the South African Communist Party is introduced.

1960   *January:* One of the worst disasters in mining history: 440 miners entombed at Clydesdale colliery, Coalbrook - a reminder of the hardship and suffering endured by the black worker.

February: Protests and open rebellion break out in Pondoland.

21 March: Sharpeville massacre, in which 69 people are killed and many more injured.

28 March: O. R. Tambo leaves South Africa illegally on the instruction of the ANC to carry on work outside the country. The ANC calls a nationwide stay-at-home in protest at the Sharpeville massacre. Pass books are burned in countless bonfires.

30 March: Regime declares a state of emergency and arrests over 2 000 people. Unlawful Organisations Act used to ban the ANC and PAC.

14 July: The CP, following its dissolution in 1950, announces its functioning as the SACP, operating underground.

1961   *March:* After a trial lasting over four years the Treason Trial defendants are found not guilty and discharged. All-in African Conference with 1 400 delegates held in Pietermaritzburg under the leadership of Nelson Mandela. Conference calls for a national convention to decide on a new constitution.

31 May: Country placed on a war footing to smash the nationwide strike called to protest against the establishment of the so-called Republic of South Africa.

26 June: Mandela declares the next stage of the struggle to be one of non-collaboration and states that he will remain underground to lead it. He will continue to act as the spokesman for the National Action Council.

11 December: Chief A. J. Lutuli, President-General of the ANC, receives the Nobel Peace Prize in Oslo and declares "There can be no peace until the forces of oppression are overthrown."

16 December: Formation of Umkhonto we Sizwe, the people's army.

1962 The road to South African Freedom - the programme of the SACP, is adopted at its fifth national conference held illegally in Johannesburg.

January: Mandela secretly leaves South Africa to participate in the conference of the Pan African Freedom Movement of East, Central and Southern Africa is Addis Ababa. He also visits several other countries, receives military training and returns to South Africa to continue the struggle underground.

September: The Congress of Democrats is banned under the Suppression of Communism Act.

October: ANC Conference held in Botswana. Delegates come from all over South Africa and from abroad.

1963 *January:* Regime places blanket ban on all named and banned people. ANC decides to send some leading cadres abroad to set up external missions of the ANC and reinforce the work being done by the liberation movement from abroad.

October-June: The Rivonia Trial takes place, which results in Mandela, Mbeki, Sisulu, Goldberg, Kathrada, Mhlaba, Mlangeni and Motsoaledi being sentenced to life imprisonment.

1964 *6 November:* Mini, Mkaba and Khayingo, three prominent trade union leaders from the eastern Cape, are executed.

1967 *21 July:* Chief A. J. Lutuli, President-General of the ANC, feared and hated by the apartheid regime, is killed in highly suspicious circumstances.

30-31 July: The "Lutuli Detachment", comprising ZAPU and ANC guerrillas, crosses the Zambezi into Rhodesia at the start of the Wankie and Sipolilo battles which last until late 1968.

1969 *May:* Seven-day ANC consultative conference held in Morogoro, Tanzania. The main aim is to bring about a qualitative change in the organizational structure of the movement in keeping with the new situation, namely a revolutionary people's war.

July: Inaugural conference of the South African Students Organization (SASO) held at Turfloop University.

1973 Waves of massive strikes in Natal shake the apartheid regime.

1975   *8 May:* Bram Fischer dies in prison while serving a life
sentence for his consistent and fierce opposition to the
racist regime in the struggle for the national liberation
and social emancipation of all South Africans. The
regime refuse to release his ashes to his family.

25 June: Independence of Mozambique proclaimed under
the leadership of Frelimo after a long and bitter war
culminating in the collapse of Portuguese colonialism in
Africa.

9 August: On the occasion of his seventieth birthday
Moses Kotane is awarded Isitwalandwe/Seaparankoe, the
nation's highest honour.

11 November: The People's Republic of Angola is born
during a massive multi-pronged invasion of the country
by the South African racist army and other neo-colonial
forces.

1976   *27 March:* The South African invading army defeated and
humiliated by the Angolan people's armed forces, retreats
into neighbouring Namibia.

16 June: The Soweto massacre and uprising. About 1 000
children killed in Soweto and in hundreds of other parts
of the country during the ensuing months of nationwide
resistance.

12 September: Death in detention of Steve Biko. This
murder drew attention to not only the bestiality of the
SA Police, but also to the corruption of the medical
profession, whose members had evidently been issuing,
false death certificates to cover such assassinations.

October: Banning of 17 organizations, including the
World and Weekend World newspapers, in massive state
repression of people's resistance.

1979   Declared the Year of the Spear in tribute to our history of
unbroken resistance as symbolized by the Battle of
Isandelwana on 22 January 1879.

6 April: Solomon Mahlangu, people's hero, is hanged in
Pretoria.

1980   Declared the Year of the Charter, to mark the twenty-fifth
anniversary of the adoption of the Freedom Charter at
the Congress of the People on June 26, 1955, SACTU,
on its twenty-fifth anniversary, declared 1980 The Year
of the Worker.

January: The Silverton siege: ANC guerrillas intercepted

228

en route to fulfil a mission, take refuge in a bank in Silverton, Pretoria. Explaining the policies of the ANC to the hostages, they pledge not to hurt them but demand the release of Nelson Mandela. In a bungled operation the police storm the bank, and in the ensuing shoot-out the police kill some hostages as well as the three guerrillas. But some police are also killed, a fact held as a tightly guarded secret by the regime.

March: The *Sunday Post* launches a nationwide campaign for the release of Nelson Mandela, correctly interpreting the demands of the vast majority of the people in our country and re-inforcing prior calls by the international ommunity for the release of the people's leaders and all political prisoners held in South African jails. The campaign receives tremendous support both nationally and internationally, with at least 15 million people signing the petition forms demanding Mandela's release.

13 March: Death of Lilian Masediba Ngoyi at the age of 68. Ma-Ngoyi as she was affectionately known by all her comrades in the struggle and millions of the followers of the ANC has always been in the front ranks of our revolutionary struggle, occupying leading positions as the first President of the ANC Women's League and as second President of the Federation of South African Women. She was also a leading member of the National Executive Committee of the ANC.

18 April: Zimbabwe becomes independent, marking the end of a long and bloody struggle.

1 June: Flames of freedom, the biggest ever seen in South Africa, leap into the skies as Umkhonto we Sizwe strikes at the Sasol complex, causing damage estimated at R66 million, originally announced as R6.5 million.

26 June: ANC award Isitwalandwe/Seaparankoe to Govan Mbeki and to Bishop Ambrose Reeves.

14 November: Nelson Mandela awarded the Jawaharlal Nehru Award for International Understanding, received on his behalf by President O. R. Tambo.

28 November: At a ceremony at the headquarters of the International Committee of the Red Cross, the ANC declares its adherence to the Geneva Conventions of 1949 and their Protocol one of 1977 on the humanitarian conduct of war.

'81   Declared the Year of the Youth by the ANC in tribute

229

to the heroism of South African youth.

30 January: A commando group of the South African army raids Mozambique, brutally assassinates 12 ANC members in Maputo, and kidnaps three others.

14 February: Reacting to the raid, President Samora Machel addresses a huge public rally in Maputo. In the course of his historic speech he declares: "Apartheid is a form of colonialism. For this reason we (as former victims of the colonialism) understand profoundly the just cause of the South African people; we stand in firm solidarity with the South African people, in firm solidarity with the ANC. The ANC is one of the beacons in Africa that has inspired the national liberation struggle against racism and colonial domination, true fertile ground in which our own liberation struggle took root. It is the patrimony and pride of our continent, the embodiment of the indestructible will of the people for their liberation".

11 March: Govan Mbeki is honoured by the International Organization of Journalists, and presented with the Julius Fucik Award.

May: Nationwide protest and boycotts of the regime's celebrations of 20 years of the white republic. The people declare: "There is nothing to celebrate! Racist Republic - No! People's Republic - Yes!"

June: Building on the total nationwide rejection of the regime's so-called "republic celebrations", the people mark the fifth anniversary of the 1976 uprisings, calling for a people's government based on the Freedom Charter. The demand is echoed through the length and breadth of South Africa, the flag of the regime being burnt and the black, green and gold of the ANC flag unfurling in many areas. Mass detentions and bannings of leaders and militants take place, roadblocks are set up, heavily armed police and soldiers patrol the streets and seal off the townships. A garrison state exists. Umkhonto we Sizwe strikes at strategic targets, blowing up railway lines and engaging the enemy.

30 July: The sixtieth anniversary of the founding the the CP.

6 August: The twenty-fifth anniversary of the historic march on Pretoria by more than 20 000 women of all races in protest against the pass laws for women.

16 December: Umkhonto we Sizwe, the people's army,

celebrates its twentieth anniversary.

1982	*8 January:* The seventieth anniversary of the formation of the ANC.

Apartheid regime raids Maseru, Lesotho, killing 42 people, mostly Lesotho residents.

Anti South African Indian Council Campaign marks the consolidation of community action.

Attack on Koeberg nuclear power plant, Cape Town.

1983 Buthelezi's impis (armed thugs) attack Ngoye University campus, killing for showing "disrespect" towards Gatsha Buthelezi.

Pretoria car bomb explodes killing SADF and SAP personnel, ANC claims responsibility.

14 June: The United Democratic Front (UDF) formed in Cape Town.

Pretoria raid on Gaborone, Botswana, ANC personnel are killed.

Bomb in Airforce Headquarters in Pretoria.

1984 Botha and Machel sign the Nkomati Accord.

Bishop Tutu awarded the Nobel Peace Prize.

South African Defence Force invades Sebokeng Township — marks the beginning of nationwide unrest.

The biggest stay-away since the 1950s. Over a million workers and students stage a joint protest against the troops' presence in the townships and schools, rent increases and so on.

1985 State of emergency declared.

Another Pretoria raid on Lesotho followed by a coup in which Jonathan Leabua falls.

Amamzimtoti bomb attack.

Congress of South African Trade Unions (COSATU) formed with 33 member unions and half a million members.

ANC consultative conference held in Zambia. Attended by delegates from both inside and outside the country.

1986 Second state of emergency declared.

Andrew Zondo, responsible for Amamzimtoti bomb attack, hung.

1987 ANC celebrates its 75th anniversary.

References

Preface

1 Mokgethi Motlhabi, *The Theory and Practice of Black Resistance to Apartheid: A Social-Ethical Analysis* (Johannesburg, 1984), pp. 38 and 71.
2 Tom Lodge, *Black Politics in South Africa since 1945* (London, 1983), p. 343.

A note on class and colour in South Africa

1 J. Slovo, "South Africa: No Middle Road", in R. Segal (ed.), *Southern Africa: The New Politics of Revolution* (Harmondsworth, 1975), p. 128.

Chapter 1 Sources of Inspiration

1 *Sechaba* (London) 12(4) (1978), p. 53.
2 L. Forman, "The Birth of African Nationalism", *Africa South in Exile* (London), 5(2) (Jan.-Mar. 1961), p. 49.
3 *The African Communist* (London), 44(1) (1971), p. 56.
4 L. Forman, *Chapters in the History of the March to Freedom* (Cape Town, 1959), p. 6.
5 Forman, "African Nationalism".
6 E. Webster (ed.), *Essays in Southern African Labour History* (Johannesburg, 1978), *Ravan Labour Studies 1*, p. 10.
7 Ibid.
8 Ibid., fn. 3.
9 P. Warwick, in Webster, *Southern African Labour History*.
10 Ibid., p. 21.
11 S. Moroney, in Webster, *Southern African Labour History*, p. 35.
12 Warwick, p. 25.
13 Ibid.

14 Moroney, p. 38.
15 Ibid., p. 41.
16 John Knox Bokwe, *Ntsikana: The Story of an African Convert* (Lovedale, 1914), p. 13.
17 Ibid., p. 133.
18 D. Williams, "Tiyo Soga", in C. Saunders (ed.), *Black Leaders in Southern African History* (London, 1979), p. 128.
19 Ibid., p. 133.
20 Ibid., p. 136.
21 Ibid., p. 139.
22 C. Saunders, "Tile and the Thembu Church: Politics and Independency on the Cape Eastern Frontier in the Late Nineteenth Century", *Journal of African History*, XI(4) (1970), p. 553.
23 Ibid., p. 557
24 Ibid., p. 558.
25 B.G.M. Sundkler, *Bantu Prophets in South Africa* (London, 1961).
26 Saunders, "Tile and the Thembu Church", p. 569.
27 Ibid.
28 E. Roux, *Time Longer than Rope: A History of the Black Man's Struggle for Freedom in South Africa* (Wisconsin, 1978), p. 77.
29 Sundkler, Bantu Prophets, p. 39.
30 Ibid.
31 Ibid.
32 Sundkler, Bantu Prophets, p. 33.
33 Ibid., p. 34.
34 Ibid., p. 56.
35 *Sechaba* (Aug. 1980).
36 T. Karis and G.M. Carter (eds.), *From Protest to Challenge: A Documentary History of African Politics in South Africa 1882-1964* (California, 1972), vol.1, p. 40.
37 Ibid., p. 41.
38 Ibid., p. 50.
39 See W.G. Bennie, *Imibengo* (Lovedale, 1949).
40 E. B. Rosenthal, *Bantu Journalism in South Africa* (Johannesburg, n.d.), p. 4.
41 Ibid.
42 Ibid.
43 Ibid., p. 5.
44 *Sechaba* (Dec. 1981), p. 24.
45 B. Willan, *Sol Plaatje: South African Nationalist 1872-1932* (London, 1984), p. 99-100.
46 See Rosenthal, *Bantu Journalism*.

47 Ibid., p. 6.
48 Ibid., p. 7.
49 Ibid., p. 8.
50 S.T. Plaatje, *Native Life in South Africa before and since the European War and the Boer Rebellion* (London, 1916 and Braamfontein, 1982), p. 165.
51 Rosenthal, *Bantu Journalism,* p. 8.
52 L.D. Ngcongco, "John Tengo Jabavu, 1859-1921", in Saunders, *Black Leaders,* p. 151.
53 Plaatje, *Native Life.*
54 Ibid.
55 Ibid., pp. 165-6.
56 Roux, *Time Longer than Rope,* p. 111.
57 Ngcongco, "Jabavu", p. 154.
58 Ibid., p. 153.
59 Ibid., p. 155.
60 Roux, *Time Longer than Rope,* p. 111.
61 See R.V. Selope Thema, unpublished autobiography, 1935, Institute of Commonwealth Studies Archives, London.
62 Ibid., p. 47.
63 Ibid.
64 L. Kuper, *An African Bourgeoisie: Race, Class and Politics in South Africa* (London, 1965), p. 193.
65 Cited in S. Marks, "Harriette Colenso and the Zulus 1874-1913", *Journal of African History,* IV(3) (1963).
66 Karis and Carter, *From Protest to Challenge*, p. 29.
67 Ibid., p. 30.
68 Ibid., p. 18.
69 Ibid., pp. 35-6.
70 Ibid., p. 42.
71 Ibid., p. 9.
72 Ibid.
73 L. Bown and M. Crowder (eds.), *The Proceedings of the First International Congress of Africanists, Accra 11-18 December 1962* (London, 1964), with a foreword by K. Onwaka Dike, President of the Congress 1961-66, p. 12.
74 Ibid.
75 Sundkler, *Bantu Prophets,* p. 43.
76 P. Walshe, *The Rise of African Nationalism in South Africa: The African National Congress 1912-1952* (Berkeley, 1971), p. 14.
77 Xuma Papers, Institute of Commonwealth Studies Archives, London.
78 Walshe, *African Nationalism in SA.*

79   Karis and Carter, *From Protest to Challenge*, p. 53.
80   Walshe, *African Nationalism in SA*, p. 22.
81   H.J. and R.E. Simons, *Class and Colour in South Africa 1850-1950* (Harmondsworth, 1969), pp. 111-12.
82   Lionel Forman papers.
83   Ibid.
84   Ibid.
85   Ibid.
86   Ibid.
87   Ibid.
88   Ibid.
89   Ibid.
90   Ibid.
91   *Sechaba* (Feb. 1985), p. 21.
92   Ibid.
93   Cited in the Forman Papers.
94   S. Marks, *Reluctant Rebellion: The 1906-8 Disturbances in Natal* (Oxford, 1970), p. 214.
95   In B. Bozzoli (ed.), *Town and Countryside in the Transvaal: Capitalist Penetration and Popular Response* (Johannesburg, 1983), *History Workshop 2*, p. 241.
96   Ibid., p. 267, fn. 75.

Chapter 2 The Formation of the African
National Congress

1   D.D.T. Jabavu, *Native Disabilities in South Africa* (Lovedale, 1932).
2   *Imvo Zabantsundu*, 24 October 1911, in T. Karis and G.M. Carter *From Protest to Challenge: A Documentary History of African Politics in South Africa 1882-1964* (California, 1972) vol. 1, p. 72.
3   Ibid.
4   B. Willan, *Sol Plaatje: South African Nationalist 1872-1932* (London, 1984), p. 139.
5   Ibid., pp. 150-1.
6   Ibid.
7   P. Walshe, *The Rise of African Nationalism in South Africa: The African National Congress 1912-1952* (Berkeley, 1971), p. 14.
8   S. Marks, *Reluctant Rebellion: The 1906-8 Disturbances in Natal* (Oxford, 1970), p. 365.
9   Willan, *Sol Plaatje*, p. 155.
10   *Sechaba* (Dec. 1981), p. 26.
11   *The African Communist* 48(1) (1972).

12   Xuma Papers, Institute of Commonwealth Studies Archives, London.
13   Sol T. Plaatje, *Native Life in South Africa before and since the European War and the Boer Rebellion* (Cape Town, 1982), p. 21.
14   Ibid., pp. 89-90.
15   Ibid., p. 199.
16   Ibid., p. 202.
17   Ibid.
18   See I.L. Walker and B. Weinbren, *2,000 Casualties: A History of the Trade Unions and the Labour Movement in the Union of South Africa* (Johannesburg, 1961), pp. 32-58.
19   Plaatje, *Native Life in SA*, p. 203.
20   Ibid., p. 209.
21   *Sechaba* (Dec. 1981), p. 27.
22   Willian, Sol Plaatje, p. 177.
23   Ibid., p. 177.
24   Plaatje, *Native Life in SA*, p. 300.
25   Ibid., p. 301.
26   Ibid.
27   A.C. Jordan, *Towards an African Literature: The Emergence of Literary Form in Xhosa* (Berkeley, 1972), pp. 112-13.
28   Willan, *Sol Plaatje,* p. 212.
29   Deutsches Zentralarchiv (Potsdam), R. Kol AII., Gr. 13, Bd 3., B1.95.
30   *Umsebenzi,* 1 August, 1932.
31   Walshe, *African Nationalism in SA.*, p. 53.
32   Willan, *Sol Plaatje.*
33   Plaatje, *Native Life in SA,* p. 133.
34   Ibid., p. 115.
35   Ibid., p. 114.
36   Ibid.
37   Ibid., p. 115.
38   *Sechaba* (Aug. 1980), p. 24.
39   L. Forman, *Chapters in the History of the March to Freedom* (Cape Town, 1959), a *New Age* pamphlet, p. 19.
40   Karis and Carter, *From Protest to Challenge.*
41   Xuma papers
42   J. Simons "Our Freedom Charter", *Sechaba* (June, 1985), p. 9.
43   Karis and Carter, *From Protest to Challenge,* p. 76.
44   *The African Communist,* 15 (Oct.-Dec. 1963).
45   Willan, *Sol Plaatje,* p. 124.
46   Ibid., p. 244.
47   Ibid., p. 203.

48   G.M.E. Leistner and W.J. Breytenbach, *The Black Worker of South Africa* (Pretoria, 1975), pp. 87-8.
49   Forman, *March to Freedom*, p. 24.
50   *The International* (Johannesburg), 10 September 1915.
51   M. Harmel, "Trade Unions Face the Future", in *Liberation: A Journal of Democratic Discussions* (Johannesburg), 10 (1954).
52   Ibid., p. 6.
53   Forman, *March to Freedom*, p. 28.
54   Ibid., p. 29.
55   Ibid., p. 30.
56   A. Lerumo, *Fifty Fighting Years: The Communist Party of South Africa 1921-1971* (London, 1971), p. 104.
57   Forman, *March to Freedom*, p. 31.
58   T.D. Mweli Skota, *Black Folks Who's Who* (Johannesburg, 1931).
59   *The International* 18 June 1917.
60   Willan, *Sol Plaatje*, p. 224.

Chapter 3 The ANC and Workers' Organizations

1   C. Kadalie, *My Life and the ICU: The Autobiography of a Black Trade Unionist in South Africa* (London, 1970).
2   Ibid., p. 31.
3   Ibid., p. 33.
4   Ibid., p. 40.
5   Ibid.
6   P. Walshe, *The Rise of African Nationalism in South Africa: The African National Congress 1912-1952* (Berkeley, 1971), p. 72.
7   E. Roux, *Time Longer than Rope: A History of the Black Man's Struggle for Freedom in South Africa* (Wisconsin, 1978), p. 156.
8   Kadalie, *My Life*, p. 51.
9   H. Reinhardt, "Die Entwicklung der verarbeitenden Industrie in der Sudafrikanischen Union von 1910-1960: Eine wirtschafts historiche *Untersuchung*" PhD thesis, Leipzig, 1965, p. 45.
10   Roux, *Time Longer than Rope*, p. 158.
11   Kadalie, *My Life*, p. 18.
12   G. Coka, "The Story of Gilbert Coka" in M. Perham, *Ten Africans* (London, 1936), p. 275.
13   Ibid., p. 295.
14   Ibid., p. 297.
15   Ibid., p. 14.
16   Ibid., p. 16.

17   Ibid., p. 79.
18   Roux, *Time Longer than Rope*, p. 160.
19   Ibid., p. 300.
20   Ibid., p. 310.
21   Ibid., p. 163.
22   Ibid., p. 165.
23   *Sechaba* (Nov. 1979) pp. 28-32.
24   T. Zania, "The ICU", in *The African Communist*, 38 (1969).
25   Ibid., pp. 77-8.
26   *Sechaba* (Nov. 1980), p. 5.
27   R.V. Selope Thema, unpublished autobiography, 1935, Institute o
      Commonwealth Studies Archives, London.
28   *Sechaba* (Dec. 1982).
29   *Das Flammenzeichen vom Palais Egmont. Offizielles Protokoll des
      Kongresses gegen koloniale unterdrückungund
      Imperialismus* . . . Brüssel 10-15 February 1927 (Berlin, 1927),
      p. 95. See also H.J. and R.E. Simons, *Class and Colour in South
      Africa 1850-1950* (London, 1969), p. 353.
30   Simons, *Class and Colour*, p. 392.
31   Walshe, *African Nationalism in SA*, p. 175.
32   *Sechaba* (Dec. 1982).
33   A.F. Plate, "I Knew Gumede", interview with the author, Moscow
      July 1977. For details about James La Guma, see the unpublished
      biography written by his son, Alex La Guma.
34   Simons, *Class and Colour*, p. 402.
35   W.E.B. Du Bois, *An ABC of Colour* (Berlin, n.d.), p. 51.
36   D.F.L. Broderick and W.E.B. Du Bois, *Negro Leader in a Time
      of Crisis* (Stanford, 1966), p. 132.
37   N. Mandela, *The Struggle is My Life* (London, 1978), p. 169.
38   "Workers' Confidence in the Communist Party - Cape Town ANC
      resolves Support Answers to Disrupters" in *South African
      Communists Speak: Documents from the History of the South
      African Communist Party 1915-1980* (London, 1981), p. 88.
39   Roux, *Time Longer than Rope,* p. 211.
40   Ibid.
41   See *South African Communists Speak*, pp. 91-7.
42   L. Forman, "Background to the National Question in South
      Africa", in the Forman Papers.
43   S. Marks, "The Ambiguities of Dependence: John L. Dube of
      Natal", *Journal of Southern African Studies,* 1(2) (April 1975).
44   Ibid.

Chapter 4 Fundamental changes

1 P. Walshe, *The Rise of African Nationalism in South Africa: The African National Congress 1912-1952* (Berkeley, 1971), p. 179.
2 See *Sechaba* (Aug. 1981).
3 Xuma Papers, Institute of Commonwealth Studies Archives, London.
4 T. Karis and G.M. Carter, *From Protest to Challenge: A Documentary History of African Politics in South Africa 1882-1964* (California, 1972), vol. 2, p. 46.
5 Ibid., p. 57.
6 Ibid.
7 Ibid., p. 55.
8 Ibid., p. 56.
9 J.H. and R.E. Simons, *Class and Colour in South Africa 1850-1950* (London, 1969), p. 501.
10 Ibid., p. 504.
11 Xuma Papers.
12 Ibid.
13 Ibid.
14 Ibid.
15 Ibid.
16 Ibid.
17 Ibid.
18 Ibid.
19 Ibid.
20 Walshe, *African Nationalism in SA*, p. 125.
21 Xuma Papers.
22 Ibid.
23 *ANC Africa Claims in South Africa*, (Johannesburg, 1945), *Congress Series No. 11.*
24 *International Organisations and Integration* (Leyden, 1968), pp. 20-1.
25 M. Benson, *The African Patriots* (London, 1962), p. 98.
26 *Africa Claims in South Africa.*
27 E. Pahad, unpublished biography of Dr Dadoo.
28 Ibid.
29 Ibid.
30 Ibid.
31 *Sechaba,* 12(2) (1978), p. 72.
32 *The African Communist,* 78(3) (1979), p. 56.
33 Karis and Carter, *From Protest to Challenge,* vol. 2, p. 286.
34 Ibid., p. 287.

35 See P.L. Bonner (ed.), *Working Papers in South African Studies, Papers presented at the AST African Studies Seminar* (Johannesburg, 1979), p. 75.

36 Ibid., p. 190.

37 Ibid., p. 193.

38 Xuma Papers.

39 Ibid.

40 Bonner, *Working Papers*, p. 203.

41 Ibid., p. 204.

42 Benson, *African Patriots*, p. 99.

43 Ibid., p. 100.

44 Karis and Carter, *From Protest to Challenge*, vol. 2, p. 319.

45 Benson, *African Patriots*, p. 105.

46 M. Harmel, "Trade Unions Face the Future", *Liberation: A Journal of Democratic Discussions* (Johannesburg), 10 (1954), p. 13.

47 Xuma Papers.

48 T. Singh, review article of Gail Gehardt's *Black Power in South Africa: The Evolution of an Ideology* (California, 1978), in *The African Communist,* 81(2) (1980).

49 Ibid., p. 49.

50 *ANC Youth League Manifesto*, in N. Mandela, *The Struggle is My Life* (London, 1978).

51 Molema Papers, Institute of Commonwealth Studies Archives, London.

52 B. Bunting, *Moses Kotane: South African Revolutionary* (London, 1975), p. 138.

53 G.M. Gerhart, *Black Power in South Africa: The Evolution of an Ideology* (California, 1978).

54 Karis and Carter, *From Protest to Challenge*, vol. 2. p. 318.

55 *ANC Youth League Basic Policy Document*, in Mandela, *The Struggle is My Life.*

56 Karis and Carter, *From Protest to Challenge,* vol. 2, p. 321.

57 Ibid., p. 312.

58 L. Forman, "Background to the National Question in South Afric in the Forman Papers.

Chapter 5 Defiance and new strategies

1 A. Lerumo, *Fifty Fighting Years: The Communist Party of South Africa 1921-1971* (London, 1971), p. 85.

2   P. Walshe, *The Rise of African Nationalism in South Africa: The African National Congress 1912-1952* (Berkeley, 1971), p. 403.

3   A. Lutuli, *Let my People Go: An Autobiography* (London, 1962), pp. 128-9.

4   D. Nokwe, "The Great Smear: Communism and Congress in South Africa", *Africa South in Exile*, 6(1), (Oct.-Dec. 1961), p. 8.

5   See Z.K. Matthews, *Freedom for my People: Autobiography of Z.K. Matthews - Southern Africa 1901-1968, Memoir by Monica Wilson* (Cape Town, 1981).

6   *ANC Speaks: Documents and Statements of the African National Congress, 1959-1976*, p. 17.

7   Ibid.

8   Ibid.

9   *The African Communist*, 63(4) (1975), p. 37.

10 *Sechaba*, 12(3) (1978), p. 5.

11 Ibid.

12 Ibid.

13 *Mayibuye* (Lusaka, ANC), 2(6), 31 July 1967, p. 16.

14 *The African Communist*, 48(1) (1972), p. 30.

15 Lutuli, *Let my People Go*, p. 160.

16 Mandela, *The Struggle is My Life* (London, 1978).

17 Ibid.

18 *Sechaba* (Aug. 1981).

19 Ibid.

20 Ibid.

21 B. Hirson, "Rural Revolts in South Africa 1937-1951", in *L'Afrique du Sud aujourd'hui* (Paris, 1978), p. 61.

22 *Fighting Talk,* 12(1), (Feb. 1958), p. 3.

23 Ibid.

24 Ibid.

25 Ibid.

26 Ibid.

27 Ibid.

28 G. Mbeki, "Backwards to Bantustans", *Fighting Talk*, 14(1), (Feb. 1960).

29 P.N. Raboroko "The Congress and Africanists - the Africanist Case" in *Africa South,* 4(3) (Apr.-June 1960).

30 *Sechaba.*

31 *Africa South*, 4(3) (Apr.-June 1960), p. 34.

32 See Speeches of Mangaliso Sobukwe 1949-1959, published by the PAC.

33 Ibid.

34 *Africa South* 6(1) (Oct.-Dec. 1961), p. 6.

241

35 *Africa South* 3(4) (Jul.-Sept. 1959), p. 34.
36 Ibid.
37 *The Pan Africanist Congress of South Africa - Whom does it Serve* (Morogoro, ANC, 1968), p. 1.
38 *Fighting Talk*, 14(7) (Dec. 1960), p. 5.
39 Mandela, *The Struggle is My Life*.
40 Ibid.
41 Ibid., p. 120.
42 *Walter Max Ulyate Sisulu - Leader of the African National Congress and Man of the People* (London, Southern Africa - The Imprisoned Society, in cooperation with the UN Centre Against Apartheid, 1982), p. 5.
43 Mandela, *The Struggle is My Life*.
44 Ibid.
45 Ibid.
46 Author interviews with T.T. Nkobi, September 1984.
47 G. Mbeki, *South Africa: The Peasants' Revolt*, 2nd edn (London, 1984), pp. 128-34.

Chapter 6 Armed resistance and ANC strategy 1961-69

1   T. Karis and G.M. Carter, *From Protest to Challenge: A Documentary History of African Politics in South Africa 1882-1964* (California, 1972), vol. 3, p. 716.
2   N. Mandela, *The Struggle is My Life* (London, 1978).
3   Ibid.
4   Ibid.
5   Oliver Tambo, interview in the *Guardian*, June 1983.
6   Mandela, *The Struggle is My Life*.
7   Ibid.
8   Ibid.
9   Ibid.
10 Ibid.
11 ANC Archives.
12 Ibid.
13 Ibid.
14 Ibid.
15 Ibid.
16 Ibid.
17 Ibid.
18 J. Kantor, *A Healthy Grave* (Berlin, 1969).
19 Mandela, *The Struggle is my Life*.

20   Ibid.
21   Ibid.
22   Ibid.
23   Ibid.
24   Ibid.
25   *Sechaba.*
26   *ANC Speaks: Documents and Statements of the African National Congress, 1959-1976*, p. 97.
27   Their short autobiographies are included in Kantor, *A Healthy Grave*. See also *Sechaba* Jan. through to Sept. 1981.
28   *Mayibuye* (June 1969).
29   Ibid.
30   Ibid.
31   *The African Communist*, 95(4), (1983), pp. 88-9.
32   ANC Archives.
33   *ANC Speaks*.
34   Ibid.
35   Ibid.

Chapter 7 The re-emergence of the ANC
(1969-85)

1   Quoted in *Documents of the Second National Consultative Conference of the African National Congress, Zambia 16-23 June 1985.*
2   *The African Communist* 102(3) (1985), p. 60.
3   In *Documents of the 1985 ANC Conference.*
4   S. Biko, *I Write What I Like: A Selection of his Writings edited with a personal memoir by Aelred Stubbs, CR* (London, 1978), pp. 155-6.
5   Ibid.
6   H. Bernstein, *No. 46, Steve Biko* (London, 1978), p. 11.
7   Biko, I *Write What I Like*, p. 157.
8   Hilda Bernstein, *Steve Biko*, p. 6.
9   Ibid., pp. 23-4.
10   Biko, *I Write What I Like*, p. 158.
11   Ibid.
12   Ibid., p. 162.
13   Bernstein, *Steve Biko*, p. 20.
14   Biko, *I Write What I Like*, p. 182.
15   Ibid., p. 185.
16   *Sechaba* (Feb. 1977).

17 R. Suttner, *The Freedom Charter: The People's Charter in the Nineteen-Eighties - The Twenty-Sixth T.B. Davie Memorial Lecture, delivered in the University of Cape Town on 26 September 1984* (Cape Town, 1984), p. 2.

18 *The African Communist*, 102(3), (1985), p. 31.

19 "Statement on the Expulsion from the ANC", issued by the expelle eight members, London, 1975.

20 Suttner, *The Freedom Charter*.

21 Biko, *I Write What I Like*, p. 148.

22 *Sechaba* (Feb. 1979).

23 Ibid.

24 Biko, *I Write What I Like*.

25 In *Documents of the 1985 ANC Conference*.

26 An ANC document with the author. For a history of SACTU, see K. Luckhardt and B. Wall, *Organize or Starve! The History of the South African Congress of Trade Unions* (London, 1980), p. 9.

27 Ibid.

28 J. Ya Otto, *Battlefront Namibia: An Autobiography* (London, 1982), p. 142ff.

29 S. Friedman, "Political Implications of Industrial Unrest in South Africa", in D.C. Hindson (ed.), *Working Papers in Southern African Studies* (Johannesburg, 1983), vol. 3, p. 126.

30 Suttner, *The Freedom Charter*.

31 Friedman, *"Industrial Unrest in SA"* p. 125.

32 Ibid., p. 126.

33 Ibid., p. 128.

34 Ibid.

35 In *Documents of the 1985 ANC Conference*.

36 An ANC document with the author.

37 Ibid.

38 P. Walshe, *Church versus State in South Africa: The Case of the Christian Institute* (London, 1983), p. 207.

39 Ibid.

40 *Dawn* (Journal of Umkhonto we Sizwe), 8(5), (1984), p. 13.

41 P. Walshe, *The Christian Institute and the Resurgence of African Nationalism* (London) p. 7.

42 *Sechaba* (June 1983).

43 Ibid.

44 Ibid. (Dec. 1984).

45 A. Stadler, "The Politics of Subsistence: Community Struggles in War-Time Johannesburg", in Hindson, *Working Papers*, p. 61.

46 *Sechaba* (June 1979), p. 11.

47 Ibid. (Jan. 1983).

48 Ibid. (Aug. 1980).
49 Ibid. (July 1980).
50 Ibid.
51 Ibid. (May 1984), p. 3.
52 Ibid.
53 *The Sowetan* (Johannesburg), 5 July 1985.
54 *Sechaba* (December 1985), pp. 11-12.
55 *National Forum* (Johannesburg, National Forum Committee, 1983).
56 *The Sowetan*, 24 June 1983.
57 Quoted in *Sechaba*, (2) (1978).

Select Bibliography

African Claims in South Africa, Johannesburg, ANC 1945, Congress Series No. 11.

ANC Speaks: Documents and Statements of the African National Congress, 1959-1976.

The *African Communist* London 1960-1987.

Barnett, U.A. *A Vision of Order: A Study of Black South African Literature in English (1914-1980),* London, 1983.

Bennie, W.G. *Imibengo,* Lovedale, 1949.

Benson, M. *The African Patriots,* London, 1962.
— *The Struggle for a Birthright,* London, 1985.
— *Nelson Mandela,* Harmondsworth, 1986.

Bernstein, H. *No. 46, Steve Biko,* London, 1978.

Biko, S. *I Write What I Like. A Selection of his Writings edited with a Personal memoir by Aelred Stubbs, CR,* London, 1978.

Bokwe, John-Knox, *Ntsikana: The Story of an African Convert.* Lovedale, 1914.

Bonner, P.L. (ed.) *Working Papers in South African Studies,* Johannesburg, 1979.

Bown, L. and Crowder, M. (eds) *The Proceedings of the First International Congress of Africanists, Accra 11-18 December 1962,* London, 1964.

Bozzoli, B. (ed.) *Town and Countryside in the Transvaal: Capitalist Penetration and Popular Response,* Johannesburg, 1983, *History Workshop 2.*

Bunting, B. *Moses Kotane: South African Revolutionary,* London, 1975.

Das Flammenzeichen vom Palais Egmont. Offizielles Protokoll des Kongresses gegen koloniale unterdrückung und Imperialismus Brüssels 10-15 February 1927. Berlin, 1927.

Documents of the Second National Consultative Conference of the African National Congress, Zambia 16-23 June 1985, Zambia, ANC.

Du Bois, W.E.B. *An ABC of Colour,* Berlin n.d.

Forman, L. *Chapters in the History of the March to Freedom,* Cape Town, 1959, a *New Age* pamphlet.

Gerhart, G.M. *Black Power in South Africa. The Evolution of an Ideology,* California, 1978.

Hindson, D.C. *Working Papers in Southern African Studies,* Johannesburg, 1983.
Hooper C. *Brief Authority,* London, 1960.

Jabavu, D.D.T. *Native Disabilities in South Africa,* Lovedale, 1932.
Jahn J. *Who's Who in African Literature,* Tübingen, 1972.
Jordan, A.C. *Towards an African Literature: The Emergence of Literacy Form in Xhosa,* Berkeley, 1974

Kadalie, C. *My Life and the ICU: the Autobiography of a Black Trade Unionist in South Africa,* London, 1970.
Kantor, J. *A Healthy Grave,* Berlin, 1969.
Karis, T. and Carter, G.M. (eds), *From Protest to Challenge: A Documentary History of African Politics in South Africa 1882-1964,* California, 1972, 4 vols.
Kuper, L. *An African Bourgeoisie: Race, Class and Politics in South Africa,* London, 1965.

L'Afrique du Sud au jourd 'hui, Paris, 1978.
Leistner, G.M.E. and Breytenbach, W.J. *The Black Worker of South Africa,* Pretoria, 1975.
Lerumo, A. *Fifty Fighting Years: The Communist Party of South Africa 1921-1971,* London, 1971.
Lodge, T. *Black Politics in South Africa since 1945,* London, 1983.
Luckhardt, K. and Wall, B. *Organize Or Starve! The History of the South African Congress of Trade Unions,* London, 1980.
Lutuli, A. *Let My People Go: An Autobiography,* London, 1962.

Mandela, N. *The Struggle is My Life,* London, 1978.
Marks, S. *Reluctant Rebellion: The 1906-8 Disturbances in Natal,* Oxford, 1970.
Marks, S. and Atmore A. (eds), *Economy and Society in Pre-Industrial South Africa,* London, 1980.
Matthews, Z.K. *Freedom for my People: Autobiography of Z.K. Matthews - Southern Africa 1901-1968. Memoir by Monica Wilson,* Cape Town, 1981.
Mbeki, G. *South Africa: The Peasants' Revolt,* London, 1964.

247

Mokgatle, N. *The Autobiography of An Unknown South African,* California, 1971.

Motlhabi, M. *The Theory and Practice of Black Resistance to Apartheid: A Social-Ethical Analysis,* Johannesburg, 1984.

Mutloatse, M. (ed.) *Forced Landing: Africa South Contemporary Writings,* Johannesburg, 1980.

Mweli Skota, T.D. *Black Folks Who's Who,* Johannesburg, 1931.

Odendaal, A. *Vukani Bantu! The Beginnings of Black Protest Politics in South Africa to 1912,* Cape Town, 1984.

Perham, M. *Ten Africans,* London, 1936.

Plaatje, S.T. *Native Life in South Africa before and since the European War and the Boer Rebellion,* London, 1916 and Braamfontein, 1982.

Randall, P. (ed.) *Not Without Honour: Tribute to Beyers Naude,* Johannesburg, 1982.

Rosenthal, E. *Bantu Journalism in South Africa,* Johannesburg, n.d.

Roux, E. *Time Longer Than Rope: A History of the Black Man's Struggle for Freedom in South Africa,* Wisconsin, 1978.

Saunders, C. (ed.) *Black Leaders in Southern African History,* London, 1979.

Sechaba official organ of the ANC, London, 1967-1987.

Selope Thema, R.V. Unpublished autobiography 1935, Institute of Commonwealth Studies Archives, London.

Segal, R. (ed.) *Southern Africa: The New Politics of Revolution,* Harmondsworth, 1975.

Shephard, H.W. *Bantu Literature and Life,* Lovedale, 1955.

Simons, J. *African Women: Their Legal Status,* London, 1968.

Simons, H.J. and R.E. *Class and Colour in South Africa, 1850-1950,* Harmondsworth, 1969.

South African Communists Speak: Documents from the History of the South African Communist Party 1915-1980, London, 1981.

Sundkler, B.G.M. *Bantu Prophets in South Africa,* London, 1961.

Suttner, R. *The Freedom Charter: The People's Charter in the Nineteen-Eighties* - The Twenty-Sixth T.B. Davie Memorial Lecture, delivered in the University of Cape Town on 26 September 1984, Cape Town, 1984.

Umbedesho Wamaculo Ase Wesile, Cape Town, 1926.

Walker, I.L. and Weinbren, B. *2,000 Casualties: A History of the Trade Unions and the Labour Movement in the Union of South Africa,* Johannesburg, 1961.

Walshe, P. *The Rise of African Nationalism in South Africa: The African National Congress 1912-1952,* Berkeley, 1971.
  — *Church versus State in South Africa: The Case of the Christian Institute,* London, 1983.
  — *The Christian Institute and the Resurgence of African Nationalism,* London.
  — *Walter Max Ulyate Sisulu - Leader of the African National Congress and Man of the People,* London, Southern Africa - The Imprisoned Society, in cooperation with the UN Centre Against Apartheid, 1982.

Webster, E. (ed.) *Essays in Southern African Labour History,* Johannesburg, 1978, *Ravan Labour Studies 1.*

Willan, B. *Sol Plaatje: South African Nationalist 1872-1932,* London, 1984.

Wilson, F. *Migrant Labour in South Africa,* Johannesburg, 1972.

Xuma, A.B. *Charlotte Manye (Mrs Maxeke) What An Educated Girl Can Do,* 1930.

Ya-Otto, J. *Battlefront Namibia: An Autobiography,* London, 1982.

Index

251

252

254

#47